LIGHT UP THE NIGHT

Also by Travis Lupick

Fighting for Space: How a Group of Drug Users
Transformed One City's Struggle with Addiction

LIGHT UP
THE NIGHT

America's Overdose Crisis and the
Drug Users Fighting for Survival

TRAVIS LUPICK

THE
NEW
PRESS

NEW YORK
LONDON

Published in the United States by The New Press, New York, 2022
Distributed by Two Rivers Distribution

ISBN 978-1-62097-638-8 (hc)
ISBN 978-1-62097-687-6 (ebook)
CIP data is available

The New Press publishes books that promote and enrich public discussion and
understanding of the issues vital to our democracy and to a more equitable world. These
books are made possible by the enthusiasm of our readers; the support of a committed
group of donors, large and small; the collaboration of our many partners in the
independent media and the not-for-profit sector; booksellers, who often hand-sell New
Press books; librarians; and above all by our authors.

www.thenewpress.com

We acknowledge the support of the Canada Council for the Arts.

Book design and composition by Bookbright Media
This book was set in Minion and Helvetica Condensed

Printed in the United States of America

10 9 8 7 6 5 4 3 2 1

For Spencer Pride

Contents

"Caring for myself is not self-indulgence, it is self-preservation, and that is an act of political warfare." —Audre Lorde

"I've never had a problem with drugs. I've had problems with police." —Keith Richards

Prelude

When Jess Tilley showed up at the address she was given on a quiet street in Northampton, Massachusetts, the door was already open a crack. This made her nervous. Though it wasn't uncommon for Northampton residents to leave their homes unlocked during the day, this slightly ajar door was a signal that something was wrong.

Jess didn't know the owner. She'd only spoken to her on the phone a couple of times before. They had connected for the first time six weeks earlier. The woman, a single mother, had found Jess's business card when digging through her 20-year-old son's backpack. Alongside the card was a bag of syringes and a small amount of heroin. The woman had called the number on Jess's card, upset. "First, she was angry, then she had a bunch of questions and she was crying," Jess says. Jess isn't a drug dealer. She distributes harm reduction supplies. Jess had given the woman's son the syringes, but not the heroin. After answering the woman's questions, Jess offered her Narcan (generic name naloxone), a miracle drug that quickly reverses the effects of an opioid overdose. The two talked further and Jess had brought the woman to understand that if her son was going to use heroin, it was better he do so with clean needles and with Narcan on hand. Now, six weeks later, the woman had used that dose of Narcan and called Jess to ask for a refill. So Jess was standing outside her home, wondering why the door was ajar.

"Help!" Jess heard the woman scream. "Somebody help me!" Jess had arrived at the house to deliver supplies. Now she realized she was responding to an overdose. She snapped into action and ran into the house. A boy—18 or 19, Jess guessed—was sitting on the edge of his bed. She ran past him. Down the hall, she found the woman banging on a bathroom door. Her son had overdosed an hour earlier. That's where the Narcan had gone. Now he had overdosed a second time and lay unconscious on the other side of the bathroom door, which was locked.

It was September 2019 and before the year was out, some 71,000 people would die after taking drugs—a number approaching the total deaths from car accidents and firearms combined (and to increase to 93,000 by 2020, compared to an annual average of 15,000 deaths some two decades earlier).[1] Jess silently prayed this young man wouldn't be one of them.

"Do you have a screwdriver?" Jess asked. "We'll take this door right off its hinges." The woman ran to the kitchen. Meanwhile, Jess took a step back from the door, gathered some momentum, and gave it a powerful kick. Three more kicks and the lock snapped off. But the door still didn't open. The boy inside had fallen against it and now his unconscious body kept it shut. The woman returned with a screwdriver and together the two of them managed to push the door open a crack and squeeze Jess through.

"I get in and I immediately clear his mouth," Jess recounts. "And I start breathing for him. I ask, 'How long has he been out?'"

"Five minutes," the woman replied. "It happened just after I called you."

"So I'm calculating the time it took me to get there," Jess says. "I'm breathing for him. And he's not coming around. So I hit him with Narcan." Jess took the medication's nasal administrator, shoved it into the boy's nose, and hit the release button. Then she waited a minute. Then two minutes. Two very, very long minutes. But nothing happened. Next, Jess loaded up a syringe, stuck a dose of intramuscular naloxone into the boy's thigh, and hit the plunger to inject it. Finally, he regained consciousness. "Where am I?" the boy asked. "Shit, where's my mom?"

That's when Jess heard the boy's mother calling from down the hall. "He's out! He's out!" the woman screamed. "No, he's not out," Jess thought to herself. "He's here with me and I know he's conscious because I'm watching him puke." Then Jess remembered the second boy who she'd caught out of the corner of her eye on her initial run through the house. "Fuck," she thought next.

Jess grabbed the boy she'd just revived, ran with him toward the bedroom, and thanked God she always carries more Narcan than she expects to use. By the time they made it into the bedroom, the second boy was on the ground and already turning blue. There was a syringe in his arm and a green powder all over the place. Jess put the pieces together. The kids were injecting crushed OxyContin pills, she realized, or at least what they thought were Oxy pills. Jess knew this was actually fentanyl. A batch of the dangerous synthetic opioid was causing overdoses all over Northampton, disguised as green OxyContin pills.

"So now the second boy is out," Jess says. "And this woman is doing what parents do when this happens: she's panicking. She's wailing on his chest. I'm like, 'You're going to break his ribs. What are you doing?'" Jess took charge of the situation, responding to her second overdose in about as many minutes.

"I revived the other kid so they both lived." She says it nonchalantly, but such situations are traumatic and extremely stressful. Every life Jess saves takes a toll on her.

The same week that Jess saved those two boys' lives, Louise Vincent was finishing up for the day at the Urban Survivors Union (USU) needle exchange on Grove Street in Greensboro, North Carolina. It was around 9:30 p.m. when a weathered old man let himself in and walked over to the desk where Louise was working on her computer. There was an infection in his right arm, Louise could see. "How can we help you?" she asked.

The man had just spent a week in the hospital, where he was treated for that infection. "It almost took the arm off," he told Louise. Now the man and his wife were living in a hotel, he wasn't working, and every penny his wife made at McDonald's went to paying rent. They couldn't afford the antibiotics that he needed to keep his arm on the mend. "Alright," Louise said. "Let me see what we can do about that." She picked up the phone and placed a call to the North Carolina Harm Reduction Coalition, a nonprofit that provides services for drug users across the state, and asked if they could help. No luck. But Louise told the man that she would stay on it, place a couple of more calls, and that he should check in with her the next day. "Come on back and we'll see," she said.

"God bless," the man said. "God bless your family."

"Hey, man, you're not alone," Louise said.

"I feel like it, sometimes," he replied.

"You're not," Louise said. "We've got a Tuesday-night group. Stop by. You're not alone. There's no need to feel shame. We all need help sometimes. You're not alone." The man took a bag of injection equipment that Louise had prepared as they'd talked, and then walked out. "God bless," he said again.

Louise stepped out a few minutes later. "Going to grab smokes," she said. Don Jackson, Louise's partner—in life, business, and everything else—took over. A group of three women had entered the exchange and sat on a ring of couches near the entrance. Don asked them what they were looking for before providing them with syringes, cookers, ties, cotton, and alcohol swabs. The exchange had prepackaged bags that contained everything but the drugs. Whereas a couple of years ago, Don mostly worked in the background at the USU—there since its establishment but always behind-the-scenes—he'd recently grown comfortable running the show. "Y'all be safe," he said to the women as they left.

By this time, Louise was back. A heavyset guy walked in. "Is there someone who can tell me how this works?" he asked. "I've never been here before." Louise began to fill out a registration form for him. "My wife and I were clean for seven years but fell off recently," the man said. "She's out in the car with our kid." Don replied quickly: "Kids can come in here. Why don't you go get your wife, because she might need to hear some of this too." The man left and returned a minute later with his wife and a little girl in his arms. She was four or five and bubbly and outgoing. Staff at the exchange instantly fell in love with her. While they played with the girl, Louise ran through what the exchange offers and what supplies the couple could leave with that night. They took a few boxes of clean syringes, a couple of Narcan kits, and a pack of fentanyl test strips. "Thank you so much," the man said. "We'll be back next week." Staff followed the family outside, enamored with the child.

The exchange was way past closing now, but the door was still unlocked and a young woman wandered in. She was nervous and looked lost. Twenty years earlier, this girl could have been me, Louise thought. If only a place like the exchange had existed back then. Louise gave a quick glance up from her laptop. "You need something?" she asked. When there was no answer, Louise raised her head to meet the young woman's eyes, and saw that what she needed was to talk. Whatever it was, Louise had been through it before. She made up a bag of harm reduction supplies. Then Louise asked if she was safe, and let her know that she was there for her.

1
Tough Love

Louise Beale was a rebellious teenager. In the late 1980s, in Greensboro, North Carolina, she was skipping school, experimenting with drugs, and riding around in cars with the town's older boys. At the same time, she was very much still just a child. Louise's parents had given her a sheltered upbringing. "I went from Barbies to crack," she says, only half joking. Louise wasn't equipped to deal with what was coming.

It's past three in the morning one night in 2018 and Louise is at her computer in her modest one-bedroom house in a residential neighborhood not far from downtown Greensboro. Louise—Weezie, to her friends—is always at her computer, answering emails and taking calls from activists around the country. She is petite, a little over five feet tall and maybe 100 pounds. Her hair is long and straight, dark red with a streak of gray where she usually lets it fall over her left eye. A cigarette hangs from her mouth as she uses both hands to type.

Louise's partner, Don Jackson, is in the living room with her, his shoulder-length hair dangling over his eyes. A special breed of Prince Charming, Don sometimes acts rough and can crack an abrasive joke, but there's not a mean bone in his body. Don followed the Grateful Dead around for half a decade in the late 1990s. Then he was somewhat hardened around the edges by three years he spent in prison for a nonviolent drug charge. He and Louise have known each other since high school.

———

"I feel like I had a normal childhood," Louise begins. "I grew up with a mom and a dad and I think that they both loved me a lot. They were professors. We went to church on Sundays."

But adolescence brought a change in Louise. "There was something way wrong at 12 or 13," she recalls in her light Southern accent. "I wanted to die. Just darkness."

Louise was depressed and, increasingly, she was angry. She fought with her parents over her curfew, her friends, her clothes, how she wore her makeup—everything. "Shut the storm windows if you're going to yell at one another," her mother would say. And then her father would smile for the neighbors and act as if all was well inside the Beale household. Louise could not handle this sort of duplicity. "My entire life, there's a story that we're telling, and then there is what is really happening, and nobody is talking about what is really happening," she says. "The hypocrisy of that was eating me up." Seeing that her parents didn't understand what she was going through—unable to understand herself—Louise acted out. She was an attractive teenager, and acting out often meant fun with boys. "I was trying to find acceptance," Louise says. "I wanted to escape and be saved."

Greensboro, population 296,700, is an unremarkable midsized city. There's a small downtown core with a few low-rise skyscrapers. Other than that, it's mostly residential sprawl. There's a real Southern charm to the town. The people are exceedingly welcoming, friendly, and generous. For many, social life revolves around the church or a weekly backyard barbecue. Greensboro has a prominent spot in the country's history with civil rights. In February 1960, in the Woolworth building on South Elm Street, four Black men took seats at the department store's lunch counter and catalyzed the civil rights movement's pivotal sit-in campaign, which successfully desegregated stores and restaurants throughout the South. Despite that, a

racial divide persists. There's a white side of town and a Black side
of town and nobody talks about it much.

Greensboro is decidedly typical, similar to a hundred other cities its size, located in a state where the overdose crisis has played
out in an average way. When all 50 states are ranked for overdose
deaths, North Carolina is almost right in the middle, at spot number 23 in 2019. Most years, the state's rate of overdose deaths per
100,000 citizens falls between 20 and 25, which equates to a little
more than 2,200 deaths per year.[1] As in most states, first it was pills,
then heroin, and now fentanyl.

When Louise began to ride around town with Greensboro's older boys, heroin was just beginning to become available there. She
didn't know anything about it. She didn't know much about drugs
in general. She had huffed butane a couple of times, and it made her
curious, but that was it. Louise's first boyfriend, a guy a couple of
years older named Corey[†], lived alone with an alcoholic father who
never knew or cared what was going on around the house. It was in
Corey's bedroom that 13-year-old Louise was offered her first illicit
substance. He brought out a small amount of cocaine and told her
they could get a stronger high if they smoked it. Corey handed her a
straw and they freebased cocaine and giggled like little kids. Before
that afternoon, Louise barely knew what a drug was. After, she
understood that they were something that could let her feel okay
with the world. Louise wasn't immediately addicted, or even all
that into it. "The relationship aspect of drugs was way more important to me than the actual drugs themselves," Louise explains. Her
struggle with depression made her feel intensely alienated, and she
longed for a sense of belonging. This longing made her especially

---

† Corey is one of five pseudonyms in this book. Each one is denoted by this
  symbol.

susceptible to Corey's crew of older boys doing drugs, a crew she could belong to. "When you do illegal things with people, when you are all in pain together, when you are all in a struggle together, you're bonded in a way," Louise says. "And I liked the way that bond felt."

Louise began huffing butane and then dropping acid. In many ways, she was a typical troubled teenager of the suburban 1980s, hanging out behind the grocery store or at the back edge of the local driving range, where the town meets the surrounding forest. "A mob of teenagers, just hanging out and up to no good," she says. The relationships Louise forged through drugs was why she was there, but she did also come to like the drugs themselves. "I liked the way that felt," she says plainly. "I liked to laugh and I liked this idea of an alternate reality."

Once Louise started using drugs, her parents, Sarah and Walter Beale, tried their best and did what they thought was right. They took Louise to one psychiatrist and then another and another. Eventually, Louise was diagnosed with a "conduct" disorder, whatever that meant. In her freshman year of high school, she was sent home for punching a girl in the face. That was her parents' breaking point. They sent her to an institution for troubled youth.

"It was the 1980s and it was all the rage to use tough love," Sarah recalls. "That seemed like the only thing one could do when we were first facing what was happening with Louise." Sarah and Walter were desperate to put their daughter back on track. "I even went to a support group called 'Tough Love,'" Sarah says. "They told us, 'All you have to do is put their things out on the front porch, and that will take care of that problem.' And this was when Louise was still in high school. It was a joke. That didn't work."

Louise ended up locked inside a North Carolina psychiatric facility called Charter Hills. "It was like a fucking insane asylum," Louise says. "That little stint at Charter Hills made me angry and I decided, from then on, I was not going to be good."

"I don't think I was that bad before they sent me to Charter," she continues. "Yeah, I had some issues going on. But whatever happened there catapulted me in a negative direction. It was at that point that I said, 'If you think I'm bad now . . . '" Louise trails off. "After that, I wanted to kill them [her parents]. I hated them."

When Charter Hills didn't work, Louise was shipped from Greensboro all the way to Escalante, Utah. There was an isolated ranch there that promised to correct troubled teenagers' behavior with the boot camp approach that was about to gain popularity on 1990s daytime talk shows such as *Montel Williams.*

"It was a cattle ranch that was going under," Louise says. "Nobody had psychology degrees. It was just one guy who was shell-shocked from the Vietnam War and his domineering wife. And I guess they practiced some strange version of Alcoholics Anonymous's 12 steps." Louise spent her days there marching aimlessly around the desert with a heavy bag strapped on her back for no reason but its discomfort. Nights passed sleeping in bunk beds with a bunch of other delinquents in a barn with nothing but a woodstove and a few old sleeping bags to keep them warm. "I was barely even a teenager," Louise says. "I was terrified. And I felt abandoned, thrown away."

On the long drive back from Utah, she was excited to see her friends and reconnect with her crew of teenage outcasts. But when she returned to North Carolina, there was another betrayal waiting for her. Desperate to keep Louise out of trouble, her parents had moved the family out of Greensboro, 30 minutes down the highway to the sleepy town of Asheboro. It's a suburb, essentially, far enough from the city that a young couple can afford a yard for the kids but close enough to commute in for work. Sarah and Walter hoped everyone could start over. But Louise hated being so far away from her friends, so she hated Asheboro. "I didn't know anybody. I was stuck in the house, there was nothing to do. I was miserable and I was angry." Shy and awkward, Louise was terrified at the prospect of venturing into an unknown high school to make new friends.

"So I snuck back to Greensboro, didn't come home," she says. "I won't do what you tell me to do. You can't make me."

Louise was sent back to Utah. The ranch offered a guarantee of corrected behavior or a return visit free of charge. Louise's parents became the first clients to take advantage of that offer. "This had become a pattern: we get upset with Louise and then we send her away," Louise says. "Sending me to Utah, that made me feel abandoned. Every time they tried to do something, I hated them worse and I became more determined to act out."

Lying on her top bunk in the barn one evening, curled up in her ratty sleeping bag, Louise received a letter. A week or so earlier, she had written her mom, begging for a plane ticket home. "No, you can't come home," Sarah's response read. "We love you, but you can't come home." Louise's eyes welled up with tears. Somehow, she hadn't expected that. "I felt stupid abandoned," she says. "That was a defining moment, a moment when I felt like I really needed her."

Boot camp did not work. This should have been expected, we know now. A wave of research on the subject through the early 2000s shone a light on a troubled industry. Adolescents who have gone through coercive treatment found such methods to be counter-productive, at best, harming relationships between young people and the adults trying to help them. At worst, even just a few weeks in these programs can catapult a young person from experimentation to a lifetime of interactions with "control systems," including social services, juvenile detention, and prison.[2]

Programs like the Utah camp that center on "tough love" are guided by a commonplace punitive logic. It is the same logic that is behind confrontational interventions, the imprisonment of people who use drugs, and the entire system of prohibition itself. In most situations, humans do respond to threats and punishment. But a drug addiction is, by definition, not one of those situations.

According to the National Institute on Drug Abuse, addiction is a chronic disorder, meaning its symptoms are recurring and persistent, characterized by compulsive drug seeking and, importantly, continued use *"despite harmful consequences."*[3] And yet punishment is America's typical response to a drug addiction. Society expects negative outcomes—abandonment, expulsion, coerced treatment, and imprisonment—to end one's addiction to drugs, which is a psychological disorder that is defined by a resistance to negative outcomes. By its very definition, America's primary approach to addiction will not work.

The result of Louise's time in Utah was therefore predictable. Tough love is punitive. Tough love is kicking your daughter out of the house or forcing your son to spend his weekends doing manual labor. It embodies the very sorts of harmful consequences that an addiction is known to defy. Note, however, tough love should not be confused with boundaries. Boundaries—limiting financial support, for example, or refusing to interact with a family member when they are high—are healthy, and often required for the mental health of an addicted person's loved ones. But tough love is different. Its punitive nature makes it counterproductive, less likely to resolve one's addiction than it is to intensify it.

A dislocation theory of addiction can help further explain why tough love so often backfires. Pioneered by Canadian psychologist Bruce Alexander and more recently popularized by bestselling author Johann Hari, this understanding of addiction suggests that people use drugs to compensate for a lack of connection, whether it's to one's parents, community, or environment. Now think of a common parental response to a teenager's drug use: "Cut them off." But if addiction is a response to broken connections, what good can we expect from this manifestation of tough love? The severed connection will lead many addicted people to seek more drugs.

Sarah and Walter acted out of desperation and felt their actions, though now understood as misguided, were justified. By the age of 16, Louise had all but dropped out of school, was huffing a lot of butane, dropping a lot of acid, and experimenting with cocaine. "I had found a group of friends, mostly men, and we hung out and did whatever we wanted," Louise says. Her parents' efforts were understandable, but every punitive action only made Louise's situation worse. When she returned from Utah to North Carolina for a second time, all bets were off.

Louise's parents were naïve but, by this time, they knew she was using drugs. The folks who ran the ranch in Utah had found a couple of joints Louise had hidden in the soles of her shoes. "My sweet child," Sarah thought. As difficult as it was to deal with Louise's out-of-control behavior, Sarah says perhaps the worst aspect of it was not having any understanding of why it was happening. The toll it took on the family was terrible. Sarah was a history professor at the local college and in her spare time worked with dropouts and troubled youth to get them back into school. "And now they were asking me, 'Do you know where your daughter was last night?'" Sarah recounts. "My high-school dropouts were with my daughter. So I quit my job there. I couldn't face my students laughing about what I didn't know about my daughter. That was really painful. It was something I had done for 20 years and something I was good at." Why was this happening to Louise and the parents who had raised her in a stable home that went to church on Sundays?

Louise had despised Charter Hills and hadn't forgiven her parents for the time she spent there. But something good had come of it. She had found a psychiatrist with whom she got along well enough. Sarah had kept in touch with her and now Louise was once again seeing her regularly. And finally, Sarah found part of the answer she was looking for.

"I would spend hours at the library," Sarah says. One evening there, she came across a medical-reference book that included a section on something called bipolar disorder. "My aunt is bipolar," Sarah thought. "And her life was strewn with hospitalizations and trouble." Sarah took this idea to Louise's therapist and eventually they discovered that Louise was bipolar, too, and quite severely.

"It has a name," Sarah thought. "It isn't just insanity. There is a reason for this and a reason for which I can feel some compassion."

Bipolar disorders are identified by abnormally high highs and extremely low lows. There are two main categories. The first, bipolar I, is characterized by manic episodes that include hyperactivity, euphoria, trouble concentrating, and impulse control, followed by periods of depression and fatigue. The second, bipolar II, similarly involves hyperactive periods, though not as intense as with bipolar I, and major depressive episodes, more severe than those of bipolar I.[4] About 40 percent of people who engage in problematic drug use struggle with a mental-health issue,[5] and 20 percent of people with a mental illness also struggle with a substance-use disorder.[6] For people who are bipolar, like Louise, that number rises further. A prominent study on this issue found that 61 percent of patients with bipolar I disorder and 48 percent of those with bipolar II will also meet the criteria for a drug addiction during their lifetime.[7] (For someone without a mental-health disorder, the chances they will develop a drug problem are just 6.1 percent.) Some psychiatric professionals go so far as to describe drug addiction as a part of the "bipolar spectrum" and "best considered under a unitary perspective."[8]

Louise was self-medicating. Stimulant drugs such as cocaine and methamphetamine are often sought by people who experience attention-deficit hyperactivity disorder (ADHD), for example, because those drugs can increase focus. Drugs that depress the central nervous system, such as benzodiazepines (Xanax and Valium) and alcohol, can provide temporary relief from anxiety, elevate one's mood, and ease uncomfortable social tensions. And pain medications and especially opioid-based painkillers such as heroin, OxyContin, and fentanyl, will alleviate emotional pain, just as they do physical discomfort.[9] Because the symptoms of a bipolar disorder oscillate wildly, from extreme highs to depressing lows, the door is left open for a myriad of mind-altering substances with varying propensities for addiction.[10]

As a child, Louise was never sexually abused or physically mistreated. But how she experiences the world is different. While most people fit comfortably in mainstream society, Louise wasn't quite built for that. "Sure," drug use is a choice, Louise acknowledges. But the transition from drug use to addiction is less of a choice, and especially so for people who struggle with a mental illness. When Louise was down, she was tormented by feelings of inadequacy, failure, and self-hate. "That fucking narrative, the internal critic or whatever it is that is in there, it is talking to me goddamn constantly, and it is fucking mean, man," Louise says.

"I don't think that I have ever used drugs because it was fun. My whole life, I've just been trying to be."

2

Trauma Was My Gateway Drug

"Someday I will look back and say, 'I did heroin for a summer,'" Jessica Tilley thought. *She never imagined how it would change the rest of her life.*

In the early 1990s, when she was 16 years old, Jess was just beginning to grapple with the years of sexual abuse that she suffered as a child. "Six and then eight, and eight to ten," Jess says. "It was through a family member, and a neighbor. And it was severe." By the time she was a teenager, Jess had gotten good at blocking out what had happened to her. She was seeing a therapist in her hometown of Northampton, Massachusetts, and her historically rocky relationship with her parents was improving. "And then I got raped, and nobody knew about it," she says. "That reawakened everything I had experienced as a child. Then I went to New York City and I did heroin for the first time."

With wild black hair and wearing her usual mix of punk and goth clothes, Jess looked mature (and cool) for her age. She and a few older teens were on the roof of an abandoned building. Her parents had let her travel into the city for a concert and Jess relished the freedom this allowed. It was a beautiful evening. One of them loaded up a small shot for Jess and she accepted it. "I finally feel normal," she thought. "And what's wrong with feeling normal? I feel safe, and what's wrong with feeling safe?" It was the first time that she consumed a drug of any sort, save for alcohol, the first time she injected drugs, and the first time she tried opioids.

The rape Jess suffered earlier that year forced back to the surface terrible memories from her childhood. Then she was introduced to heroin and learned of its power to gently push the trauma of her childhood down far enough to where she could again forget that it existed. Nearly 30 years later, Jess recalls dates and locations with photographic accuracy. She is intensely self-aware and discusses her struggles with addiction like a therapist presents their analysis of a patient. Assessing her history of drug use, Jess points to something called the Adverse Childhood Experiences (ACE) study.

It is almost impossible to overstate the impact that the ACE study has had on our understanding of trauma as it relates to childhood development, mental health, addiction, and health issues ranging from headaches to obesity and diabetes. The simple yes-or-no questionnaire asks patients if, before the age of 18, they experienced any of 10 categories of abuse, neglect, or household dysfunction. Each category is worth one point, and the total is an individual's ACE score. ("Was a biological parent ever lost to you through divorce, abandonment, or other reason?" a sample question reads.) The original ACE study was led by co–principal investigators Vincent Felitti, then a physician with Kaiser Permanente and today semi-retired with a clinical professorship at the University of California, San Diego, and Robert Anda, an epidemiologist with the U.S. Centers for Disease Control and Prevention.

In the early 1980s, Felitti was a doctor with Kaiser Permanente's department of preventive medicine. He was working mostly with patients who struggled with obesity and became intrigued when a new drug, Optifast, led to significant weight loss. It wasn't the drug that fascinated him; rather, it was some of his patients' reactions to its effectiveness. "We discovered that this was a terrifying experience to many," Felitti says. "They fled the program in the midst of their success, rapidly regaining all of the weight." Investigating this unexpected result, Felitti interviewed one woman about when exactly it was that she first identified as overweight. "I was raped at

21 and gained 105 pounds afterward," the woman told him. Then she muttered to herself, "Overweight is overlooked, and that's the way I need to be." Felitti thought: "My God, what we've been seeing as the problem, she is seeing as her solution. A solution to a problem that we knew nothing about."

Felitti began asking more of his obese patients about any experience they had with sexual abuse and, to his shock, "it seemed every other person was acknowledging such a history." A small study followed and then a larger one. To handle the massive amounts of data, Felitti partnered with the CDC and Anda. Some 17,330 patient interviews later, the pair were staring at astonishing results. The Adverse Childhood Experiences study revealed that abuse—trauma that occurred years or even decades in the past—often led to significant changes later in life. If you were beaten or raped as a child, if your parents divorced when you were young, or if you went hungry growing up, you were significantly more likely as an adult to experience clinical depression, come down with cancer, and smoke cigarettes. The strongest correlation was with a suicide attempt. The second was injection drug use.

In 1998, Felitti and Anda published the results of their study, which were eye-opening. Compared to someone who underwent no significant trauma, a person who experienced four or more categories of traumatic events as a child is 7.4 times more likely to develop a problem with alcohol. For illicit drugs, the number is 4.7; for injection drugs, it is 10.3.[1] "The behaviors such as alcohol or drug abuse, smoking, or sexual promiscuity are likely the result of the effects of ACE on childhood development, which we now know to be neurodevelopment," Felitti and Anda found. "In many, if not most cases, the behaviors may act to alleviate the emotional or social distress that results from ACE. Thus, these behaviors, typically considered to be problems, continue because they function as short-term solutions, even though they have detrimental, long-term effects."[2]

Researchers subsequently built on the initial ACE study and

continue to today, with findings that are immensely useful to the way we understand addiction and treat addicted people. For instance, a history of trauma is especially common among drug users who favor opioids.[3] Academics surveyed hundreds of drug-using psychiatric patients and learned that of those who experienced physical abuse, sexual abuse, or both, 62.5 percent reported "heavy" opioid use.[4] In addition, a higher ACE score not only corresponds with a higher rate of illicit-drug use, but also makes a person more likely to begin using hard drugs like cocaine and heroin at a younger age, more likely to use drugs intravenously, and more likely to experience an overdose.[5]

Felitti marvels at their results. "The relationships are extraordinary," he says. Drug use is an abuse victim's attempt to self-medicate, he explains; therefore, the police persecution of someone who uses drugs becomes a case of victimizing a victim. "What we perceive as the problem turns out to be, yes, a societal problem," Felitti says. "But from the patient's standpoint, it is often an unconsciously attempted solution." Albeit an imperfect solution, Felitti adds. "We had a sign painted on the wall at the obesity program: 'It's hard to get enough of something that almost works.'"

Prestigious medical professionals who continue to advance Felitti's work include the Child Trauma Academy's Dr. Bruce Perry, celebrated author Dr. Gabor Maté, and Dr. Nadine Burke Harris, who was appointed surgeon general for the state of California in 2020. All three have written important books on the subject. Maté's *In the Realm of Hungry Ghosts: Close Encounters with Addiction*, for example, posits that the sort of abuse Jess suffered beginning when she was six years old physically rewired sections of her brain to program a proclivity for problematic drug use. It explains how the four systems of the brain most relevant to addiction—the opioid attachment-reward system, the dopamine-based incentive-motivation apparatus, the self-regulation areas of the prefrontal cortex, and the stress-response mechanism—are affected by a person's environment. "To various degrees, in all addicted persons these systems are out of kilter," the book says. "The less effective our own internal chemical happiness system is, the more driven we are to seek joy or relief through drug-taking or through other compulsions we perceive as rewarding."[6]

It's estimated that 80 percent of women with a substance-use disorder previously experienced physical abuse, sexual abuse, or both, and between 30 and 59 percent subsequently struggle with posttraumatic stress disorder (PTSD).[7]

Despite Jess's awareness of the ACE study and the phenomenon it describes, keeping at bay its worst consequences remains a struggle she concedes she often loses. "If you look at ACE, I score 8 out of 10," Jess says today. "Trauma was my gateway drug."

Of course, this clarity didn't come until many years after Jess's first experiences with drugs. Attending high school in the early 1990s, she was simply confused. A fashionable teenage goth, Jess rarely wore anything that wasn't black or white. The same went for her hair and nails. Her lips were usually red, though. She was different, an outcast, but also the sort of high-school kid who could lead a clique of her own. Jess returned to school from summer break after having injected heroin for several consecutive days. She hadn't used for long enough to feel the pain and anxiety of full-blown withdrawal, but she wasn't feeling great, either. She looked around the classroom and saw the other kids in high spirits, dressed in sharp clothes for the new school year, excitedly catching up with friends they hadn't seen since the spring. Meanwhile, Jess pulled away, into her own head. "I wasn't sick but I had a hangover. And I wondered, 'I don't think anybody else at school shot heroin this weekend.'"

The mental-health issues that Jess experienced as a result of childhood trauma intensified as she moved through adolescence. "I was really, really suicidal, begging my parents for help," she says. "I tried to cut my wrists but it was more passive. I couldn't bring myself to do it, but I was so sad. There were so many instances where I was obviously crying out for help."

Eventually, her parents did intervene. Toward the end of 1993, Jess was sent to Manchester Memorial Hospital's psychiatric unit in neighboring Connecticut. "It was horrible," Jess begins. When she received attention from staff, it was often with the same sort of "tough love" that defined Louise's time in Utah. Because she had tried to kill herself, Jess was placed inside a black body bag as some sort of twisted plan to scare her straight. Such treatment was the exception, however, because during her time at Manchester, Jess seldom received much attention of any kind. She was largely abandoned in a padded cell, forced to remain alone with her thoughts. "That was one of the more traumatic events I've been through," she says. "It left me with this impression: Do not ask for help. This is how society will treat you if something is wrong with you. If you feel depressed, if you are not competent enough to get through life, if you act too sensitive, you are screwed."

Through ups and downs, Jess continued to attend classes at East Hartford High School. Despite her fragile emotional state, Jess excelled academically and was placed in the school's gifted program. When she graduated from high school in 1994, it was with honors. "I had this very double life," Jess says. "I did well in school but I was amazed: how did nobody know that something is wrong?"

Her parents' second attempt to help their troubled teenage daughter went better than the first. Jess started therapy the following year and actually enjoyed it. "I truly believe that saved me," she says. "I did stop feeling suicidal after I started confronting a lot of my childhood trauma." But feelings of teenage isolation stuck with her and Jess increasingly embraced the life of an outcast. The second she could, Jess moved out of her parents' house and into a sort of misfits' paradise. She left home with $600 in her pocket and nothing else. It was a carefree time, living with other teenagers in an artsy neighborhood on the west side of Hartford, working minimum-wage jobs and not thinking much about the future. She lived with another runaway named Tonya and whoever else needed a place to stay for a while. Tonya was more experienced with drugs and used heroin in the house they shared. "Why can't you just stop using?" Jess asked her over and over again. "If you loved me, you would stop." Instead, the two began using together.

Slowly, a crew formed around them. A childhood friend named Chelsea joined in, then a girl named Shana. "Her mother had died of a heroin overdose when she was eight," Jess says. "Shana would always say that she tried heroin because she wanted to know what her mother loved more than her." The group experimented with drugs until they weren't experimenting anymore. Ever so gradually, things began to unravel. Tonya started taking money from a few guys for sex. Within a year, Shana was looking completely strung out. They had started by using together on weekends, but soon enough, they were getting high on weekdays, too. Still only in their late teens, there weren't a lot of places for the group to hang out. Jess and Tonya's place became the home base for other kids their age who used opioids. The pointlessness of it all began to get to Jess and she decided she'd had enough. "I fucking hate heroin," she thought. "I don't want it anywhere around me." The coming September, Jess was scheduled to attend university. Rather than wait for the end of the summer, she packed her things that July and drove one hour north, back to Northampton, Massachusetts, and there moved into "a hot mess."

Northampton is perfectly representative of small-town New England, about as American as it gets. There's a Main Street with a prominent town hall at one end of it and a couple of tall church spires within view from there. With a population of 28,500 and almost all of them with left-leaning political tendencies, Northampton has so far managed to hold back most corporate chains. Its shops and restaurants remain largely independent, family-owned businesses. While picturesque with its thick surrounding forest and folksy charm, Northampton is also emblematic of the decline of factory America and the pain that followed. A 20-minute drive from Northampton is Springfield, where there once was a sizable manufacturing sector. As that industry declined there and throughout the greater New York Capital District, Northampton suffered. While Springfield still produces Smith & Wesson handguns, as it has since 1852, many other large factories that once offered Northampton residents steady union jobs shuttered their doors many years ago. Since then, however, Northampton has reinvented itself as a bit of a college town and enjoys a youthful energy.

Close enough to New York for heroin to have always been a bit of a problem, Northampton also had fentanyl early. Massachusetts ranks near the top of states most affected by the overdose crisis, most years coming in just below spot number 10. In 2019, it had an overdose death rate of 32.1 per 100,000 people, which equated to 2,210 deaths.[8]

When Jess moved back to Northampton, she began dating a musician named Jesse and together they rented one-third of a three-bedroom house. Jesse's best friend, Ian, took the second room, two girls took the third, and a fifth roommate slept wherever he could find enough space to lie down. Another guy, Walt, had grown close with everyone and became another unofficial roommate. The house got crowded and then complicated. Jess fell for Ian and moved out of Jesse's bedroom and into Ian's, which was just across the hall from Jesse's. A scuffle promptly followed. Ian was left with a broken arm and Jesse a black eye; there were bruises but nothing else came of the fight. The house dynamic was filled with free love and no judgment, or at least not to anyone's face.

One night, Jesse asked Jess if she could get him heroin. Jess wasn't using at the time, having successfully left the drug in Hartford. But she knew where to get it and, feeling guilty for leaving him, told Jesse she would pick up the drugs he was after. Jesse split the bag with her and Ian and now the three of them were using together on weekends. "It was that feeling I missed so much," Jess says. "Being present without having to be present. I felt safe. I felt warm. I felt comfortable in my own skin."

Again, things were okay until they were not. Jess was working at a little grocery store and noticed she was having trouble showing up on time for work. She began feeling sick when she wasn't using heroin, and so she began using heroin more often. It was time for a change. Jess moved into a different apartment with Ian and together they got on methadone, a synthetic opioid agonist that relieves cravings for heroin and similar drugs while blocking their euphoric effects. They were doing really well until, coming home from the grocery store one night, Jess found her good friend Josh waiting for her on their front steps. "You want to take a trip?" he asked her, using the group's nickname for heroin. "Sure, why not?" Jess said. "And that started the cycle all over again." Josh moved into the house with them and he was small-time dealing so now Jess had a steady supply without having to walk to the corner or even put on pants.

They were young, had few responsibilities, and it was still mostly all fun and games. Then Ian overdosed. Jess had just left work and was walking up Main Street, back to the house they shared, and an ambulance sped past her. Something told her it was headed to the same place she was, and a bolt of panic shot through her. She ran. Jess made it home just in time to see her boyfriend carried out on a stretcher into the back of that ambulance. Most of his face was covered by an oxygen mask but Jess could see that his eyes were closed. Standing on the sidewalk at the edge of the property, she struggled to take in what was happening. A cop stood a few feet away, similarly surveying the scene. He turned to Jess. "Your boyfriend's dead," he said. "You still think heroin is cool?"

Jess crumbled. The next few hours passed in a blur. Police searched the house. They didn't have a warrant, but no one was in any state to think of asking for one. "They threatened to arrest us," Jess says. "They wanted us to work with them to get the dealer." Of course, none of that mattered. Ian was dead. That was all Jess could think about until the house phone rang. It was Ian. He was at the hospital and needed a ride home. Ian was alive. With indescribable relief, Jess realized that the police officer had lied to her, trying to teach her a lesson or just messing with her because he could. "For four hours, I thought Ian was dead," Jess says.

Ian was alive and that was a very good thing. But his trip to the hospital and the cops ransacking their apartment was only the beginning of the blowback that his overdose would bring on the group. When Ian had turned blue, one of their roommates called 911. The subsequent commotion—the ambulance and two police cars that arrived shortly after—had caught the attention of their landlord. Twenty-four hours later, they were evicted. Not only that, they were made into an example. Their landlord told everybody in the building, "They're being evicted because they were using drugs." Northampton is a small town so the news spread quickly. A couple of days later, Jess's boss heard about what had happened and the grocery store fired her. Jess wondered if it had been a mistake for them to call 911. Were they supposed to have let Ian die? What was the message here? "It was really messed up," Jess says.

An eviction remains a too-common consequence of a drug addiction. In many jurisdictions, "Chronic-nuisance ordinances" (CNO) hold a landlord accountable for a tenant's 911 calls and therefore give landlords an incentive to evict a tenant who calls 911.[9] When people are regularly evicted for using drugs, it amounts to a system of housing regulations that systemically penalizes individuals who struggle with a substance-use disorder. Dangerously, CNOs can deter people from calling 911 in the event of an overdose, impeding access to emergency care.[10] What's more, an eviction for using drugs does not discourage drug use. Instead, the drug-using victim of an eviction usually continues using drugs and does so in riskier circumstances that increase the likelihood of a fatal overdose.[11]

Losing her home and her job did not prompt Jess to stop using heroin. "My drug use got a lot worse because of all that," she says. "I wouldn't have hit rock button if I hadn't been shoved down." It all reminded her of the time she had spent inside Manchester Psychiatric Hospital: "Do not ask for help. This is how society will treat you."

Jess was 19 years old and these experiences—how police treated her, the eviction, and the stigma that now seemed to follow her around Northampton—were piling up and feeding into Jess's budding identity as an activist.

Four years earlier, when Jess was just 15, she had grown close with an older girl named Jen, "this 1970s-looking punk-rock chick," and the two began spending time in New York City, which is a three-hour drive from Northampton. In addition to style, Jen also had a driver's license and a father who had an apartment in the city. Jess had a lot of freedom as a teenager. She and her mom had a deal: sleepovers are okay and you can stay out as late as you want, but no lying and I always know where you are. She spent a lot of time in New York City with Jen and her punk-rock friends. It was the music that interested her most. They would hang out at clubs like the Limelight, Coney Island High in the East Village, or Cathedral if it was a Tuesday. As Jen pulled Jess into Manhattan's punk-rock scene of the 1990s, she also introduced her to activism. One afternoon, the pair ducked into a meeting down the street from Coney Island High convened by ACT UP, the legendary activist collective that accomplished so much for AIDS awareness and LGBTQ rights. Jess recalls she could literally feel her eyes growing wide as she listened to whoever was speaking that day. "I want to do this," she thought. "I *need* to do this. How do I do this?"

It was on one of these teenage trips to New York that Jess learned she wasn't alone. One evening, she was at ABC No Rio, another beloved venue from the 1990s. She was there for a U.K. Subs concert, but was distracted from the music, preoccupied with falling in love. Across the club was a girl wearing black lace, a 1920s dress, Doc Martens, and lots of silver jewelry. "Who is this girl?" Jess thought. The girl spotted Jess, walked over to her, and said, "I need this." She gently removed the wide-brimmed black hat that Jess was wearing, the sort a widow wears to a funeral, and placed it on her own head. And they struck up a conversation. "My name's Rachel," she said. "Rachel Auspitz."

The two were separated as the concert got a little rowdy but connected again the following morning. Jess had used heroin after the show and couldn't hide how rough she was feeling in the harsh light of the new day. "You've got to be careful," Rachel, nine years Jess's senior, told her. Rachel was an activist, on-again-off-again drug user, HIV-positive, and not afraid to talk about it. For the next few years, Rachel became something of an older sister to Jess, like the kind who's away at university. They exchanged letters and Jess tried to find Rachel anytime she made a trip into New York. "I was dealing with a lot of trauma and she would give me advice," Jess says. Then Rachel disappeared. "I never knew what happened." It would be nearly a decade before she found her again.

At another ACT UP gathering, this one in Central Park, Jess joined in a large demonstration that called for housing for people with HIV/AIDS. Those in attendance were mostly members of the city's punk-rock subculture, like Jess was by this point. She admired the group's one rule: no judgment. This was 1992 and the "gay cancer," as it was still sometimes referred to, was burning through LGBTQ communities and, though they received less attention, people who used intravenous drugs. Public service warnings about HIV/AIDS were on billboards, in magazines, and seemingly interrupting every television show on the air. "Anyone can get it," Americans were told over and over again during those years. Though the message was true and shared with good intentions, because the disease was so closely associated with the LGBTQ community and drug users, it had the effect of raising not only awareness but also stigma. People were afraid to touch anyone who was gay. Anyone with visible symptoms of HIV/AIDS could not even find stable housing. This wasn't right, Jess understood. She marched with ACT UP that day and felt pride for the aspects of her life for which she had previously been taught to feel shame. "Whose blood? Our blood," Jess shouted with the group. "We're here, we're queer, get used to it." It was her first taste of activism, "and I was in love with it," she says.

Back in Northampton, four years later, Jess was sleeping on a friend's couch after she was evicted and fired from her job because her friends had called 911 for Ian's overdose. This wasn't right, either, she thought. Jess saw a reason to raise her voice for people stigmatized because they used drugs.

3

A Moment of Need

Louise did not like taking medication for her bipolar disorder. For starters, nothing worked. And anything that did have an effect left her numb. "I still don't take meds," Louise says. "I have never found meds that didn't dumb me down. I don't want to be Seroquel'd out in a corner somewhere, you know?" She pauses a moment and adds, "And anyway, by that time, I had already put together my own regimen."

Louise was self-medicating with alcohol, hallucinogens, and increasing amounts of cocaine. She stumbled through her later teenage years and hooked up with an older guy named Reggie Vincent who sold drugs. That took care of her cocaine supply but brought on a bunch of other problems. Reggie was Black and not everybody close to Louise approved of their mixed-race relationship. Some friends deserted her, eroding a support network that was already very thin. For a while, things were still all right. "At first, he was an amazing guy who offered me the safety and fun I always wanted," Louise says. "We ran the streets and he protected me." Before long, however, Reggie was cheating on her. "He turned abusive and insane," she says. "And my ability to cope with any of this was zero. Growing up, I was sheltered. This wasn't a part of the script for my life. And now here were these bad people who were appearing in my life and doing awful shit." It wasn't like Louise could call the police. She used drugs. That meant that option for help was closed.

Then, on October 25, 1996, things got complicated, in the most wonderful way possible. Louise gave birth to her first child, Selena, and fell in love. "The drugs were still there but I was a good mom," she says. "I was doing all of the things that I needed to do."

Louise knows what people will think of her time as a new mother who used drugs. People will argue that authorities should have taken her daughter from her as soon as she was born. But what does more harm to a child: leaving them in the home of a loving mother who uses drugs, or removing them from that situation, but severing the bond between the child and their mother? A growing body of scientific research indicates that Selena would have likely fared worse without Louise's care.

Neonatal abstinence syndrome (NAS) is the medical term for an infant born experiencing drug withdrawal. Studies have found that punishing women for using drugs while pregnant discourages them from seeking treatment for a substance-use disorder and from securing prenatal care, which in turn results in higher rates of NAS among their babies.[1] One paper states that when infants dependent on drugs were kept with their mothers, the percentage of them administered medications for withdrawal declined from 68 percent to 9 percent, and the duration of hospital stays declined from 17 days to 6.5.[2] Other studies have replicated those results.[3] Simply by remaining with their mothers, babies experiencing withdrawal can be sufficiently soothed to the point where they need less medication and fewer days in the hospital.

Regardless of a mother's drug use, she remains the best person to provide care for her newborn baby, and depending on the severity of circumstances, this generally holds true as the child progresses in age. Even short-term stays in foster care, for example, can severely harm a child's mental health, resulting in lifelong trauma that we know can lead to the very sort of drug use that the original placement in foster care was presumably intended to prevent.[4]

Louise embraced motherhood, if imperfectly. Reggie was, however, tragically unprepared to raise a family. He was immature, coming and going as he pleased, and he was at a point with his addiction where it controlled most of his life. Meanwhile, Louise's parents were not entirely ready to see their first grandchild born of mixed race in the American South. "We had no support," Louise recalls. "We were homeless. We were living in crack hotels with Selena. We had no way to take care of her." Their drug use spiraled and Reggie began abusing her physically. Then he was diagnosed with a kind of kidney cancer, renal medullary carcinoma. The disease was detected very late and Reggie was told he would likely die within a matter of months.

On Selena's second birthday, Louise married him and became Louise Beale Vincent. "It's complicated," Louise says. She was torn by mixed emotions. Reggie hit her. At the same time, he was Selena's father and Louise was still only 22. She believed she could make it all work. Meanwhile, Reggie was getting sicker. The drugs he was doing didn't help his cancer, and he never received proper medical care.

Louise was not a socially conscious person during this period of her life. Maintaining her cocaine addiction and caring for Selena took up just about every hour of the day. But when Reggie was diagnosed with cancer, Louise noticed differences in the way North Carolina's health care system treated Black people compared to how it cared for people who looked like her. Her mom had cancer at the same time that Reggie did and Louise witnessed the care she received versus how Reggie was treated. "They wouldn't give him pain pills. They were worried he was going to sell them, which was insane. He had been given two months to live and they wouldn't give him a fucking Percocet. It was infuriating."

Reggie was a Black man addicted to drugs and, in the eyes of his doctors, that's all he was. Implicit bias factors heavily in interactions between care providers and patients, affecting treatment decisions and health outcomes. The result: during interactions with the health care system, people of color consistently fare worse than white people.[5] They are also less likely to find adequate treatment for pain. Studies show that fewer Black people are prescribed opioids for pain and, when they are, they are prescribed less of them.[6] Louise watched how Reggie was treated and never forgot it.

"That was my first view of the system, and there being some shit there that doesn't make any sense," Louise says. "Up until then, I had thought people were the same."

At the same time, Louise didn't have a lot of sympathy for the man. Reggie never grew into his role as a father. He only cared about himself, or at least that's all the cocaine would allow him to care about. He also continued to be abusive. Meanwhile, the cancer ate him alive. Toward the end, Reggie found Jesus and everyone was very impressed, except for Louise. Two months later, Reggie did succumb to the disease. He passed away in November 1998. Louise was left a single mother living in poverty with bipolar disorder and a vicious addiction to cocaine. "Cocaine was the first drug that I was introduced to, but I never really liked it. I get too high, I get weird," she says. "I don't feel good. I do it, and I hate it. And if I don't have something to come down on, then it's a phenomenal mess." Chaos swept through her life in waves.

Her mom did try to help. "When my mother is in my life is when my life is better," Louise says. Sarah even bought Louise a small house just a few blocks from her own, which went a long way to provide a healthy degree of stability for Selena. An artist friend visited and painted the baby's room like a jungle with tall trees and elephants. "It was really pretty," Louise says. "I was trying to be a cool mom. Selena was happy. We had a little cocker spaniel. We made it fun. We tried to make it as normal as we could."

While at first Sarah disapproved of Louise having a baby at such a young age, any reluctance she felt toward Selena was by this time rapidly dissipating. "She wouldn't give her back!" Louise says with a laugh.

A precarious support system fell into place while Louise continued to struggle with her addiction. "A drug-using mother, that's despicable to people," she says, very much aware of the judgment she commonly faces. "Boys will be boys but girls are still sluts and crack whores. A woman who uses drugs, that's just the most hated thing in the world." But by all accounts, Louise was a good mom. Not perfect. Sadly, the state of her drug addiction did affect the amount of attention she gave to her new baby. But Louise was in love with Selena and, with Sarah's help, Selena was always fed, into bed on time, and raised as a happy-go-lucky toddler. "I was a cool mom," Louise says, allowing herself the small compliment.

Part of Louise's problem was that there was never a shortage of drugs. After Reggie, she fell for a guy named Tommy. Tommy wasn't exactly a dealer, or not a real dealer, anyway. But he kept himself in close proximity to a lot of dealers and moved enough drugs to cover his own habit. Tommy gave Louise access to free coke and this took a lot of hassle off Louise's plate. But then Tommy got too far into his own supply. He started smoking crack and let the drug take him to a bad place. "Tommy wouldn't act right," Louise says. "He wouldn't leave the house. Every time I would come home with coke, he would take it. I couldn't get him to act right. He wouldn't come out of the bathroom. Tommy was on crack and it was a fucking mess."

Louise took over his business. She was good at it. Very good. She already knew just about every hard drug user in Greensboro. In no time at all, she had a small crew working under her and was making enough money to maintain her own habit plus pay the bills. But it wasn't long before Louise began to go as crazy as Tommy, she admits. "I had enough money and enough people around me stealing that I installed cameras," Louise begins. "We had all these cool contraptions because people hawked all their shit to us. I had all this surveillance equipment everywhere and I started watching what people are doing. And it's insidious. You start watching what people are doing when they don't know you're watching and you hear what they're saying when they don't know you're listening. . . ." Louise trails off. "It messes with you."

This was 1998 or 1999, and, somewhat remarkably, Louise had still never taken an opioid. There wasn't much heroin around North Carolina at the time, at least not in Greensboro's Guilford County. But soon, prescription painkillers began showing up on the street. A couple of women who Louise sold cocaine to were short on cash one day and offered a pair of OxyContin pills instead. When she accepted the pills, it changed her relationship with drugs forever.

Up until this point, her drug use was more about the people she was using with as opposed to the drugs themselves. She had always felt alone in life, like no one understood her. But with a crew using cocaine together, there was camaraderie. Of course, it was mostly imagined. "I was beginning to really realize that my friends in the community that I had developed through dealing were not real friends," she says. But it was still enough for her to feel a part of something. "For a long time, it was about relationships and stuff. Then, when I did opiates, it was about the drugs. Then, yeah, it did become about the drugs."

Louise felt better on cocaine than she did sober. But cocaine still didn't let her feel okay. It brought her mental state closer to what most of society considers a baseline, but not all the way there. Issues likely related to her bipolar disorder left Louise feeling intensely uncomfortable in the world. She felt alone, isolated, and misunderstood. She could not tolerate bad vibes. An uncomfortable room could make Louise feel like she had to escape from her own skin. These feelings crawled through her, prickling every inch. Louise simply did not feel right in this world. Until opioids.

"I loved it. There's just nothing better. Those kinds of things are indescribable," Louise says. "I just felt right. And for somebody who is never happy, always anxious, and never okay, that was love. That was love and I was safe. I wanted it from then on."

The pharmaceutical industry played a role in America's opioid epidemic, but not exactly as it's usually ascribed. The accepted narrative goes like this:

Pharmaceutical corporations such as Purdue Pharma convinced doctors that a new generation of opioid-based pain medications, including OxyContin, were less addictive than earlier medications. Meanwhile, pain was categorized as the "fifth vital sign," joining temperature, blood pressure, respiratory rate, and heart rate as part of a doctor's basic assessment of a patient. The medical community was pressured to treat pain with the same seriousness it did a high fever. This resulted in doctors overprescribing addictive painkillers, not only hooking some patients, but also allowing a glut of pills to pour over onto the black market.

From 1991 to 2005, the number of opioid prescriptions filled in America more than doubled, from 76 million to 163 million.[7] Overdose deaths subsequently climbed a similar trajectory, nearly tripling, from fewer than 10,000 in 1991 to 29,800 in 2005.[8]

The consequences played out at the local level. In Louise's home county of Guilford, for example, precisely 149,372,831 opioid pills were distributed over the course of eight years until 2014. That's 34 pills for every man, woman, and child, each year. Around Jess's hometown of Northampton, 44,652,920 pills were sent to Hampshire County, or 31 pills per person per year.[9]

During the same years, drug overdose deaths in North Carolina increased from 906 to 1,150. In Massachusetts, they rose from 876 to 1,213.[10]

Across the country, fatal overdoses climbed from a rough annual average of 15,000 deaths through the 1990s to 29,800 deaths in 2005.[11]

This popular narrative is true, but it is a story removed from context that is crucial to understanding who uses opioids and why they are using them to the point of overdosing. Many people who use heroin today did start with prescription opioids—about 75 percent[12]—but a majority of that group did not obtain those pills legally. Patient case files from 157 addiction treatment facilities reveal that 78 percent of those who used OxyContin never received the drug legally.[13] In 2013–14, people who use prescription painkillers where similarly asked where they got them from, and just 22.1 percent reported their regular doctor was the source. Meanwhile, 65.9 percent said it was a friend or relative (whether given, purchased, or stolen), 4.8 percent conceded they used a dealer, and 3.6 percent said "some other way."[14] While a lot of people who use opioids did start with legal pills, only a minority obtained those legal pills legally.

Overprescribing played a role in the current crisis, but not the way it's explained in 90-second segments on the evening news. Pills are significantly less stigmatized than heroin, and it was pharmaceutical companies and doctors who made pills more widely available. But the reality of America's opioid epidemic is that it is and largely always was one of *illicit* drug use. This does not make anyone less deserving of the public's sympathy, nor does it erode the need for reformed drug policy. But it does mean that, contrary to popular belief, the first wave of the opioid epidemic was people using drugs *illegally*. This is significant because it suggests that if it hadn't been prescription pills, it probably would have been something else. This notion is supported by more recent data showing that as doctors prescribe fewer opioid painkillers, more people are not only turning to heroin, but also using more cocaine and methamphetamine.[15]

People are hurting. They are learning that the American Dream is no longer a promise made to everyone. Corporate executives are paid more, employees are paid less, and economic inequality is approaching levels not seen since the Great Depression.[16] Adjusted for inflation, today's federal minimum wage is roughly one-third what it was in the late 1960s.[17] For the vast majority of Black Americans, generational wealth remains elusive. From 1983 to 2016, a white household's income rose by one-third while a Black household's declined by as much as half, bringing racial inequality to a point where the average Black household possesses one-tenth the wealth of the typical white one.[18] Since the end of the Great Recession in 2009, America's stock market has soared, but the richest

1 percent of the country's population controls as much as 80 percent of the stock market's total value.[19] Until the COVID-19 pandemic, the country's unemployment rate remained relatively low, at less than 5 percent; however, how the American government calculates the unemployment rate has become less meaningful. The official unemployment rate only includes people as unemployed if they are actively looking for work. As factories moved overseas, blue-collar jobs were lost to automation, and intensifying inequality left workers feeling like the game was rigged, many people conceded defeat. This group is no longer looking for work and, therefore, is technically not unemployed, but rather is officially considered to have dropped out of the market entirely. From 1999 to 2019, the civilian labor force participation rate declined from 67 percent to 63 percent.[20]

These people have given up. They sit at home with feelings of inadequacy and uselessness, and with access to drugs that can provide some escape. What researchers call "deaths of despair," consisting of fatalities attributed to suicide, alcohol, or a drug overdose, increased for whites aged 45 to 54 from 30 per 100,000 people in 1990 to 92 per 100,000 in 2017.*[21] The overall effect is so significant that it is dragging down life expectancy for the entire United States. From 2014 to 2017, the average life expectancy for an American citizen declined from 78.9 years to 78.6.[22] The difference might seem small, but in the world's wealthiest nation, where sanitation, nutrition, and health care generally only improve, a decrease in life expectancy is simply not supposed to happen. The fact that it did, three years in a row, in the United States of America, is an unprecedented and profoundly troubling indicator of the nation's over-

---

* Anne Case and Angus Deaton's provocative book on the subject, *Deaths of Despair and the Future of Capitalism*, focuses on middle-aged non-Hispanic whites but notes similar trends exist in younger age groups and in Black populations.

all health, and the toll inflicted by drugs, and the despair driving people to use them.

Given the severity of Louise's cocaine addiction and the level of paranoia that was setting in, it wasn't actually such a bad thing for Louise to find opioids. Mainstream American discourse demands any respectable person parrot the supposition that drugs are bad, at least most of the time. But at this point in Louise's life, opioids provided some balance and brought a bit of much-needed sedation. "I could never get the combination of my drugs right," she says. "It was hard for me to sell drugs once I'd get all jacked up on cocaine. I needed to be awake to sell all the drugs, but I'd get so high I wouldn't want to go out of the house. So I'd drink. But if I drank, I'd lose all the money and get all fucked up like that. So opiates were really exactly what I needed. They just made things perfect."

Or almost perfect. Amidst so much turmoil, Louise had somehow missed that she was pregnant again. She was on birth control, and so this development was a complete surprise. "How far along is it?" Louise asked during her first meeting with an OB-GYN. "Do you want to know whether it's a girl or a boy?" the doctor replied. Louise was already at five months.

Summer was born on June 19, 2001. "I knew Tommy was not in a good place to have a child," Louise says. "Shit hit the almighty fan."

Louise suffered from postpartum psychosis, a psychiatric condition that is relatively rare, but less rare if you are bipolar.[23] Deeply paranoid, manic, and disassociated from reality, Louise grew convinced that four-year-old Selena was out to kill newborn Summer. To protect the infant, Louise stopped sleeping. "I was worried about her safety while I was sleeping and so I stayed up for nine days," she says. "I really think I was just insane."

The cocaine didn't help. Louise had connected with a woman in her mid-20s named Amanda[†] and the two of them were making money. "We sold dope out in the country to guys who didn't want to deal with Black men," Louise explains. "Redneck motherfuckers." Their phone was always ringing. Louise felt important, and like she had friends. By now, however, she had also gotten herself addicted to heroin. "I snorted it for a long time," Louise says. "Then, eventually, there was some sort of drought, and all we could get was tar.* So I couldn't snort it anymore. Then someone said, 'Here, shoot it.'"

"At that point, I was sick [experiencing withdrawal] and I didn't care," Louise continues. "Whatever. So I shot that up. And then it was like, 'Oh, wow, I can put everything in there.' I didn't inject for a long time. Then, when I did inject, I injected everything [cocaine and heroin]."

It's difficult to comprehend how much Louise was dealing with at one time. Baby Summer was usually with her grandmother on Tommy's side, and that took some pressure off. But even with Sarah's help, five-year-old Selena was a full-time job. Louise was bipolar and not on medication. She was addicted to cocaine and now heroin, too. Her boyfriend was unreliable, unpredictable, and abusive. By this point, Louise was a midlevel dealer managing a small crew. Miraculously, she was also attending Greensboro College, working toward a master's degree in public health. She was holding everything together, but only by a thread.

"Selena still went to school," Louise notes. "Somehow, life goes on." Selena also got along well with Amanda, Louise's new partner in dealing. They adored each other, and so Louise's "co-worker" often doubled as a babysitter. They read Selena bedtime stories together and ensured Selena always had a "magic blanky" that helped her sleep.

Meanwhile, Tommy was a growing problem. He had fallen in love with Selena and was trying to make an honest living for her and

---

* There are two main types of heroin. Black tar heroin, more common on the West Coast, looks and feels like its name suggests: tar. It is sticky and its viscous quality makes it impossible to snort. Powder heroin, more common on the East Coast, sometimes comes in small rocks but is easy to break up and snort. Both types can be cooked with water and injected.

Summer, Louise says. "He had a painting business so he was trying to get things together and calm down." But at the end of the day, it just wasn't working. Worse, he wouldn't leave. To get rid of him, Louise enlisted the help of a dealer friend named Brice[†]. "I'll make sure that he doesn't bother you," Brice told her. "Alright, cool," Louise thought. Brice was good to her, at first. When, a month later, the police caught her with an ounce of cocaine, it was Brice who paid to bail her out. Before long, Tommy was gone, and before much longer after that, Louise was in a relationship with Brice. And it was worse than Louise ever could have imagined.

Brice was sadistic. He beat Louise, unpredictably, not particularly out of anger or for any reason at all. He was cruel. He once poured a drink over her in public, just to show people that he could. He raped her. Every interaction was a manipulative play for power. Louise ran from Brice but friends would rat her out, which messed with Louise's head as badly as any physical abuse. "People would tell him where I was for a $5 piece of crack, knowing what the deal was going to be [that he would beat her]," Louise says. "So I really saw horror. What people would do." Brice would lock Louise in the bathroom, forcing her into withdrawal cold turkey with nothing but a couple of towels to comfort her. "I had to sleep on a mat while I detoxed. Just cruel stuff. Using dope sickness to really keep you in pain and torture you."

"So I learned really quickly the power of heroin," Louise adds. "And the power of needing heroin."

Finally, Louise found the strength to leave him. They had a blow-up one night and Louise thought of a way out. Brice claimed that she owed him money and wouldn't let her leave him until that debt was paid. There was no debt. Brice had made it up. But they were arguing about it when Louise realized she happened to have the money. Still enrolled at Greensboro College, she had $10,000 in the bank that she had received as a student loan.

"In your fucked-up mind, how much money do I owe you? $5,000?

$10,000? How much is it?" Louise screamed at him. In response, Brice destroyed her living room. For him, it wasn't about money. He knew Louise didn't actually owe him anything. It was a mind game, only about power. So he screamed back at her, flipped over furniture, and left Louise badly beaten. He also took the $10,000, but Louise didn't care about that. She was free. "Fuck you," she told him. "I fucking hate you."

The next morning, Louise awoke to the largest man she had ever seen leaning over her. He was inside her bedroom and the shock and then fear instantly forced her eyes open wide. "You're coming with me," the man told her as the situation entered her sleepy mind. "The bail bondsman," she realized. The giant of a man dragged her through her house and out the front door. It was about the bail money that Brice had put up a few months earlier to get Louise out of jail after she was caught with an ounce of cocaine. Now that Louise had told Brice that they were through, he had called the bail bondsman, took his money back, and told the bondsman, "She's all yours."

Little Selena watched as this unknown man carried her mother outside and threw her into the back of a black SUV. It was one of the single worst moments of Louise's life. "My daughter was left there crying and I wasn't there to calm her."

Still a young woman who hadn't gone before a judge very often—there had been a couple of charges for possession but nothing more serious than that—Louise was able to convince the court to release her on probation. But that's only where her problems began. Brice was an expert at inflicting pain and knew exactly how to hurt Louise. He made sure she lost her girls. Selena was to remain in Sarah Beale's custody and Summer went to live full time with her grandmother on Tommy's side. Louise was heartbroken. "It *destroys* women when their kids are taken from them," she says. Brice's torture and manipulation continued. Brice had filled Sarah's head with every sort of lie about Louise and convinced Louise's parents to change the locks on the little house they had purchased for her. This meant that when Louise was released on bail, she was homeless. So when Brice told Louise that he had rented her a little place outside the city, Louise felt she had no choice but to accept. "I just took pills," Louise says. "Handfuls of pills. Just so miserable. I got beat up every goddamn day. And not just beat up. He was huge. I'd wake up and just be flying into the fucking air. I'd be all high and he'd find me wherever I was. I was never safe. I was terrified. By this time, I am terrified of this man. Pure, honest terror."

Separated from her children and living in fear of Brice, Louise fell into a dark and total depression. She had no friends, no one she could trust for anything, and nowhere to go. She only had drugs. Louise lost months of her life hiding inside a bathroom stall at a nearby McDonald's. She never took a magazine or a book with her. She didn't have a phone to help her pass the time or even anything that could play music. Nothing but heroin and depression. "I'd get picked up [by dealers] every day, go to McDonald's because I wanted to get out of the house and get away from everybody, and I'd just shoot dope in the McDonald's bathroom, all by myself, all day long," Louise says. It was the unlikeliest of people who kept her alive those days. "I was having no contact with anyone else [but dealers] for a long time. Maybe the only person I talked to in a day was the person selling me drugs. And some of those conversations saved me. Some of those guys saved my life. Just by asking, 'Louise, how are you doing?'" Louise's dealers kept her alive, but barely.

"All I wanted to do was spend my days in a McDonald's bathroom. That's what I preferred. That felt like peace. And that is so miserable," Louise says. "All my life, I'd wanted people to be around me. I had this need for people. I liked people. I liked relationships. I wanted to be liked. I just wanted to be loved. Now, it was total loneliness."

Throughout all of this, Louise had been getting sick. "I needed to go to the hospital and was too afraid to go."

Methicillin-resistant *Staphylococcus aureus*—MRSA, for short—

is a nasty bacterial infection, says Dr. Kim Sue, a physician and medical director with the National Harm Reduction Coalition, America's leading nonprofit organization advocating for the rights and improved treatment of people who use drugs. It lives on the skin of many of us, she explains. "In most cases, it doesn't do anything. But once it gets into the bloodstream, it can wreak havoc. It can give you pneumonia, it can give you cellulitis, and it can be really, really difficult to treat." A case of MRSA infection can require antibiotics and other medications administered via an IV for an extended period of time, and that's what was now required for Louise. As a result of her reluctance to seek treatment, the infection was severe. Without commenting on Louise's case directly, Sue argues that someone who uses drugs should not take the blame for delaying care. "For people who use drugs, there is a common belief that the medical and psychiatric consequences of substance use, and the complications related to substance use, are deserved, that people who use drugs deserve to be punished," Sue explains. "So they are, in many ways, denied access to evidence-based care, compassionate care, and respectful care." Sue says this can take the form of a tone of voice, body language, or something as subtle as a look, but these minor interactions that might not register for a doctor can leave an impression on a drug user that lasts a lifetime. "And then they come into a hospital too late," Sue continues. "They come in very, very late, they are very sick, and then they are blamed for it."

Louise forced herself to visit the ER only when she was sure that she was actually going to die. And, exactly as she feared, she was treated horribly there. The MRSA infection that Louise contracted injecting drugs was so severe that hospital staff conducted their examination wearing the sort of hazmat suits one sees in a movie about a plague. "Here I am at 20-whatever years old and there are people coming into my room with yellow suits on, nobody telling me shit and using big words like 'methicillin-resistant Staphylococcus,' and telling me I have hep C," Louise says. "I was lying there, pulling up my sleeves, and man, I was stripped with infection. The totality of it: 'I'm a junkie.' Here I am, not proud of myself. This is a disaster. That was a monumental moment in my life."

Months passed before Louise was well enough to leave the hospital. Eventually, she was transferred to a nursing home for the elderly. It was a strange situation. But finally, for the first time in nearly a decade, she could breathe.

Louise got along well with many of the older women living there. She was on methadone, a drug prescribed as part of a medication-assisted treatment (MAT) program that is effective in reducing cravings for illicit opioids and minimizing symptoms of opioid withdrawal.[24] "I was maintained," she says. "And I was shooting dope through a PICC line [a thin tube inserted into her arm]. No more missing veins. I'm enjoying myself. I'm playing dress up, pushing old ladies around, playing the piano. And I have no men around. No goddamn abuse. Nobody telling me what to do. I cried when I had to leave."

Louise recuperated at the nursing home. She continued injecting heroin and some cocaine but, on methadone, she was using fewer illicit drugs. And with access to clean needles and even a PICC line, her body began to heal. It was peaceful—the first period of calm that Louise had experienced in many years. They took decent care of her at the nursing home. But, Louise says, she's never been able to forget the time she spent in the emergency department and the ways doctors there treated her during her initial intake for MRSA. Lying in a hospital bed sick and scared, with nobody telling her what was wrong, with nobody even acknowledging her as a human being. It's kept Louise afraid of the health care establishment to this day.

"If we want to know where activism started, it was maybe in that moment of horror and despair," she says. "In that moment of need."

4

A Safe Space for People Who Use Drugs

By 1996, Jess had been using on and off for a couple of years and already had a strong desire to quit. She fully believed that heroin was a word that she would soon leave behind. But that's not what happened.

All this time, Jess had been snorting heroin. The only time she had ever injected drugs was four years earlier, the very first time she tried heroin in New York City. "I never want to put a syringe in my arm again," she had told herself. "But then I meet this kid, Sam." Laid-back West Coast vibes, easygoing confidence, "a fatally cool kind of guy," Jess says. She liked him. Sam had a casual way of convincing others to join his adventures. "And he made fun of me because I didn't shoot." A couple of nights later, a deal went bad and Jess got ripped off for $100. She was left with no money, no dope, and the early pangs of withdrawal. While walking down Northampton's Main Street, not knowing what to do, she bumped into Sam. "What's wrong?" he said. "Come back to my house."

At his apartment across the Connecticut River, in neighboring Hadley, Sam handed Jess a syringe. "I don't shoot up," Jess told him. "Well, you either shoot up or you're sick," Sam replied. Jess didn't know how to inject. But she extended her arm and Sam took it. "I go out, immediately," Jess says. "I hit the ground." She didn't exactly overdose. Jess never stopped breathing that night. But she was out cold for a while. "Hey, I only have to do a quarter of what I'm doing," she thought. The next morning, Jess asked Sam, "Can you shoot me up again?"

Jess's good friend Josh was furious when he found out that Jess had started injecting and actually hit Sam. Jess had asked Josh about injecting before, when the dope was weak or when there wasn't much to go around. He always refused. "Your whole life will change," Josh told her. And now it had. "The difference between sniffing and shooting up is like the difference between throwing a bullet with your hand and shooting it at someone," Jess explains. "The ways my life changed in that instant, the whole ritual—the finding, the getting, the using—became so much more desperate. And the sickness and the withdrawal."

Once Jess started using needles, however, Josh accepted it and supported her as best he could. He was a little bit older and had seen a little bit more of the world. "If you want men to control you and to control your drug use, that's fine. That can be your life," he said to Jess. "But I've been watching this happen to women for 10 years. What you need to do is learn how to shoot yourself up." Josh wanted Jess to have the knowledge and ability to exercise autonomy over her own body. If she was going to inject drugs no matter what, he wanted her to learn how to reduce the harm that was associated with her injection drug use.

"And I did," Jess says. In Josh's room, sitting on the bed one evening, Jess realized that just because this was about how to use drugs, it wasn't necessarily bad information to have. It was an epiphany that would come to define Jess's life as a budding activist. Josh took her through the process, step by step. By teaching her how to inject, he freed her from a reliance on men that so many other female injection-drug users are forced to endure, sometimes for years. Jess would never have to watch a man steal from her cut or negotiate a blow job for assistance injecting. Josh gave her the tools she needed to control what she put inside her body. "It was very empowering," Jess says. "That was one of the best gifts that was ever given to me."

Jess's increasingly close relationship with Sam led her to use more heroin. Then Josh moved to Oregon. It was Josh who usually made drug runs for them, so in his absence, Jess had to figure out something else. "I start making runs for people," Jess says. She wasn't a dealer. It wasn't like Jess was picking up kilos or anything like that. But she was buying more than a couple of grams at a time and hooking up friends and a few other Northampton kids who came around when they needed something. Usually, Jess was making just enough of a profit to cover her own habit. During this time, she was living in the dorms at a Massachusetts university, but that didn't last long. Pretty quickly, the administration noticed the constant traffic in and out of her room. Before the second semester was over, Jess was asked to leave. She moved in with Sam and, with school out of the way, there was more time to do heroin. "This is when my use got really, really bad," Jess says.

In small towns, everyone talks to and about everyone else. By this time, Jess had a reputation in Northampton. "I'd been accused of running a brothel, prostituting, and breaking into people's houses," she says. "All of this stuff that comes with being a drug user. Somebody said I was walking around a house party with a needle hanging out of my arm. It was ridiculous. You don't do stuff like that." Jess was young and an avid reader of William Burroughs, the Beat generation author whose lurid books about drugs pushed the 1950s boundaries of free speech, but she wasn't proud of using heroin. "I was terrified that I was going to lose my friends, that they were going to die," she recalls. "I was totally embarrassed that I was using. It was spread around town that I was a junkie." Jess was hurt by the rumors, the looks she began to notice, and how people who once said hi now looked toward the ground and avoided eye contact. "It was my introduction to how drug users are treated." She had heard about stigma and this was it, she realized, and she was ashamed. To stop feeling that way, she used more heroin.

Jess took another shot at therapy. It didn't go well. Her therapist never wanted to talk about anything but her drug use. "I'm sorry," Jess said to her, "I wasn't shooting dope when I was six years old. Obviously, there is more to it than this." She made a couple of attempts at detox and began attending Narcotics Anonymous meetings.

Narcotics Anonymous (NA) is the de facto treatment program for drug addiction in America. It's so widespread that you can find a meeting in just about every sizable town anywhere in the country, and so well-established that a court of law will order a convicted criminal to attend NA meetings in lieu of going to prison. Either free to attend or incorporated into a larger for-profit treatment program, NA and its antecedent cousin, Alcoholics Anonymous (AA), consist primarily of meetings where people with a substance-use issue confess their addictions, share their struggles, receive support from fellow members, and work to maintain their abstinence through the program's "12 steps." The 12 steps provide structure and serve as a guide. They require that participants admit they have no control over their addiction, embrace a higher power, acknowledge past harms they have inflicted, attempt to make amends, and maintain a lifestyle free of drugs. Low-bar treatment is what this country needs. But there are problems with NA. Some people can't stomach the parts infused with religion. Many spurn NA for its prohibition of medication-assisted treatments like methadone. Others find the 12 steps less a path to sobriety as they are incantations. Others still are wary of the sponsor-system's susceptibility to abuses of power. It is not uncommon for women to be preyed upon by older men in the program. Finally, despite its popularity, NA doesn't actually work that well, at least not for the majority of people who try it.[1] And because NA is pedestaled as America's path to recovery, failing with NA can leave few places to turn.

Retention is a primary issue of concern. If you attend NA meetings regularly, the literature shows, you stand a better chance of maintaining sobriety than if you don't stick with any sort of rehab program at all.[2] But the vast majority of people who try NA don't stick with it. And even if it's beneficial, how successful can you call a program that only a minority actually continue to attend? According to one study, just 19 percent of people who attended an AA meeting continued with meetings after one month.[3] Then, among those who do remain with NA or AA, relapse is very common. AA's success rate stands somewhere between just 5 and 10 percent, meaning that only one out of every 15 people who attempt abstinence with AA remains sober for the long term.[4]

There's another issue. Whenever NA or AA is the subject of an academic study, the specific support group reviewed is almost always part of a larger, more regimented treatment program, usually involving therapists, case managers, and the like. There's actually very little analysis of the effectiveness of the stand-alone, more casual 12-step programs that dominate the real-world treatment landscape of America.

As for Jess's experience with Narcotics Anonymous, she sums it up like this: "I was told to come back when I wasn't nodding out."

"Everywhere, I was treated horribly," Jess adds. She was learning that the treatment world simply does not treat people who use drugs very well. Her next lesson would come from the health care system at large.

A year or so after Jess started shooting up, in 1997, she got her first abscess. Then a second abscess developed and then a third. All three were on her left arm and each one was further up her arm than the last. "There was a red line running," Jess says. She became terrified that an infection was moving toward her heart.

An abscess is the result of a soft-tissue infection. The immune system sends white blood cells to the infected area and they mix with bacteria and dead tissue to cause swelling. A pocket of pus forms beneath the skin. Before long, the surface breaks, and if aggravated or left untreated, the wound remains open. It's very painful and can quickly turn serious, requiring a limb's amputation and even resulting in death. An abscess is not caused by drugs. There is nothing in cocaine that will prompt an abscess to form. This infection is caused by bacteria that are introduced to the body via the equipment that one uses to inject drugs.

Dr. Kim Sue notes that an abscess is one of the most common reasons for which an intravenous drug user will seek medical care. However, Sue emphasizes, when intravenous drug users have low-barrier and affordable access to sterile injection equipment, abscesses are rare and there is little chance of contracting HIV or any other virus. But in the 1990s and still in many jurisdictions today, that equipment is difficult to find or prohibitively expensive. Pharmacies are allowed to sell syringes to diabetics, for example, but if a pharmacist is proven to have sold a syringe knowing that it would be used to inject drugs, they can be legally subject to fines and additional penalties. This means that many people who are addicted to drugs are forced to share and reuse needles and other equipment. Sue also places at least some of the blame on health care professionals. "No one interfaces with a doctor to learn sterile technique and many doctors don't even know how to teach it," she says. "So users pick up tips from each other."

Jess remembers understanding this even though she was barely 21 at the time. It made her angry. The entire situation made her angry, afraid, and isolated. But as frightened as Jess was by the infection, she was equally scared of hospitals. It was only when the pain became unbearable that she dragged herself to the emergency room at Cooley Dickinson Hospital. "I tried lying, saying I had gotten cut on some dirty glass," Jess says. "You sure it wasn't a dirty needle?" the nurse replied. "The way she said it was so disdainful." Jess rolled up her sleeves to reveal long red track marks. The nurse saw them and then made a big deal of wearing gloves and a face mask, putting them on with exaggerated motions to signal her disapproval. Next, she asked Jess what school she went to, if she injected drugs, and if she had AIDS. Each question lacked concern or sensitivity. "It wasn't done in a prevention or education sense," Jess says. "It was like, 'Let me see how bad I can make you feel about yourself.'" It was just the two of them in a small examination room, but Jess found the embarrassment and shame to be unbearable. "You're going to lose your arm," the nurse told her. As soon as she stepped out and Jess was left alone for a moment, she grabbed her things and ran. "Then I started getting really sick. This wasn't just something that felt bad. Thinking back, I could have died."

Research on drug users' interactions with health care systems suggests Jess's experience was a typical one. Even one negative experience can have lasting consequences. People who use drugs can be denied pain medications, subject to confrontational treatment by staff, harassed by facility security guards, and demeaned with stigmatizing language and institutional racism.[5] Patients who have had such experiences will then trust their doctors less, and those doctors will in turn perceive their mistrustful patients as less cooperative.[6]

Sue has seen this firsthand. "People have died because they haven't accessed care because they've been stigmatized and haven't gone back to a hospital after being mistreated," she says. "They haven't been able to access the medication that they might need, or help that they might need, or counseling, because we created a lot of barriers for them. That definitely has consequences that are very significant. People have died."

Back at home with a fever and vomiting, Jess knew she had to do something. But she could not bring herself to return to the hospital. "I realized I needed to go to the needle exchange," she says.

If you've never heard of needle exchange, it can sound counterintuitive. How does giving people equipment to inject drugs in any way improve their health? Doesn't it enable drug use and therefore perpetuate one's addiction? These are valid and important questions. Thankfully, we have their answers. Scientists and academics have built entire careers researching needle exchange. Their results:

yes, giving people clean needles improves health outcomes in myriad ways, and no, it does not lead to higher rates of drug use.[7] Understanding needle exchange—also called a syringe services program, or SSP—becomes a lot easier when you remember one thing: substances such as heroin and cocaine cannot by themselves infect someone with a blood-borne disease or cause a skin infection. These ailments—the most common negative health outcomes associated with injection drug use—are not caused by using drugs; they are caused by using drugs in ways that are unsanitary. Needle exchange provides for conditions of improved cleanliness.

During the HIV/AIDS epidemic, syringe exchange programs were deployed in New York City and the disease's prevalence among injection drug users declined from 50 percent in 1990–1992 to 17 percent in 1999–2002. The greater the number of syringes distributed each year, the lower the estimated incidence of HIV.[8] A decade later, a systemic review of more than 1,800 papers on syringe exchange similarly showed a clear decline in the spread of HIV or hepatitis C (depending on what was studied).[9]

On the question of whether syringe exchange programs enable or promote drug use, intravenous drug users have been shown to inject less frequently after they begin using a needle exchange,[10] are more likely to enter a detox facility,[11] remain in drug treatment longer than those who have never used an exchange, and are more likely to eventually stop using intravenous drugs altogether.[12]

Finally, what about the community? When comparing syringe disposal practices in a city with low-barrier access to needle exchange (San Francisco) to one where exchange was still illegal (Miami), a study found that 13 percent in San Francisco said they improperly disposed of needles while in Miami, this number was 95 percent. Eight times as many used syringes were found discarded in Miami compared to San Francisco.[13]

Even the Centers for Disease Control and Prevention (CDC)—a cautious and conservative bureaucracy by nature—has nothing but support for this harm reduction intervention. "By providing access to sterile syringes and other injection equipment, SSPs help people prevent transmitting blood-borne and other infections when they inject drugs," a CDC website reads. "New users of SSPs are five times as likely to enter drug treatment as those who don't use the programs."[14]

Yet as of April 2021, syringe exchange remains illegal in eight states.[15] It is understandable if people do not like syringe exchange because it involves a behavior that they categorize as bad, or if people oppose syringe exchange on ideological grounds, arguing it violates family values or antidrug principles. But it is impossible to factually claim that syringe exchange does not work to reduce the spread of infectious diseases. If one opposes the establishment of syringe exchange in their community, they are advocating a prohibitionist policy that is proven to result in higher instances of HIV and hepatitis C. The data are clear.

In 1997 western Massachusetts, needle exchange was still a new thing. Jess had heard about it and, as an injection drug user, understood the benefits of access to clean syringes. But she regarded needle exchange as a component of the health care system that now incited fear. Meanwhile, her arm throbbed with pain. Jess began asking friends what they thought about the one place in Northampton where she'd heard users were treated all right: Tapestry Needle Exchange. Josh had returned from Oregon and started making trips there. "I want you to meet this guy," he said. Jess agreed to go along and mentally prepared herself for the worst, fully expecting to receive the same stigmatizing treatment that she'd experienced earlier that week in the ER.

The first person Jess met at Tapestry was Luciano Colonna, a short Italian guy who was manning the front desk that day. Before she could really get to know the place, Jess told Luciano about her arm. She felt safe with him. But that feeling was quickly tested when

Luciano said Jess needed to return to the hospital. It was late in the day and Luciano would be off soon. "I'll go with you," he told her. "If you can wait until 5 p.m., we'll go together."

As Luciano finished up for the day, Jess's eyes wandered around Tapestry, taking everything in. There was a Kerouac poster on one wall, romanticizing the Beat writer's travels across America, and quotes by Allen Ginsberg and other poets taped here and there. "Not promoting drug use, but this was our world," Jess thought. "You could feel very comfortable here." Northampton was a town that teenage transients passed through regularly and those who used drugs often found their way to Tapestry. Many of those kids would stay in touch and send postcards from Amsterdam, Tangiers, and wherever else they traveled. Those messages adorned Tapestry's walls, offering a sense of community. Jess's eyes swelled with tears as she began to understand what she was seeing. Staff were kind and warm with everyone they assisted. Clean syringes and other supplies including condoms were available and free to those who asked. It was a safe space for people who used drugs.

In the end, Jess didn't have to return to the emergency room. She met a boy at Tapestry who was recently treated for an abscess and had a 10-day supply of antibiotics that he no longer needed. "He gave me the script, so I skipped returning to the ER," Jess says.

The afternoon's brief introduction to Tapestry revealed a new world. It was an epiphany around the idea that a drug user could improve their life without total abstinence. Another friendly employee named Tim Purrington explained harm reduction to her: "Any positive change," she heard for the first time. This had never occurred to Jess before. The idea that injecting drugs with a clean needle instead of sharing a dirty one, while still injecting drugs, was a step in a positive direction. That you could improve health outcomes for people who use drugs without entirely ending their drug use. But more than that, Tim continued, harm reduction is public health with an activist streak and a social justice movement that seeks to end the war on drugs. It was more than a lightbulb going off. "This was one of those defining moments that people have in their lives," Jess says. "When they realize what gives them passion and fire."

From her visit to Tapestry, Jess had antibiotics for her infection and enough clean needles to last for a while. But she couldn't stay away from the place. "My life was getting so chaotic and each visit was this quiet moment for me," she says. "I was like, 'I like this. What is this? What is this harm reduction thing?'

"Being the good overachiever that I was, I went to the library and began pulling microfilm, reading articles about drug-user unions in Australia and harm reduction in England in the late '80s, in response to the AIDS epidemic," Jess continues. It saved her life. "Before I walked into the Tapestry office, I was sure that I would be dead within a year and had no desire to live," she says. "Then, that first week, I went into the needle exchange every day. I already had my syringes but I just wanted to be back in that feeling."

Jess immediately became a familiar face. "I started off doing a little bit of volunteer work," she says. "I would go into the needle exchange every day. Then they got me involved in this weekly meeting that they did."

Jess didn't realize it at the time, but she was just as useful to Luciano as Tapestry was to her. The drug scene in Northampton was scattered and inconspicuous. It wasn't like in a big city, where there's a dealer on the same corner every day and a visible collection of customers hanging around the surrounding block or two. Northampton drug users arranged meets on the phone and made quick buys wherever their dealer happened to be that day. The people who needed harm reduction in Northampton were hidden in basements and cheap apartments. "So how could we reach those people?" Luciano asked. The answer was Jess. She began helping Luciano and other Tapestry staffers tap into Northampton's underground, introducing them to other injection drug users who could benefit from a needle exchange.

Tapestry noticed Jess's value and began paying her a stipend. "They paid us $35, so you had enough to get two bags of heroin, a pack of cigarettes, and then 10 bucks for whatever you wanted on top of that," Jess says fondly. In return, Jess walked Northampton's vacant lots and back alleys, letting street kids know about Tapestry and the programs offered there. Tapestry also had Jess and her friends conduct basic surveys related to HIV and intravenous drug use, equipping them as junior epidemiologists. "We would go into a house full of drug users and collect their information," she continues. "They were doing community participatory research before we had a name for it. We were getting real data."

Luciano began thinking about what might be next for Jess. He wasn't telling her what to do. "I was a cheerleader," Luciano says. "You have that spark in you," he told her. "You have an activist in you. I see that fire in you. What can we do to foster that?" A couple of years earlier, a copy of an underground harm reduction pamphlet had landed on Luciano's desk. Called *junkphood*, it was created by program participants at a needle exchange in Santa Monica, California, with the help of a staffer there named Heather Edney. The publication quickly ran afoul of the public health department, but Luciano loved it. In addition, by this time, the National Harm Reduction Coalition was moving out of its founding city of San Francisco and growing into an organization that truly was national, and Luciano was also reading its slightly-less-controversial newsletter, *Harm Reduction Communication*, which NHRC leaders Allan Clear and Sara Kershnar created in 1995. "Why don't you do a zine?" Luciano asked Jess. "And I gave her scissors and a copy machine."

Volume one, issue one of *Junk* was published out of the back room of Tapestry during the fall of 1997. A bubbly fairy princess graces the cover, her butterfly wings fluttering as she carries a syringe to the sky. "The pages ahead are not meant to promote drug use, nor are they in any way condoning it," it begins. "The following pages simply are to inform, educate and enlighten injection drug users and the community they live in. Please read this with an open mind and take something away from it that could possibly save your life or somebody you know. Above all love it!"

Inside, *Junk* offered advice on how to minimize the spread of bacteria when injecting drugs. There was also poetry and artwork full of 1990s teenage angst, and a directory of needle exchange sites in cities across the United States, Canada, and Mexico. A letters-to-the-editor section begins, "Dear *Junk*, The only vein I can get a good hit in is the one in my cock." *Junk*'s reply: "First of all, Dan, don't shoot into your cock. If that's really the only place you can get hit you need to consider some other options (no judgment from us—visit or call the nearest needle exchange)."

Monique Tula, a Tapestry manager at the time, recalls how this little zine led to the formation of the organization's first drug-user advisory board—a group of drug-using clients who were actually given a say on the day-to-day operations of the place. "They had this project where they did a bunch of calls to detox and treatment facilities in Massachusetts, asking them questions about their programs," Monique says. "And then they put it together in a booklet, like, 'This is what you can expect if you go to so-and-so's detox.' Nobody had ever done that before, where drug users had that role."

By the start of 1998, Jess was behind the counter at Tapestry. "I started doing a couple hours of volunteer work running the syringe exchange," she says. "People would come in, I would do the exchange, and I flourished. I loved it. And our enrollment numbers were going up." Jess found she was a natural. When someone spoke to her, she looked them in the eyes and let them feel that she was listening. In their moment of vulnerability, when they were sharing a memory of trauma or shame, Jess let them know that she did not judge them, that she cared, and that she was one of them.

Tapestry's clients understood that and trusted her—women, especially. She used the lessons Josh had taught her about men using drugs to manipulate female users and shared how empowering it had felt when she learned how to inject herself. "I would watch this ritual that happened between men and women who came into the exchange," Jess says. "I'd ask a girl, 'What size syringe do you need?' And she would look over to her boyfriend. It could have been a same-sex partner, too. With gay men, there was always that glance over and their partner would answer. So I would ask, 'What happens if you guys break up? Do you inject yourself?' It was a great tool for dialogue, to say, 'Let's talk about your injection habit.'" Sometimes, men would get really upset. "They didn't want their girl to have that power," Jess explains. "It's all about power and control." In those situations, Jess deployed a secret weapon: tampons.

Tampons were another reason that women visited Tapestry. While toilet paper is free in public washrooms, tampons are not, and for women struggling with addiction, tampons can be difficult to afford. So Tapestry distributed them for free. And now, when a woman arrived with her boyfriend and asked Jess for a pack, Jess took the opportunity to separate the two and grab a moment alone with the girl. They would duck into a supply closet down the hall and, alongside tampons, Jess would tuck a flyer into their bag. "Hey girls, sick of yucky guys shooting you up?" it read alongside a comic illustration of yucky guys. "Stand up for yourselves! Learn the fine art of shooting yourself up. It's as easy as changing your tampon." On the back, there were instructions. "First, have your own clean needle," they read. "Don't share your boyfriend's! Use a tie. It's good for your veins. And will make it easier to find one. Insert the needle at a perpendicular angle, bevel tip up. Once in, pull back the plunger, release tie, inject slowly. Remember to clean your syringe. Enjoy. Remember—real women shoot themselves!" Variations on the "It's as easy as changing your tampon" slogan are still used in harm reduction programs today.

The exchange saved Jess's life, not from an overdose or an infection, but from oblivion. "My life was falling apart and I wanted to end this pain," she says. "But now there was a tiny voice in the back of my head, saying, 'You can lie in bed and be depressed and hate yourself because you feel like a bad person because you're using. Or you can go down to the exchange and spend 10 minutes talking to somebody.' And it was like, 'Why'd I even feel like that this morning?'

"Any time I hit that low, I still had harm reduction to lift me back up."

5

The Wright Focus Group

By 2008, Louise had begun to pull herself out of the chaos that had dominated her life for the previous decade. She was living at a treatment facility in Burlington, which was down the highway from Greensboro, just far enough away from the city to keep her out of trouble. She was sober, doing the NA thing. She made a bit of money doing menial jobs at the treatment center. She was also enrolled at the University of North Carolina at Greensboro, taking courses online, and was just a few credits shy of completing a master's degree in public health.

Things were looking up. But she hated Burlington, and she still couldn't bear living without her daughters, Selena and Summer. Then her mother offered Louise a deal. Sarah suggested that Louise come live with her and Selena at the family home in Greensboro. Louise wasn't thrilled with the plan. She and her mom had a tough time getting along when they were living under the same roof. Summer was still living with her grandparents on Tommy's side of the family, and Louise was crushed by her absence from the arrangement. But Louise decided she would give it a try.

Packing up her life in Burlington, she purchased an old Mazda 323 with a few hundred dollars she had saved. Insurance would be the bigger expense, she learned at the DMV later that day. "Louise Vincent?" the clerk asked. "Are you aware that the last time you had car insurance, you wrecked one vehicle every month?" The woman paused for a moment. "And two in November?" There were stumbles and unanticipated hurdles to clear, but Louise's life was coming back together.

At the University of North Carolina at Greensboro, Louise's history as an intravenous drug user led her to infectious-disease prevention, which led her to syringe exchange, and then to the entire field of harm reduction. Louise learned there was a small but energetic group of activists already advocating for the types of programs that she was quickly coming to envision for Greensboro. They were just down the highway, in neighboring Jamestown, with a group calling itself the North Carolina Harm Reduction Coalition (NCHRC), led by a woman named Thelma Wright.

Thelma Wright is where Louise intersects with the birth of harm reduction in North Carolina. Thelma was born in Huntsville, Alabama, in 1948, and raised on a farm there in rural Madison County. "My parents were sharecroppers. Cotton," she says with a warm Southern accent. "I was in the cotton field before I was in the first grade," she adds. "It was a white folks' farm. We didn't have nothing." Thelma became pregnant on her fourteenth birthday and dropped out of high school shortly after. But she obtained a certificate in auto mechanics, which let her find a decent job at the Huntsville Sears. Looking to supplement her income, Thelma also tried her hand at bootlegging. "Quart beer," she says. "And selling wine by the bottle." Thelma was making money. Then, working the third shift at Sears late one night, she received a call from a friend who told her that the police had arrested her bootlegging partner. "After that, I decided I needed to get out of Alabama. Because I wasn't going to stop bootlegging. Once the money starts coming in, it's hard to let it go."

In 1973, Thelma moved to Louisville, Kentucky, beginning a long career with the Lorillard Tobacco Company and a lifelong friendship with a man she worked alongside named George Henderson. As luck would have it, the two of them were transferred together to the Lorillard factory in Greensboro. Thelma has called North Carolina home ever since.

Life was pleasantly boring, for a while. Thelma was busy working 40 hours a week for Lorillard plus Saturdays at Sears. She was earning enough to keep her boys fed so she was happy. George lived just across the street, making it easy for them to visit one another often. "He loved my cooking," Thelma says. "Then he started losing weight, got sick on the job a couple of times. Then he confided in me that he was HIV-positive." This was the late 1980s and the stigma inflicted on a Black LGBTQ man with HIV was terrible. She took care of George as best she could until he passed away in 1993. "He's the reason I got involved in harm reduction," Thelma says. "I promised George, on his deathbed, that I was going to do everything I could about HIV."

In his final years, George received support from the Triad Health Project, a nonprofit that supports people living with HIV/AIDS. They brought groceries to his home and helped ensure he made his doctors' appointments. "So after George died, I really wanted to do my best for that particular agency," Thelma says. But she and George had always felt that Triad was really only interested in delivering HIV support to gay men who were white. The experience of a Black gay man living in the South was very different, Thelma understood, and Triad wasn't showing any interest in her efforts to make the organization more inclusive. So Thelma began doing HIV education on her own, visiting Greensboro's Black barbershops and leaving educational pamphlets wherever business owners would allow her. She shared her concerns about existing services one day with a couple of especially receptive barbers and they responded with an idea: "Thelma, you know the community," one said to her. "Why don't you start your own organization?"

The Wright Focus Group began meeting in Thelma's living room in 1999. Among its earliest supporters was a man named Steven Daniels, better known by his nickname, Gator. "That's where I learned everything that I know about needle exchange," Thelma says. "We started knocking on doors in public housing, talking to people with HIV and AIDS. Then we realized that we were missing this whole other group of people. That whole group of people was the injection drug users." At 49, Gator was a few years older than Thelma and, as a former IV-drug user who was HIV-positive, he taught her about how the two worlds overlapped. Performing community outreach for the Wright Focus Group, he met HIV-positive heroin users in housing project stairwells, and Thelma learned about the unique needs of HIV-positive women from sex workers whom she approached with options for family planning. Together, the pair of them attended a harm reduction conference in Portland, Oregon, and there connected with a man named Dave Purchase. Dave had pioneered needle exchange in Tacoma, Washington, and, in 1992, co-founded the North American Syringe Exchange Network, a sort of underground railroad for unsanctioned needle exchange programs across the United States. "My name is Thelma Wright, and we have founded the Wright Focus Group," Thelma said, introducing herself. "We need some supplies." To which Dave replied, "That's no problem." He started sending them.

In North Carolina, supplying someone with a syringe for the known purpose of injecting illicit narcotics was illegal, so the Wright Focus Group's volunteer board of directors was not in full support of the organization's newfound friends. "Everybody was good with educational outreach but then we started doing needle exchange," Thelma says. "That's just the way it is with harm reduction; you know you're doing a good job when someone says you're doing wrong." Thelma wanted the Wright Focus Group to continue with its HIV prevention programs that by now were well established in the community, and realized that the organization's underground needle exchange was putting all of that at risk. To save what she and Gator had created, she would have to abandon the organization that bore her name.

"Next came the North Carolina Harm Reduction Coalition, NCHRC," Thelma says. "Dave Purchase supplied us with the needles, the caps, the cookers, bleach, cotton balls—not always for free," she adds. When clean syringes are scarce, it's a harm reduction practice to clean used syringes with bleach, which kills bacteria, hepatitis C, and the HIV/AIDS virus.* Thelma, Gator, and a pair of volunteers cleared Thelma's kitchen counters and went to work like an assembly line. One of them opened a bag and dropped a pack of needles in, the next person on the line added cookers and cotton balls, and the third was in charge of bleach.

Being the first to provide harm reduction services in conservative North Carolina was sometimes lonely work. The health care establishment refused to support them and law enforcement considered them criminals. They were cautious, Thelma notes; for example, they never kept syringes around the new NCHRC office that they had moved into. Instead, injection drug users would visit the office and Thelma would connect them with Gator. Then he would meet them somewhere off-site and provide clean equipment there. Still, people heard about what the pair of them were doing and some weren't happy about it. "One morning, I went in and my computer had been thrown through the window," Thelma says. "The keyboard and everything, out the window. My files were all over the place. And I just sat down and cried."

Gator, however, kept spirits high. Although he was getting older and relying on a cane to get around, his enthusiasm was limitless. He and Thelma began holding twice-monthly meetings for drug users at the NCHRC office. "Everybody would talk about what they experienced with the police," Thelma says. "They would talk to me about what they were facing out there. And from there, I'm trying to figure out what we can do to help." At these meetings, Thelma

---

* While using a new needle for each injection is best practice and the most effective way to prevent the spread of infectious diseases when using intravenous drugs, one Yale University study showed that washing a used needle with bleach, if done thoroughly, will reduce the chances of spreading HIV by as much as 99 percent.

realized the organization was evolving beyond her areas of expertise. She knew HIV, but while she was sympathetic to people who used drugs, she didn't have any experience with addiction herself. They put an ad in the paper announcing that NCHRC was looking for someone who knew something about injection drug use. Louise had some experience, and she and Thelma met for coffee. "I thought she was just the smartest little woman I had ever seen," Thelma says. "She knew the community of users, and chaotic users, and she also knew what she needed to know from all them degrees she got. That's a real strong mix. I love that girl. Never did I think I would say that about white folk."

Thelma gave Louise her first job in harm reduction. "My intention was just to write a school paper," Louise says. "Thelma hired me that day."

As she waded into activism, Louise grew aware of racism and of race as a social construct. When Thelma and Gator added Louise to their little crew, she felt welcomed into Greensboro's community of Black harm reduction advocates. This was part of a pattern for her, where Black people embraced her while white people distanced themselves or abandoned her. When Louise began dating Reggie and then gave birth to Selena, white people she had previously counted as friends stopped talking to her. Meanwhile, Reggie's family received her warmly. Then Reggie was diagnosed with cancer and Louise observed how North Carolina's health care system treated him poorly while providing her mom proper care. "I didn't understand that people weren't all equal until Reggie got sick," Louise says. "Since then, my whole life has been on this racial division, because I've got the kids." Louise realized that she was privileged, but not as privileged as she was before she gave birth to two half-Black children. "I was abandoned for something that I felt was so wrong," she says. "The veil was lifted off of me and I was able to see all of these things that I was never able to see before."

The impact was profound. As a child, Louise believed that people were equal and treated equally. Then she learned that the adults who had taught her that didn't believe it themselves. They had lied to her, and if she had been lied to about this, how could she trust anything that she was taught about the world? She began to challenge what she had been told about her mental illness—about how it recategorized her as someone who was not "normal" and how it should cause her to reconsider her ambitions in life—and, more than anything else, she began to challenge dominant beliefs and societal norms around addiction, illegal drugs, and prohibition.

For Louise, the war on drugs became the war on people who use drugs, and especially on Black people who use drugs. This was a war that that was waged against Black people in entirely different, inconceivably more intense ways than it was against whites, Louise realized. She would likely never fully grasp the extent of those differences or what it was like to live through them as Black people did, but she told herself this was something of which she would always keep herself aware. "I was determined to figure out what the fuck was going on," Louise says. This is how she entered the world of activism: looking for truth in the world and aware that things were not always as they appeared.

Less than a month after Thelma hired Louise, they traveled together to the 2008 National Harm Reduction Coalition conference in Tacoma, Washington. "I was very nervous. I did not like it," Louise says. "We had a good time, but it was nerve-wracking." Though she didn't know it at the time, it was in Tacoma that Louise would first meet harm reduction connections that would remain with her for the rest of her life.

"I met Dan Bigg," Louise says. Dan Bigg is affectionately referred to as the "godfather" of America's harm reduction movement—not its founder but an elder statesman, admired with great respect, and who could make things happen. Dan had established the Chicago Recovery Alliance, an influential harm reduction organization that operates by his mantra, "Any positive change." He championed the idea that abstinence was not required for a drug user's life to be considered a success. Drugs were healthier in moderation than used daily to maintain a full-blown addiction, and snorting drugs was less harmful than injecting them, and if a person transitioned from the latter to the former, those were changes that were positive. Though new to harm reduction, Louise had heard a lot about Dan, and what she had heard excited her. If a law was unjust, Dan was willing to break it. He arranged for the distribution of syringes in jurisdictions where they were still illegal, for example, which made Louise think: "That might be a good person to know." Needle exchange remained illegal in North Carolina. Though intimidated during their meeting, Louise mentioned that to Dan and he replied with his phone number. She tucked it into her pocket and was very careful not to lose it.

Louise was nevertheless torn in two directions. "I had drunk that NA Kool-Aid," she explains. "I had been taught that you don't put yourself around drugs. And now I'm in a situation where I'm thinking, 'Holy shit, I'm not supposed to be here.'" Despite knowing her sponsor would disapprove (to put it mildly), Louise remained at the conference and kept her nerves in check. "And I'm amazed. Blown away. Floored," she says.

"I got sent to Tacoma, found out about needle exchange, and that was sort of the birth of all of it," Louise continues. "It was the first time that I realized that maybe I was not a bad person. Before that, I had no idea other people thought like me. I had no idea there was a movement. I mean, I was born again."

Upon returning from Tacoma to Greensboro, Thelma asked Louise if she would be the NCHRC's first program director. "You're what we need," Thelma told her. Louise was pleased to accept the offer. Next, Louise and Thelma traveled to Atlanta, Georgia, where they were taken under the wing of Mona Bennett, a Southern harm reduction pioneer who, like Thelma, got her start during the HIV/AIDS crisis in the early 1990s.

"We started hearing more about HIV spreading through injection drug use," Mona says. "So I got involved with ACT UP Atlanta, and we were acting up." Mona was also working with a group called Prevention Point Atlanta (which later became the Atlanta Harm Reduction Coalition, which Mona still works for today). "We knew certain nurses, certain low-income clinics, and they would leave a drawer open and there would be a box of ten-packs of syringes peeking out. That was harm reduction." Mona was also getting needles from Thelma's connection, Dave Purchase, and doing outreach via a van that Prevention Point drove into Atlanta's poorest neighborhoods. When Louise visited, she was taken along on these rides, her eyes growing wider.

They spent most of the week in a community called the Bluff. "'Better Leave U Fucking Fool,' I think it stands for," Louise remarks. "I'd never seen a ghetto quite like that." The Bluff is a low-income residential area not far from Atlanta's downtown core. It has a proud tradition of civil rights and was once the home of Rev. Martin Luther King Jr. and Coretta Scott King. Decades of government neglect have, however, left the neighborhood dilapidated and devoid of economic opportunity.[1] Small houses and low-rise brick apartment complexes line narrow streets. Many homes are boarded up. The area has trees, but vacant properties go unkempt and tall grass and weeds grow wild. Young men with little to do collect on street corners. "There weren't even children running around," Louise says. "All the children had been taken off to social services. I was watching this guy by the fence selling dope. You could see the whole fucking scene."

Mona similarly describes the Bluff of the 1990s as the "wild, wild west" and "a neighborhood with a lot of needs." She recalls taking Louise into project stairwells, to a typical "spot." They found an overturned bucket and concrete blocks set up as a table and chairs and a "'carpet' of orange and white" beneath it. (The cheap syringes favored for drug use usually have a white plunger with an orange cap over the needle.)

Louise gained hands-on experience working the mobile needle exchange that operated out of Mona's van. She loved the outlaw element of it. "It was tolerated by local authorities but it was illegal," Louise says.

Prevention Point Atlanta maintained an unspoken working relationship with the government of the day and then pushed the limits of that arrangement. The organization was forced to follow a one-for-one exchange requirement for needles, meaning that for anyone to get a clean syringe, they had to bring a used one back. But Mona knew that a one-for-one requirement defeats the entire purpose of a needle exchange and contributes to higher rates of infectious diseases.[2] "Nobody left empty-handed," she says. "Plus cookers, cotton, alcohol pads, ties, and all that kind of stuff. And our 10-gallon cooler of ice water, which is as much harm reduction as any needle." Mona taught Louise and Thelma that harm reduction doesn't have to be as complicated as supplying syringes and working through all the red tape that entails. If Prevention Point's participants were injecting cocaine in the roasting heat of a Georgia summer, keeping them hydrated could mean the difference between life and death, so basic harm reduction was access to clean and cold water.

With half a public health degree under her belt, Louise was able to assist with on-site HIV and hepatitis C testing. Mona appreciated how Louise and Thelma made themselves useful. "They had the right attitude," Mona says. "No judgment. They were in it for the people. They were about the people. They were soaking it up."

In Atlanta, Louise also volunteered at a drop-in center that made a profound impression on her. It was the first time she witnessed a brick-and-mortar space for drug users where staff treated every client with total nonjudgment and respect. "They had phones there and people could actually use them, even if they were calling the

ways to obtain naloxone outside of the medical system, where it remained hopelessly overregulated and criminally underutilized. "Old-school guerrilla tactics," Jess says.

In addition to the wider world of harm reduction, the Cleveland conference introduced Jess to the idea of drug-user organizing. She met Ann Livingston and Bud Osborn, a couple who earlier that year had created Canada's first drug-user union, the Vancouver Area Network of Drug Users, or VANDU for short. Just across the border from Seattle, Ann, Bud, and their group of mostly homeless people had quickly become a force in local politics. They were holding street protests and sit-ins at city hall, demanding health care services for people who use drugs.* Jess had heard of user unions before. There was a lengthy article about them in the very first issue of *Harm Reduction Communication*, which Luciano had shared with Jess a few months earlier. But reading an article was one thing; actually meeting activists like Ann and Bud in the real world and hearing them share news about what they were accomplishing—accomplishing *as drug users*—this was something else.

Jess never slept in Cleveland. A pioneering drug-user organizer from California named Sheila O'Shea took her under her wing and Jess soaked up every minute of it. "I spent hours holed up in Sheila's hotel room," Jess says. "I had this big black hardcover sketchbook I used to bring everywhere. It had pages and pages and pages of what a union is. What is a bylaw? These are bylaws. What is a constitution? How do you write one? What is a board of directors? What is its purpose?" It became her blueprint. "I carried that book around for years. It was my life." When they parted ways, Sheila left Jess with an article she had written titled "Being a Drug-User Union

---

* For a history of VANDU and Canada's harm reduction movement, see the author's first book, *Fighting for Space: How a Group of Drug Users Transformed One City's Struggle with Addiction* (Arsenal Pulp Press, 2018).

of One." "Which is not a union, if you think about it," Jess says. "But she had me convinced I could go back to Massachusetts and be my own drug-user union." At Tapestry, working on their little zine, *Junk*, and listening to other drug users recount experiences of neglect and abuse, Jess decided that that's what she was going to do. "The advocacy bug had taken off in me," she says.

There were only nine or ten of them at first, Jess remembers. She and Josh and a few other close friends. Jess brought her dealer along to a couple of early meetings. And there were two 19-year-old girls who had really taken to the zine. "The club that nobody wants to belong to," Jess says with a laugh. "The group of people I used with back then, we were so tight, we were like family. We were all so young. These uber-goth, gutter-punk kids." Producing *Junk* brought drug users together on a regular basis and in a semis-tructured way that let them feel like they were a part of something. "People may not show up every week, but you pick a time and you take an hour," Jess says. "You throw a bunch of supplies on the table, and you say, 'Who's good at writing? Who's good at spelling? Who's good at editing? Grab a razor and start cutting.'" The back room at Tapestry became a place where Jess and her small group of user friends shared stories and compared notes on the ways that they were treated as drug users.

It was this little group of street kids that formed the Massachu-setts Drug Users Union, the original incarnation of the New England Users Union (NEUU), which is still going strong today. Jess remembers their very first meeting. "Luciano had given me petty cash to get Chinese food," she recounts. "And the union was like, 'We want to vote. We want to use this money for drugs.' And I was like, 'We can't use this money for drugs.' And they were like, 'We're not meeting quorum!' Everyone was throwing out all these words that didn't mean anything. But it was interesting, how everyone fell into it, like, 'Let's vote.'"

The little union began looking for a cause. One area in which they made progress was education. "I felt it was really important that people know their rights," Jess explains. They made up flyers that stated in plain language the rights that someone who was caught with drugs could exercise during interactions with police. "Simple stuff like 'Do not speak unless spoken to,' and 'You have the right to not answer questions.'" The larger idea was to create a sense of belonging. To let teenage runaways know that they were not alone. "If there was anything that a union could move forward in the community where we lived, it was that drug users care about drug users," Jess says. In the eyes of so many people who looked at them with disdain, they were nothing but despicable junkies. But in the back room at Tapestry, they were activists fighting for health care and their human rights. Slowly, word spread about what they were up to and the drug scene in Northampton grew a little softer. "I'll always buy into the adage 'Reach one, teach one,'" Jess says.

In a similar vein, Jess and her crew had the idea to put everything they knew about injection drugs and harm reduction into a film. *User Friendly: A Documentary on Peer-Driven Interventions and Injection Safety* was recorded in 1998 and serves as a wonderful artifact from the New England drug scene of the late 1990s.

The film begins with one of the teens wearing a Richard Nixon mask, using a spoon to cook a shot of heroin. He loads the liquid into a syringe, ties himself off, and then injects the drugs into his left forearm. Radiohead's "High and Dry" begins to play and then there's a lighthearted montage of the crew goofing off and just hanging out. "No one else is going to look out for your health, so you take care of you," one of the teens says as the film gets going. "If you are unsure of your needle or your cooker, bleach it. There is no need to take any unnecessary risks." Then *User Friendly* gets to the meat: "The 12 Steps to a Safe Hit."

The obvious ones are all there. "Don't share needles" is inevitably step one. And step six, "Find a safe place to hit," includes warnings against repeatedly using the same vein. But there are also clever tips that even seasoned users might not have thought of. One of Jess's friends recommends using a sharpie after each injection to mark the vein that was used and then, to prevent veins from collapsing as a result of frequent use, refraining from hitting that marked vein again until the pen has worn off.

To prevent the spread of bacteria, of course avoid sharing needles, but also make sure you're not sharing cookers or water, the film instructs.* "Sharing water out of a bottle is almost as bad as sharing a needle," another of the boys explains. "If somebody else sticks theirs in there to draw water, and they have blood residue from their shot left on it, you're going to have that. When you suck it up, you'll be sucking up their blood." Another tip: to avoid careless mistakes, mark each piece of your equipment with your initials or a burn mark. There's also this piece of wisdom, from Jess: "Men, you do not want to shoot anywhere near your penis."

"The most important thing we can do as IV drug users is to educate others and let them know about our lifestyles and how to make our lifestyles safe, instead of contributing to society's effervescent hidden junkie, shooting up in the closet alone, overdosing," Jess says later in the film. "We need to prevent those overdoses and people hiding their lifestyles. We need to share our experiences with others, with non–drug users as well, so that they can learn to accept people like us."

User Friendly doesn't advocate for drug use. "Every time I was high, I would wonder why I did it," a young woman recounts. "Stopping was the best thing I ever did. The only advice I can really give is that if you don't physically need it right now—if you aren't

---

* A cooker is anything metal that will hold a small mixture of drugs and water and to which one applies heat for the drugs to dissolve. A spoon is the stereotypical tool that appears in movies. Today, however, it's more common for a cooker to be specifically designed for the purpose of drug use, consisting of a tiny metal cup with low walls and a small handle.

dependent on it—then stop. Because it takes over who you are. It kills your soul, if you believe in souls. It kills that person you were born into. You become the drug."

The film is a plea for people who are going to use hard drugs to do so in a way that is as safe as possible. "Even if you're jonesing, if you don't want to share, if you don't want anybody else to know that you're using or that you've got a bag, have someone else there when you do a shot," another of the teens says. Then Sonic Youth's "Junkie's Promise" starts up. The credits roll.

Recorded more than 20 years ago by a bunch of teenagers, it's remarkable how smart and accurate *User Friendly*'s advice remains today.

Later the same year, the National Harm Reduction Coalition published a document that focused on the same themes, with a little more authority behind it. Describing itself as a "compilation of medical facts, injection techniques, junky wisdom, and common sense," the 89-page booklet details best practices for intravenous drug use.

Topics include what materials one needs to inject drugs, how to set everything up before getting started, and how to cook your drugs and administer an injection in as safe a manner as possible. "Insert the needle into your vein with the needle bevel opening facing up, at a 15 to 35 degree angle, and always in the direction of the heart," it reads. "Once you think you're in a vein, pull the plunger back to see if blood comes into the syringe. If so, and the blood is dark red and slow moving, you know that you've hit a vein. You can now untie your tourniquet and proceed to inject your drugs."

Health considerations and potential negative outcomes are explained at every step. "If you proceed to inject without being properly positioned in a vein, you'll be putting your drugs into the tissue surrounding the vein, under the skin, or some other place," the booklet continues. "It will probably be painful and become swollen, and the effects of your drugs will come on much more slowly. You also risk abscess formation and other possible problems." It treats drug users as intelligent adults and assumes people want to take care of their bodies as best they can. The book includes advice on how to engage in riskier injection practices—hitting in the groin or neck, for example—but explains why specific behaviors are riskier and how to make those behaviors a little less risky. Other topics include wound care, overdose response, and how to safely store and dispose of injection equipment. Illustrations make instructions easy to follow. The old guidebook remains online today, easily found with the search term "getting off right."[3]

Jess was becoming more comfortable in her skin as an activist and as someone who used drugs. People addicted to heroin faced hatred everywhere they looked, but the confidence Jess felt at Tapestry increasingly let her stand tall beyond the drop-in's walls. Then stigma hit her in the face.

Jess was doing needle exchange in Hartford one night, working out of a backpack, doing outreach where she knew the city's down-and-out congregated. A pair of police officers stopped Jess, asked her what she was doing, and, when she told them, began a search. The contents of Jess's bag were dumped onto the pavement, and the more aggressive of the two officers rattled off questions littered with curse words. "Be respectful," the second cop said. "She's a woman." His colleague replied: "That's not a woman. That's a junkie." The search continued.

"If I put my hands in your pocket, am I going to get anything?" one of the officers asked, implying that Jess was HIV-positive. Jess, admittedly escalating the situation, replied to the officer: "I don't know. Are you going to go home and fuck your mother tonight?"

The officer grabbed the back of Jess's head and slammed her face into the hood of their police car. Jess remembers how it bounced back off the soft metal. Then her face was thrown down a second time and again bounced off the car. Jess stayed quiet and refused to let the officers know she was in pain. She didn't go to jail that night but went home with a bruised face and a bloody mouth. "I was 21 at the time," she says. "And I hated police."

With every step that Jess took toward stability, it felt like the world pushed her two steps backward. During the summer of 1999, Jess made another attempt to quit heroin. The warmth she felt at Tapestry had her in a good place and she thought she could do it. On June 21, she was almost one month sober but, despite her progress, couldn't escape the repercussions of past drug use.

Jess had received a court order to remain in the state of Connecticut, where a few months earlier she had been arrested for possession. She was living in an apartment with a guy she didn't like because the court mandated that she live in Hartford and she didn't have the money to do that alone. Jess didn't feel safe and took the bus 45 minutes to her parents' place, in Northampton, to tell them that. This violated Jess's court order. A fight with her parents ensued and Jess was driven back to the apartment in Hartford. Once there, every bad vibe Jess felt about the place and her roommate came to life. "He brutally raped me that night, repeatedly, and left me in a pool of my own blood," Jess says. After the man went to sleep, Jess was able to get to a phone. She called her father, he called the police, and Jess waited. It felt like an eternity but shortly after, officers kicked in the door. The roommate was arrested and Jess was taken to a hospital where she was treated horribly.

She sat in the emergency room with a split lip and a black eye, waiting for a detective to arrive to take her statement. When one finally did, it was a man, causing Jess to feel sick to her stomach. "Are you sure this isn't a trick gone wrong?" he asked her. "Did he not pay you? Because you know, crying rape isn't a way to get back for not getting paid." Jess couldn't manage to reply. She was only 23 years old. She told the police she wouldn't file charges. If this was how a hospital treated her, she couldn't imagine how terrible it would be moving a case through the criminal justice system. "I knew who the guy was. We had him. But the whole thing was too horrifying," Jess says.

As soon as the cops had finished with her, Jess fled the hospital against medical advice and, for the second time that night, caught a ride to her parents' home in Northampton. "They were devastated," Jess says. "It was them who had driven me back to that house."

Her mother and father were acting strange, but Jess attributed that to shock and extreme guilt. Then the phone rang. Jess's mother tried to grab it before she could, but Jess noticed and made sure she got there first. On the line was her friend Careena and she was crying. "Josh is dead," she told Jess. "And I just dropped the phone." Jess's mother had known all night but had tried to hide it because of the attack Jess had suffered earlier that evening. Hysterical, Jess called Luciano to ask him why nobody was with Josh when he overdosed. Before she could get her question out, Luciano attempted to console her. "I can't believe he shot himself," Luciano said. Jess fell apart. Luciano told her what had happened. Josh's mother had found him in their backyard with a gunshot wound to his head. "He committed suicide as a direct result of being addicted," Jess says.

After Josh died, Jess felt like she had little reason to stick around. "At this point, I'd had one friend commit suicide because of heroin and one friend die of an overdose, so there's already been two deaths," she says. "But Josh's death . . . she trails off. Jess had gone three weeks without heroin, but after the rape and Josh's suicide, she knew that wasn't going to last. Not in a town where everyone she knew was still injecting. "I had this idea that if I just got away from Connecticut and Western Mass., I would be okay," Jess says. "I decided to go to Arizona, to sort of start over."

7

All Practice up to Now

The brief time that Louise spent in Atlanta and at the Bluff changed her life. She had found a community and now was excited to start her new position in Greensboro as program director for the North Carolina Harm Reduction Coalition (NCHRC). It was something of a fresh start. She had a new job and had also just dealt with a number of small-time drug charges, avoiding prison with a promise to attend NA meetings and obey a long list of additional conditions. With enthusiasm, Louise excelled at NCHRC, demonstrating the singular focus and obsessive dedication that people in recovery often apply to new interests after they stop using drugs. Out of a small office, NCHRC offered whatever harm reduction supplies were then legal under state law—condoms, for example, and Chore Boy copper scouring pads that recipients used to assemble crack pipes. Louise was also hosting harm reduction training sessions, teaching overdose response, and helping other nonprofit service providers understand how best to cater to drug-using clients without stigmatizing them. "We're teaching people in North Carolina about harm reduction," Louise says. She also didn't mind that NCHRC was increasingly engaging in illegal syringe exchange. "You know, whatever. Just got rid of all those old pending charges so let's get some new ones," she says with a laugh.

On the surface, life was good. Methadone was working for her and Louise had remained off cocaine and heroin for a while now. She was also still working through a master's in public health at the University of North Carolina at Greensboro and, with NCHRC, had a legitimate job that, for the first time in her life, she actually enjoyed going into. Beneath a recovery that looked perfect on paper, however, Louise was feeling internal tensions that went right to her core.

She was still attending NA meetings several times a week, and every word she heard there was in total opposition to the harm reduction work that was becoming her whole life. "I had to lay down an entire belief system," she says. Living in two worlds was intensely destabilizing.

Meanwhile, things at the NCHRC office were getting complicated. Tension was developing between her and Thelma. For Louise, always intensely sensitive to bad vibes, this was unbearable. She had slipped up and smoked crack with a poor choice of a temporary boyfriend and then found herself struggling with renewed cravings for opioids. Louise began to dabble back into heroin. Thelma realized something was up.

"I relapsed," Louise says. "And I was trying to hide it, and hiding an addiction is a huge job. Trying to hide an addiction is all-consuming." A new hire to the organization named Jill found out that Louise was using again and held it over her, threatening Louise, not outright but in subtle ways that Jill used to manipulate her. "You are never safe as a drug user," Louise says. "You always have something that somebody can use against you." The walls were closing in.

Thelma says she simply did not know how to respond to an employee who she discovered was using hard drugs. "I might have not been totally professional about it," she concedes. Thelma began asking Louise why she did or didn't do one thing or another. Louise felt the accusations and stigma in her questions and, after a couple of minor confrontations, fell to the floor of the NCHRC office crying. "She felt like she'd disappointed me," Thelma says.

Louise did feel like she had let Thelma down, and this feeling overwhelmed her. "I had too much to do, was just working too hard," she says. "I'm trying to assert some boundaries and realizing

I can't. People get mad, and then I go to work the next day and can feel the hostility. And I am really sensitive to it. Everywhere I'm going, I'm feeling fucking uncomfortable as fuck. I can't take it."

In addition to Louise's bipolar disorder, this heightened sensitivity could have played an important role in her addiction to opioids. Sensory processing sensitivity, or SPS, is a common thread among people who use drugs. In *Unbroken Brain: A Revolutionary New Way of Understanding Addiction*, Maia Szalavitz, a journalist who was formerly addicted to heroin and cocaine, writes that, from the time she was a child, sensory experiences overwhelmed her. Bright lights, loud noises, and, especially, uncomfortable social situations, caused Szalavitz to feel like "the world was always on the verge of erupting into chaos and engulfing me." It was one of the reasons she used heroin, to "simply turn the volume of my emotions and senses down," and to feel safe.[1] Judith Homberg, a researcher of behavioral neurogenetics at Radboud University in the Netherlands, says that SPS is a condition identified by heightened sensitivities to one's environment and external stimuli such as interactions with friends and colleagues. "These people get more details or are more empathetic or have a very well-developed intuition. They are also very adaptive and reactive and so forth, because they notice things in the environment. But the disadvantage is that you can be easily overwhelmed," she says. "If something is too much or too intense, then that impacts these people more. And that leads to all kinds of stress-related problems—among them, addiction."

The research is in its early days, Homberg cautions, but these potential links are under investigation in Norway, Switzerland, France, and Italy, with Homberg's colleagues in each country working together to investigate. The goal is to understand possible associations between SPS and drug use, particularly when one begins using drugs, the amount they take, and how often they use them. Preliminary data suggest no link between SPS and cannabis but a possible link with cocaine use and a probable link with opioids.

"People use drugs to self-medicate, as a kind of coping strategy," Homberg says. "They have a lot of anxiety and depression and want to use or continue to use drugs because they want to suppress those negative feelings." With sensory processing sensitivity, heightened feelings can lead one to seek to dampen those thoughts with drugs that soften emotions, like heroin and other opioids.

Overwhelmed by her feelings, Louise resigned as program director for the NCHRC. Shortly after, Thelma also stepped down from her leadership position as executive director. All this time, Thelma had continued working for Lorillard Tobacco and Sears, plus she was raising a family and by now had two teenage sons, "wrecking cars and shit." She was tired. "I needed to go," Thelma says. "I worked two and three jobs all my life. And I was just burned out."

Everyone said farewell on good enough terms. But the split left Louise without a reliable source for harm reduction supplies. Overcoming significant anxiety, Louise placed a call to Chicago's Dan Bigg, the legendary figure who in Cleveland had introduced Jess to naloxone and in Tacoma had revealed America's underground syringe network to Louise. Dan and other early advocates who were willing to break the law to save lives had established clandestine harm reduction supply chains right across the United States. In 2010, Louise became Dan's primary distributor in Greensboro. Syringe exchange was still illegal in North Carolina, and because NCHRC was receiving some money from the government, it tried to stay on the right side of the law. With Louise now at arm's length from NCHRC, the organization began using her as an independent proxy that could bend the rules in ways the organization could not. Louise called it North Carolina Syringe Access.

She was perfectly situated for the task. The years that she had spent injecting drugs made her invaluable to Dan's underground network. "I did a lot of needle distribution with myself," Louise says, laughing. "That's where a lot of needles went. As soon as I started getting high again, that whole world opened back up."

By this time, the second wave of America's opioid epidemic was underway.

The first phase was driven by prescription painkillers—pills that people obtained either from a doctor's office or, more likely, on the illicit market, from a friend with a prescription or from a dealer who had tapped into the glut of pills that had flooded America.

The drug epidemic's second wave—heroin—was sweeping through a nation that had taken a new interest in opioids and now found itself losing its supply. With overprescribing, doctors eventually realized their mistake and faced increasing scrutiny from regulators. Authorities cracked down on physicians who were still too loose with addictive medications like OxyContin, Opana, and their generic equivalents. Decision makers thought they were doing the right thing. But an unintended consequence slowly became apparent. For some patients, losing a prescription didn't end their drug use—because they were addicted. When doctors cut off a patient's supply of OxyContin, they simply went looking for a new source of opioids. Many of them found dealers on the street, and the dealers quickly turned them on to a stronger and cheaper drug: heroin. People buying pills on the black market were similarly offered opioids in a purer form.[2]

Organized crime saw an opportunity and seized on it. Sam Quinones's *Dreamland: The True Tale of America's Opiate Epidemic* recounts how Mexican cartels adopted a franchise model, expanding distribution networks beyond the likes of New York, Miami, and Los Angeles, into mid- and smaller-sized cities, like Greensboro and Northampton. In much of the country's less-densely populated interior, a cheap and consistent supply of heroin became easily available for the first time.

Drug overdose deaths surpassed the levels they had already hit with pills. In 2005, there were 29,800 fatal overdoses in the United States. Half a decade later, in 2010, there were 38,300.[3]

Center for Optimal Living in New York City, an addiction treatment organization that combines harm reduction with an emphasis on empowerment. "If we can understand the meaning and the function of a person's drug use, we might actually be able to help them come up with more effective, healthier ways of serving those functions. Which may be consistent with abstaining from drugs or might not and might be more consistent with using substances in less harmful ways."

Reading Tatarsky's work alone in Sarah's basement, Louise finally realized that if she was ever going to capture what she was after, she would have to build it herself. "They're doing this in San Francisco, they're doing this in these other places," she thought. "We could do this here. Let's do this."

Louise and Wiggs quickly grew close. Organically, they began to function as an underground harm reduction organization. It helped that they were selling drugs—just enough to cover their own habits. It kept them in close proximity to people who could benefit from harm reduction. Another reason the pair grew so close so fast is that Louise was in need of a friend. "I was moving back in with my mom after having yet another failed relationship where there was abuse," she says. This was a big step. With Reggie and then Tommy and then Brice, Louise had remained in relationships for years after they turned abusive. But not anymore.

She was also back at school, finally completing her master's degree, finding her passion in harm reduction, and mostly keeping her illicit drug use to a minimum, successfully managing her addiction with methadone. Things were going well. But her methadone clinic didn't see it that way. The U.S. government requires that the distribution of methadone occur at designated facilities, and they are notoriously unpleasant places for people who use drugs. Hours are often limited, resulting in long queues where a lack of privacy makes it obvious people are there for the treatment of an addiction.

The consumption of methadone is supervised, and random urine tests are usually a clinic requirement, which critics argue equates addiction treatment patients with common criminals. That sort of stigma is also inflicted by some clinic staff who treat patients with indifference and disrespect, similarly acting as if they have done something wrong simply because they are there.[4] Louise's clinic seemed to take any opportunity it could to kick her down a notch.

"I'm failing drug tests," Louise explains. "Actually, I'm doing much better. But the methadone clinic can't tell that. All they see is I'm failing drug tests." The clinic threw her out and cut her off methadone. Louise pleaded with them. "You don't realize that in the last six months I've left an abusive relationship, I'm back in school, I'm doing all of these positive things?" she said. "All you can see is that I'm testing positive. But my life is 100 percent better. And if you throw me out of the methadone clinic, it's all going to go to shit again."

That's exactly what happened. Off methadone, Louise resumed using more heroin. It didn't slow her work with harm reduction, though. Just the opposite, Louise's return to street drugs put her and Wiggs at the center of a community that needed exactly what they were offering.

Wiggs lived on Walker Avenue, a perfect location for their purposes. "He was right by the bars," Louise says. "Cocaine corner. It's just where people hang out. And his house was where people hang out. So, to have syringes there is to have a syringe exchange there."

Every so often, deliveries arranged by Dan Bigg would appear on the front porch of her mom's place, where Louise was still living. "We've got packages at Sarah's house!" Louise would say. When they arrived, there were so many boxes they blocked the door. "Stacks taller than me and we're trying to move everything inside," Wiggs says.

Louise gives all credit to Dan. "Anytime I need anything, I'm calling Dan and he's sending it," she explains. "Then we'd come home and there's boxes of needles all over the front porch and I'd be like, 'Holy shit. We've got to get this off the porch before Sarah sees it.'"

While Louise remained in charge of procuring supplies, she and Wiggs shared distribution responsibilities equally. "Between my having sold drugs and his having sold drugs, we knew a lot of people," Louise says. "He was 10 years younger than me so we knew two decades of people."

As heroin replaced pills in Greensboro, deaths became a more common reality. Soon, people who were calling Louise for syringes were also calling when an overdose occurred. "We didn't have enough naloxone to give out," Louise explains. "We had only enough naloxone for people to call when someone overdosed."

The first time this happened, she was hanging out at Wiggs's one night, preparing a small bag of cocaine, when the phone rang. A mutual friend named James[†] was on the other end of the line, begging for their help. "Dude, I don't know what's going on. I've got this guy and I think he's dying," James cried. "I don't fucking know!"

Louise and Wiggs leapt into action. Wiggs grabbed his keys and a naloxone kit while Louise began talking James through the basics of overdose response. "We were telling them, on the phone, 'Give him some rescue breaths,'" Wiggs says. "For every breath you take, they need to be taking a breath. Don't just give them *a* rescue breath. *Keep* giving them."

Louise and Wiggs ran outside to Wiggs's car and peeled away from the curb before their doors were closed. "Wiggs had this little fucking yellow Subaru, some little five-speed thing," Louise says. "And we flew across town in maybe five minutes."

The OD had occurred at a little two-story apartment complex. Everyone was too afraid of the police to risk calling 911. The man who had overdosed had a girlfriend there and she was in shock, on the verge of overdosing herself, and unable to follow directions. "It has all been practice up to now," Louise thought.

Meanwhile, James was somewhat disassociated from the crisis at hand. He was pacing aimlessly, appearing more concerned with doing whatever drugs were still around. The man who had overdosed was unconscious on the bathroom floor, soaked and freezing. "They'd thrown the guy in a cold bathtub with ice," Wiggs says. "Like, 'Come on guys, don't do that. You're going to put him into shock.'"

Neither James nor the girlfriend could tell them what drugs the man had taken. "We know there was some heroin, we know there was some cocaine, but we don't know which one he did," Wiggs says. The guy weighed something like 250 pounds. He was hard to move and the bathroom where they found him was small and cramped. "And they can't tell us what drugs he's on," Louise emphasizes, recalling her frustration. "This was frightening stuff." Louise began to panic but Wiggs remained cool. "Weezie, you need to slow down, you need to think," Wiggs said to her. "Louise followed his instructions and regained her composure. She began mouth-to-mouth resuscitation while Wiggs unpacked an intramuscular naloxone kit and loaded a syringe. Louise moved away from the man's head and then Wiggs inserted the needle into his upper arm and hit the plunger. Then Louise gave another series of rescue breaths and they waited for the naloxone to take effect. But nothing happened.

"You guys need to go ahead and call an ambulance right now. He's not coming back," Wiggs said. James finally put aside his fear of involving authorities and called 911. "We'd given him naloxone," Louise says. "We'd given him mouth-to-mouth—the only oxygen we had." Louise told James and the girl that it was time for her and Wiggs to leave. "We're not doctors," she said.

Wiggs hastily grabbed their things and neatly assembled their used naloxone kit where he hoped emergency responders would see it. "When the paramedics get here, tell them that he's had two of these," Wiggs told James. "We're not going to be here. We're going to disappear for this." Just then, with a quiet gasp for air, the guy came to. The authorities were still due to arrive any second, however. Louise and Wiggs ran out of the apartment, rounded a corner, and hunched down to watch the scene continue to unfold from there. "Then the girl overdosed," Louise says. They watched a team of paramedics save her, feeling a huge sense of relief that she didn't overdose while they were still inside the apartment trying to revive her boyfriend. Responding to an overdose is stressful, Louise explains, but responding to two overdoses simultaneously is terrifying.

With the paramedics finally in firm control of the situation, Louise and Wiggs headed back to their car and then to Wiggs's place. At his apartment, they both collapsed on his couch and simultaneously let out long sighs of relief. The evening was, however, not quite over.

At some point, the bag of drugs that Louise and Wiggs were sharing had fallen out of Louise's bra. After searching Wiggs's car and everywhere else, they figured it had to be somewhere at James's apartment. "They're going to the hospital and now we have to figure out how to get back into their place to get our shit," Wiggs says. "Jesus Christ." Thankfully, their second visit was less eventful. Wiggs crawled into the apartment through a window they found unlocked and located the bag of coke that Louise had dropped sometime during the confusion of the overdose. "All good," she says.

Months later, Louise bumped into the guy who had overdosed that night. She learned that at the hospital, a nurse told him that he would be dead if it were not for whoever had injected him with naloxone. "Man, I appreciate you," he said to Louise. "You saved me and my girl's lives. Thank you."

"That was healing," Louise says. "When do I feel like I've actually accomplished something?" she asks herself. "Doing syringe exchange. And the first time we reversed an overdose. The first time somebody called me and we were able to rush over there and save somebody."

Louise and Wiggs were saving lives, but that didn't stop the Greensboro police from coming down on them. Technically, it was a probation violation that Louise was arrested for, but it was her and Wiggs's harm reduction hotline that had put Louise back on the cops' radar. It was June 2011 and she was driving home from school one evening when police pulled her over, found a used syringe in the vehicle, and used that as a pretext to search her room at Sarah's, where there were boxes of supplies from Dan Bigg stacked floor to ceiling. Down in the basement where Louise was living, police officers ransacked the place. "And this was over nothing. This was harm reduction supplies. It was just syringes and stuff. But it was definitely enough to take me to jail." Louise was arrested for drug paraphernalia.

She was in good company. Women are the fastest-growing segment of America's population of incarcerated people.[5] The reason is the crackdown on drugs that began in the early 1970s and intensified through the 1980s, and, more recently, what's been termed the "feminization of the contemporary war on drugs."[6] In 2019, some 231,000 women and girls were behind bars, plus another one million were on probation or parole.[7] The vast majority of them were there for crimes related to drugs.[8] For women who use drugs, incarceration is the most likely path to both mental-health services and options for addiction treatment.[9]

After Louise was arrested, seemingly anything that could go wrong did go wrong. "My lawyer was out of town at an attorneys' convention or something. And then it was a $100,000 bond, so even if my mom would have wanted to get me out, she would have had to put up property, and she wasn't doing that. So this was going to be the longest I ever spent in jail. And I was very sick [in withdrawal]."

At Guilford County Jail, Louise was stripped naked, dressed in a prison-gray jumpsuit, and placed in an isolated cell. "Solitary was not a bad place for me at that point," Louise notes. "I would have been extremely uncomfortable in general population. I was so sick."

The walls were concrete, the door was steel, and the only blanket Louise had was scratchy polyester. There were no bars or window. For 23 hours a day, Louise was confined to a box. Her only connection to the outside world was a slot in the door through which "worse than shitty" food appeared. She had one *Harry Potter* book but was usually too sick to concentrate well enough to read it.

For a lot of people going through cold-turkey heroin withdrawal, water becomes a very important thing. "You're sweating, and in jail, you don't have any deodorant or anything like that," Louise explains. "And you stink, because you are sweating." So water is crucial, and being able to clean oneself becomes very important. But going through withdrawal inside Guilford County Jail, Louise had neither.

"The showers have got flies and larvae in them and just 20 seconds of hot water. So I'm trying to shower . . . but it is so disgusting. I want to clean the shower because there are some cleaning supplies that you can use. But I'm too weak and I'm too sick. So I'm doing the worst cleaning job. I'm just doing whatever I can, but I can't even push the mop. I'm so sick."

Back in her cell, there was nothing but intense discomfort. "You are really sensitive to any kind of touch," Louise says about withdrawal. "Your nerves are firing off. You're sensitive to temperature and it's not hot enough so I'm freezing. So I'm wrapped up in this blanket. You can't move but you have to move. Your muscles hurt. You are sweaty and gross. And you can't wipe the gross off."

Louise pulled her rough blanket up over her eyes and tried to sleep but couldn't. It was seven days before she finally was able to arrange bail. "I have never been so sick," she says. "Withdrawal is fucking horrible."

8

A Period of Calm

In Tucson, Arizona, Jess found a cozy apartment and made a home of it. Feeling rejuvenated, she embraced the activist bug that Tapestry had imbued in her. Less than a month passed before Jess connected with injection drug users in Tucson, began listening to their needs, and figured out how she could meet them. "I realize there's really a need for syringe exchange," Jess says. Friends at Northampton's Tapestry Needle Exchange were willing to go off the books and mail boxes of needles to her. "So I started running an underground exchange in Tucson, out of my house." Next, she secured a small grant to organize a support group for sex workers. Things were going great. "But I'd moved 45 minutes from the Mexican border and discovered there was tar there," Jess says. She was back into drugs. "I'd be up for four days at a time doing meth."

Jess quickly fell into a familiar pattern. She excelled in professional endeavors while her personal life crumbled. Around this time, a church cut her a check for $3,000 for condoms and other supplies for the sex workers with whom she worked. "I remember having that money sitting in a lockbox," Jess says. "They had given me a check, I had cashed it, and I was so sick on so many occasions. But I didn't touch that money. That was a source of pride."

Life in Tucson was exhilarating. Jess found a regular supply of naloxone in Mexico. The pharmacies there sold it without a prescription and so Jess began making trips across the border to purchase the medication in bulk. "It was expired and God knows where it came from, but I was excited about it," she says. "This was really my first experience with total frontline, grassroots, boots-to-the-ground street work." The needs were extreme. Friends in Northampton mailed her boxes of syringes but there were never enough. "I had to limit people. I watched people share, constantly." Jess was doing harm reduction in its most basic and crucial forms: needle exchange, support groups, and offering assistance on hygiene and nutrition.

"I learned how to make tamales from my Mexican neighbor. It was cheap to make rice and beans and tamales. That was the staple diet of many of the women [sex workers] out there, because many of them came from Mexico. So we'd have these kitchen cooking dates. We had almost 20 women doing tamale-cooking stations in my kitchen," she says. Jess and the women whom she affectionately calls "my girls" sold them on busy street corners around downtown Tucson. They used the money to purchase soap, shampoo, tampons, and other hygiene products for the group.

"I saw women brought from Mexico, beaten, and made to work," Jess says. "The men could control them because a lot of these women had drug habits. They couldn't shoot themselves up, they didn't know where to buy." Over a couple of months, Jess taught her girls those exact things, instructing the women on how to inject themselves and connecting them with dealers. In addition, some of the women had abscesses or other types of infections, and their handlers would withhold medication if they did not pay up a large percentage of the money they earned on the street. Horrified, Jess began supplying them with antibiotics she purchased on the black market. "We were removing the things that kept women under the control of men," Jess says. "I was also hooking these women up with a methadone clinic."

Prohibitionist laws and the drug war greatly endanger the lives of women who use drugs. When America criminalized drugs, women did not stop using them; instead, they adapted their behavior to hide it. The same is true for sex workers. Drug use and sex work continue under prohibition, but instead of taking place out in the open, where there is a degree of security, women hide these activities, and so there is seldom a witness who can intervene when something goes wrong. Moreover, there is significant overlap between the two groups; while not all sex workers use drugs, a high percentage do and the two behaviors are frequently linked.[1] This situation greatly increases the extent to which sex workers are exposed to violence.[2] The more repressive the laws forbidding sex work, the higher the rates of violence sex-working women endure.[3]

Jess's home was operating as a harm reduction drop-in, delivering services that were entirely unique to the region. But it wasn't sustainable. "I broke every best-practice rule there is," Jess explains. "I was going out alone, I was going out at night, I was going out in miniskirts. Because of that, I was embraced by the world of sex workers. But I was young, still in my mid-20s, and I was doing a lot of dangerous stuff I would never do now." Worst of all, she was alone.

Walking home one evening, Jess was hit with just how alone she was. She cut through a large, poorly lit park. She knew she shouldn't have, but it was getting late and going around the park would have taken longer. Then she heard a woman screaming. Far across the park but close enough for Jess to watch, two men grabbed one of her girls and threw her into the trunk of their car. The woman's hand reached up and one of the men swung into the trunk with a piece of rebar. "That image is stuck in my mind," Jess says, "her hand reaching out."

Jess was standing in the middle of an open field with nowhere to hide. The men slammed the car's trunk shut with the girl inside and then looked around to check if anybody had seen them. "They both turned and looked over at me, and I just froze, like a deer in headlights. And then I booked. I was terrified," Jess says. "She was one of our girls. She had been with me earlier in the night. I knew her name, or at least I knew her street name. And she went missing. I asked around about her. She was gone."

Jess never reported the incident. "I was terrified," she says. "Girls disappeared all the time out there. They were disposable. They had no family. I had never thought of myself like that, but at that point, I was separated from friends and my family. I could have gone missing for weeks at a time—months maybe—and nobody would have noticed."

Even more frightening, Jess suspected that she was the reason the woman was kidnapped. She was sure that her girls' handlers knew she was the one teaching them to inject and connecting them with dealers. "So these men were very angry that I was stepping in between."

Jess could no longer sleep at night and even during the daylight hours had to overcome visions of her own murder just to leave her apartment. "I was freaked out. And I was burned out," she says. "I went home to Northampton and I realized I had to go straight into detox."

By this time, Jess had spent more than a few hours of her life at Narcotics Anonymous meetings. She believed that her life was going to either continue with abstinence or end with addiction. She accepted that the only way to escape drugs was to surrender herself to a higher power. She was admitting her wrongs and was on her way to making amends. Then, in 2002, Jess did something that she didn't think was possible. She walked into a bar, ordered a whiskey sour, had a drink, and then walked out without drinking further. She didn't immediately run to buy heroin or relapse beyond that one whiskey. "The hand of God didn't come down and smite me, and I wasn't shooting heroin in 30 minutes," Jess says. Was everything she had learned in NA all a lie?

"Wait a minute," Jess thought. "This whole harm reduction thing I've been doing—why don't I apply it to my own life?" That's what she did. Jess embraced methadone maintenance and didn't beat herself up for "replacing one drug with another," as so many in the

NA world think of it. She also used heroin, infrequently, and was able to keep an occasional habit in check.

There is very little research that compares a state of abstinence to one of moderation; the vast majority only looks at abstinence versus chaotic or long-term drug use. But the little that does exist supports Jess's anecdotal report. Quality of life improves with the remission of a problematic addiction regardless of whether that remission reaches the point of abstinence.[4] Compared to the health outcomes for heavy drinkers, outcomes for low-risk drinkers are similar to those of adults who do not drink at all.[5] In a survey of addiction counselors across America, a little more than half said they find it "acceptable" for someone who abused alcohol or drugs to use their substance of choice on an "occasional" basis.[6]

A period of calm followed Jess's decision to moderate her use. She met and then was engaged to a man named Jordan. It didn't last forever. "He was gayer than I am and hated women because of it," Jess says with a laugh. But it lasted for a while. The couple moved to New Jersey and bought a house with a white picket fence. Aside from taking methadone, Jess remained mostly abstinent for nearly six years. "I used [heroin] a handful of times," she confesses. "I would go to New York City, see my friends, use for a weekend, and stop. And then I had four years of no use." It was during "the New Jersey period," as Jess refers to it, that she learned how to live like an adult. "I didn't know how to pay a bill," she explains. "I needed someone to teach me how to have electricity in my name, how to pay rent, and how to open a bank account. And that's what New Jersey was for me. I was learning skills for the first time in my thirties that most people learn when they move out of their parents' house for the first time." Jess bought a vacuum cleaner and then a living room set and then a dishwasher. "My house was beautiful," she says. "But I was really unhappy."

Struggling with suburban depression, Jess nevertheless remained mostly abstinent. She found, however, that her dedication to harm reduction was tougher to quit. She kept in touch with friends in the harm reduction world but stopped attending the community's annual conferences. She was working as a certified nursing assistant and that kept her busy and let her feel like she was doing something positive in this world. For the most part, the early 2000s was the furthest Jess had ever been from the world of chaotic drug use that she'd known for so many years. Eventually, however, she found she couldn't take the stillness of life in Pleasantville, New Jersey. She visited a friend in Boston one weekend and fell into a job at a syringe exchange and drug-user drop-in located across the river from the city's downtown core. Cambridge Cares About AIDS wanted someone who had used hard drugs—"lived experience," in the language of government and nonprofit partners—and Jess fit the bill. She was offered a job as a health educator. By this point, her relationship with Jordan had been over for some time, save for the formality of a breakup. So it was easy for her to move to Boston, and she was thrilled to return to harm reduction full time. Then things got even better.

Visiting Cambridge Cares one afternoon before officially starting the new job, Jess was hanging out, getting a feel for the place, and heard a familiar raspy voice. "That's Rachel!" she realized. It was the girl Jess had met when she was just 16 years old on one of her first trips to New York City: her "big sister," Rachel Auspitz.

For years, they had traded letters and enjoyed reunions with one another whenever Jess could make it into Manhattan. Then Rachel had completely dropped off the face of the Earth. Now she had reappeared. Jess walked over to her with a huge smile on her face. "Do you remember me?" Jess asked. "Yeah, I remember you," Rachel replied. But it was clear she didn't and Jess was heartbroken. Refusing to let it show, Jess held her in conversation for a few minutes. Finally, interrupting Jess midsentence, Rachel's voice jumped 10 levels: "Holy shit! Jess Tilley!" she exclaimed. And now they were both smiling and embraced in a hug. "From that point on, we were inseparable," Jess says.

Cambridge Cares About AIDS was established in 1988 and had a well-earned reputation as a leader of Massachusetts' harm reduction community. It was known for nonjudgmental programs and services that got condoms, syringes, and other supplies to marginalized groups who otherwise often slipped through the cracks. But when Cambridge Cares hired Jess 20 years later, in 2008, the organization was in a state of disarray. Staff turnover was a problem and duties were going unfulfilled. The gaps gave Jess and Rachel a lot of room to carve out their own space. "It was like being in a candy store for me," Jess says. "A harm reduction candy store. They gave me a budget and said, 'Do what you do.' Because for months, nothing had been done. Only the basics of ordering supplies. So I loved it." What Jess and Rachel decided they "do" was grassroots harm reduction: street outreach and drug-user organizing.

The pair began offering Cambridge Cares clients part-time jobs as stipendiary outreach team members, essentially hiring them without hiring them. This allowed Jess and Rachel to get drug-using participants involved in the work without going through the employee screening process that likely would have found reasons to disqualify them. They paid active users to walk Boston alleyways, check up on homeless people, and offer clean syringes, condoms, and other supplies. In addition, at around this time the old overdose-reversal drug naloxone—first approved for medical use in 1971—was receiving new attention. While today it is available in many states without a prescription, in the late 2000s, naloxone was still under tight government control.* Massachusetts was

---

* It is something of a mystery exactly why naloxone required a prescription and remained under government lock and key from the time it was approved for medical use in 1971 until states began to drop its prescription requirement in the mid-2010s. Naloxone involves no serious side effects. If a person

beginning to allow nonprofit partners to make the overdose antidote more widely available, but only on a trial basis and still only
with arduous and arbitrary regulations. "We got this amazing grant
for overdose outreach where we could actually distribute Narcan,"
Jess says. Institutional challenges remained. "We fought the department of public health to get it, and then they were trying to say that
nobody except people on payroll could distribute Narcan." This
was a rule created specifically to target Jess and Rachel's stipendiary outreach workers, they suspected. It was nothing more than a
roundabout way to prohibit the involvement of people who openly
used drugs. The pair pushed back and convinced the higher-ups to
allow their outreach team members to carry naloxone. "We developed a peer-driven, user-run staff," Jess says. "And the sky didn't
fall." Their team of drug users distributed naloxone efficiently and
without incident.

This was one of the earlier aboveground naloxone programs that
moved beyond the walls of an establishment health care facility in
America. "We decided to start doing what we called 'Narcan parties,'" Jess says. They would collect a group of people who used
opioids together at someone's house and teach the group how to
administer naloxone, perform rescue breaths, do chest compres-
sions, and provide care for someone resuscitated from an overdose.
They also instructed participants to give a loud warning when Narcan was about to be administered. Because the drug essentially
puts a person addicted to opioids into instant withdrawal, it is an
awful experience, and so a vocal warning is sometimes enough to
bring a semiconscious person around. Jess and Rachel had one foot
in the system and one foot out, and occupying this legal gray area

---

who does not have opioids in their system is injected with naloxone, there
is no effect at all. A probable reason for the drug's prescription requirement
lies in the stigma of the war on drugs. Many authorities view naloxone as enabling drug use and so, despite its remarkable ability to save lives, naloxone
remained under authorities' control for a very long time.

was working for everyone involved. Cambridge Cares allowed it because, as far as management was concerned, this was a "community participatory research project," and Boston drug users learned how to take care of one another in the event of an overdose.

Jess and Rachel placed themselves firmly on the side of their clients, and intermittent arguments with management served to tighten bonds and camaraderie among Jess, Rachel, and their staff of drug users. "Rachel was all about drug-user organizing," Jess says. Though she was once addicted to heroin, Rachel was now on methadone and only used sporadically. She often half-jokingly referred to herself as an "old-school dope fiend." While employed by Cambridge Cares, Jess was a bit more protective about her drug use past and, occasionally, present. She worried that if anyone learned too much, it would cost her her job, and that fear hung constantly overhead. Rachel was still an entry-level employee, and so had less to lose. But Jess was aiming for a manager's position; her hard-drug use had to remain a secret.

Next, Jess and Rachel convened a client advisory board meeting, which was really a way to form a drug-user union. "Hey, there's a meeting on Tuesday," they told clients. "We want to hear your ideas and I'll be taking minutes." There wasn't immediately a lot of enthusiasm—definitely not from Cambridge Cares upper management, but also not a lot from the drug users themselves. To Cambridge Cares' credit, however, they let Jess and Rachel do what they wanted, gave them a room for their meetings, and even provided pizza. Then people actually showed up (free pizza). Feelings of inadequacy, however, lingered. "Everybody in that room was, like, 'What can we do? We're just drug users,'" Jess says. Rachel nudged the group along with questions. "What issues are bothering you?" she asked. Jess recounted her attempts at drug-user organizing in Northampton, 10 years ago by this time. And slowly but steadily, a few members' eyes widened.

Jess and Rachel made an extra effort to ensure that women were involved in the union they were forming. "We started doing a Tuesday-night women's group where we would do nail painting and pajama parties," Jess says. Somehow, Rachel had an old copy of one of the flyers Jess had produced for Tapestry that instructed women on how to inject themselves: "It's as easy as changing a tampon!" They reprinted those old pamphlets and asked the women to share them around the neighborhood. It was exciting and it was fun.

This was Jess's second (or third or fourth, depending on how you count) attempt to establish a real drug-user union in New England. And this time, it looked like it was taking off. Again using the name New England Users Union, the group continued to do harm reduction outreach under the Cambridge Cares umbrella and inserted themselves into local debates that affected people who use drugs. "We created a space for drug users to come together," Jess says.

By this time, Jess's title had advanced from entry-level health educator to middle-management overdose prevention coordinator. She and Rachel were a force in New England's harm reduction scene. By 2010, their reputation was national, and the National Harm Reduction Coalition invited the pair of them to deliver the opening plenary address at its annual conference, that year in Austin, Texas. Together, Jess and Rachel hatched a plan for something big: Rachel would use their speech to announce that she was an active drug user.

Their work alongside street-entrenched drug users at Cambridge Cares was receiving a lot of interest and praise from addiction programs across the country. Their syringe and naloxone outreach programs were saving lives. If Rachel revealed herself as an active user, it would demolish every stereotype and stigmatizing limitation that government agencies and nonprofit partners used to minimize drug users' employment prospects. That was the plan, anyway. They knew it had risks. This was going to be a big deal. Rachel was an outreach coordinator employed by an organization that received a lot of money from the Massachusetts government. And nobody officially involved in the delivery of health care services at that level had ever openly admitted to using drugs. The pair decided they would break this barrier and use Rachel to spark a debate about internalized stigma within the movement. They were going to contribute something significant to America's harm reduction community that would, they hoped, begin to change the way it stigmatized the very people it claimed to help.

Jess had a nice apartment in a city she loved and a job in harm reduction that let her work with drug users. It was everything she wanted. But because Jess was happy, she was scared. Having things that she was happy about meant she could lose those things. At an ACT UP benefit in New York, Jess had too much to drink and fell into Rachel's arms. "I don't want to lose you," Jess told her with tears in her eyes. Rachel smiled. "I'm not going anywhere," she replied.

Two weeks later, toward the end of their workday at Cambridge Cares, Rachel mentioned she wasn't feeling well and asked Jess if she could cover for her for the rest of the afternoon. The next day, she called in sick again. "'I've got bacteria in my blood work,'" Rachel told Jess over the phone. "'I'm going to need a couple days off.'" Before the week was out, on September 5, 2010, Rachel died of sepsis as a complication of HIV/AIDS. She was 43.

Jess shut down. "I couldn't function," she says. "I had a bunch of money in a savings account and I start draining that savings account."

Cambridge Cares was supportive. It let Jess take a leave of absence and said it would hold her position until she was ready to return to work. But Jess no longer wanted the job. She didn't want anything. Another Boston harm reduction nonprofit had a deal on rooms at the Park Plaza, a grand hotel that dates from the 1920s. Jess used the nonprofit's discount code to get a room there and moved in. Under its ornate chandeliers and tucked into Egyptian-cotton sheets, Jess gave in to her pain. She drew the curtains, hung a "Do Not Disturb" sign on the door, called her dealer, asked for a delivery, and lit a cigarette. Weeks passed that way. "I'm blowing through my money and I just don't care," she says. "I was hoping every shot would kill me."

Eventually, the harm reduction community pulled her out of bed. The National Harm Reduction Coalition's 2010 convention in Austin was scheduled for November 18. Jess was still signed up to do the opening plenary address that she and Rachel had planned to deliver together.

Rachel had intended to out herself as an active drug user. Jess hadn't, because she was a program manager. But now Rachel was gone and Jess knew she had to take her place. "So I announced at the convention that I was an active user. And I watched the harm reduction world divide."

As Jess delivered the conference's opening session address, more than a thousand social workers, researchers, doctors, and activists stared up at her. "My name is Jess Tilley, and I am proud to be a drug user," she said from behind the podium. "I am proud to be alive and proud that my experience has helped keep so many others alive and safe. I am proud that I have not let the war on drugs make me a statistic. And I am proud that I have refused to be shamed because I choose to inject a substance." The room did not erupt in applause. A few people clapped, but mostly there were hushed whispers.

Over the next four days of the conference, many people told Jess she had done the wrong thing. "I was told I pushed our movement back 10 years." There were many in attendance who supported her, however. "What Jess Tilley did is speak for people who cannot speak," Mark Kinzly, a research associate at Yale University and a respected veteran of the movement, told a session he led at the conference. "I'm hearing a lot of talk about her. This is harm reduction and we don't treat our family members like this." Another big supporter was a boyish young man about the same age as Jess named

Shilo Jama (formerly Shilo Murphy). He and Jess had met only the day before but stayed up all night talking and had already grown into good friends. "Here's Jess, who's said, 'It's okay to be a drug user, it's okay to be in this movement,'" Shilo says. "Before that, I honestly didn't think there was a place for us. And now, here comes this person who said, 'There's not only a place for you, but we can do this together. You don't have to be alone.'"

Others criticized Jess for allegedly discrediting harm reduction at a time when government partners were just beginning to give serious consideration to needle exchange and similar programs. "You can't do this. You run a program," people told her in the conference hallways.

Mark says the incident underscored a growing divide in America's harm reduction community. "Jess came out and made the statement that she was proud to be a drug user and people chastised her relentlessly," he says. "They yelled at her. I mean, it was ugly." In 2010, America's drug policy reform movement was not as inclusive as it claimed or aspired to be, Mark says. "We had made space, somewhat, for drug users at the harm reduction conference. But only if you acted a certain way. Only if there were no problems and everyone was good." And in Austin, according to her critics, Jess hadn't behaved herself.

Not that she cared. Rachel would have been proud of her.

Jess returned to Boston and quit her dream job at Cambridge Cares. She couldn't handle working there without Rachel by her side. By this time, Jess had lost her apartment and, with her savings account drained, the Park Plaza was no longer an option. "I was pretty much hell-bent on killing myself," she says. "I didn't want to die, but I didn't know what to do. So I move into a loft and I'm just shooting up, shooting my life away."

9

The Urban Survivors Union

Recovery is seldom linear.

For a while, Louise was off cocaine and heroin. She was attending Narcotics Anonymous meetings. But she wasn't feeling any better about life. "I was living at my mom's. I was spending a lot of time in the basement, just studying," she explains. "It was a really dark, quiet, lonely time for me."

NA had become a big part of Louise's life and she found some semblance of community there, a few friends, but she wasn't happy. As Louise once again involved herself more in harm reduction, she stopped going to NA meetings and those friends disappeared. At the same time, outside of that NA world, Louise found it increasingly difficult to make new friends. "I was in school, on a public health track. But fellow students were running marathons and I'm on cigarettes and heroin, scratching my feet and shit," Louise explains. "Once you've had a life like mine, what do you say? One of the first things that women talk about is their children. So what do I say? 'Oh, I've got two children and I don't raise either one of them'? Or you can lie. But it gets old lying to everybody about your life."

Meanwhile, Louise's best friend Wiggs was in Taipei, completing his college degree with a year abroad, and Louise was doing her best to stay away from other old friends with hard-drug habits. She missed the camaraderie of NA, if nothing else about the program. She was lonely.

Looking for friends who were a step removed from heroin, she was spending time with a guy named Jimmy[†]. Jimmy was more into techno music and party drugs such as ecstasy. He was a relatively good influence, Louise figured. "It was all platonic," she says. "He was a DJ who made music and we could have fun. We'd do molly and hang out. He was antiheroin." They were out drinking one night and ended up back at his place, out on the edge of Greensboro, and that's just about the last thing that Louise remembers.

"I remember stopping by my house. I remember driving toward Jimmy's house. I remember crawling around in a yard out in the country, screaming and not knowing where I am, not knowing what was going on."

Louise woke up on her stomach in tall grass. One of her legs was turned around backwards. One side of her pelvis was crushed and her knee was completely smashed. Her head hurt bad. Her face hurt and would later turn black and blue. Everything hurt.

Time passed. Maybe 45 minutes or an hour, Louise guesses. Or maybe it was just a few minutes. Jimmy was inside his house nearby and finally came running out, shouting at Louise to stop screaming, for fear she would wake the neighbors. Then Jimmy saw Louise and stopped shouting. He went quiet for a moment. Louise did, too. The entire area went quiet. Louise could hear the wind through the tall grass around her. Then Jimmy snapped back into the moment. He scooped Louise's small body into his arms and carried her across the street and into his house. "He picked me up off the ground and it hurt me so bad," Louise says.

Back inside the house, Jimmy lay her down in a bathtub. "I looked down and my ankle was turned all the way around the other way," Louise says. She could see that she was seriously hurt and that scared her. And yet she begged Jimmy not to call 911. As bad as her injuries frightened her, the idea of going to a hospital scared Louise worse. Hospitals terrified her. She would do anything to avoid interacting with police or any facet of the establishment. "I'll be good," Louise sobbed. "Please, just let me stay here. I don't want an ambulance. I'll be good." Jimmy called 911.

The police arrived before an ambulance that night. Jimmy

claimed he had no idea what had happened and Louise was similarly no help. She was mostly incoherent, anyway. "I wouldn't give the police any information," Louise says. "They hadn't been a source of safety or help for me for a very long time."

To this day, Louise does not know what happened to her. She eventually decided that it was an accident. She must have been walking along the road outside Jimmy's place and a car struck her in the dark. There were no streetlights out there. Whoever was driving might not even know they had hurt someone. It was a random hit-and-run, a senseless action with no motive or connection to her life, Louise told herself. She has a number of other theories. Brice had just gotten out of prison. "But it's less painful to think that there was no purpose behind what happened. It could have been random. I finally just decided I didn't want to know."

The accident marked the onset of a long and dark period of Louise's life.

After a few weeks at Greensboro's Moses Cone Hospital, she discharged herself against doctors' orders; the hospital was a traumatic place for Louise. Despite having found a place of her own just before the accident, she was forced to move back into her mother's house. Sarah and Walter Beale had divorced a couple of years earlier. Sarah was initially reluctant to let Louise stay with her again but saw that her daughter's injury meant she truly needed help.

The health care system treated Louise horribly. "Right before my last operation, one of these doctors says to me, 'You're not going to like what you see when you wake up.' He didn't tell me anything else. Just, 'You're not going to like what you see when you wake up.'"

Out of the hospital, Louise began visiting another doctor on a weekly basis, primarily to manage and treat infections, which, with Louise's leg healing poorly, threatened to become serious. The two of them were not getting along. This doctor was responsible for pain management as well, but he refused to prescribe Louise OxyContin pills containing more than five milligrams of the opioid. It would have been a uselessly low dose for almost anyone, and the problem was only compounded by Louise's considerable tolerance for pharmaceuticals. But because of that same history of addiction, five-milligram Oxys were all that Louise was going to get. Confined to Sarah's house, unable to walk, and in constant and severe pain, Louise grew increasingly frustrated with her situation.

Although she had the connections to obtain a steady supply of painkillers on the street, she was trying to stay out of that scene. Again and again, Louise asked her doctors for help. "I was going to be honest. I was going to talk to the doctors, we were going to have trust, and I was going to get the medicine and the help that I needed. But this doctor could not see me as doing anything but seeking drugs." At one appointment after another, Louise cried and cried.

The doctor stopped returning Louise's calls and eventually she received a formal discharge order. This meant that Louise was left without a regular physician even as her leg was barely holding together and a bone periodically poked through the skin of her ankle. It was more than a full month before she finally found someone who would take her on as a patient. This period without care was extremely dangerous. Louise had an external fixator on her leg that was holding her broken bones in place. With her history with MRSA, the risk of infection was extremely high. "By the time I made it to another doctor, my leg was as big as an elephant's. The bone kept going through my skin, the metal was reacting poorly. My leg was not getting better."

By now, Wiggs had returned from his year of school abroad. He assumed the role of Louise's caretaker, acting as her nurse, assistant, and chauffeur. Getting Louise to a doctor's office was no easy feat and Wiggs took this responsibility seriously. "I had to fight her and drag her, kicking and screaming, so many times," he says. "I would say, 'We're going to the hospital,' and she would be crying. But we went. I dragged her there."

Before long, Wiggs and Louise were talking about partnering on a small-time drug operation. Louise put a stop to the idea, however. They were running an underground syringe exchange, and so dealing was no longer an option. Louise figured that if they were selling drugs, the police would be on them so hard for that illegal activity, they might not be able to continue with their other illegal activity, distributing needles. And Louise decided she couldn't do that to their participants. "But no one would give her any painkillers for her leg," Wiggs says. "Louise had told me about that for a long time, but I thought she was being dramatic. Then, finally, I saw it and it hit home: she's not exaggerating any of this."

As America's opioid epidemic caught the public's attention, there was a growing backlash against pharmaceutical companies and the doctors that prescribed their pills. As a result, people like Louise—legitimate patients with injuries and very real pain—increasingly had trouble finding a doctor who would provide adequate treatment.[1] From 2006 to 2017, the CDC tracked a 19 percent reduction in annual opioid prescribing rates. Health care providers had suddenly become more "cautious" about prescribing opioids.[2]

So Louise and people like her started using heroin—again, in Louise's case, but others for the first time. And, to pay for it, some of them started small-time dealing. Louise stuck to the promise she made to herself to protect her syringe exchange, however. Cut off of prescription painkillers and short on the money she needed to purchase medicine on the street, there were many nights Louise lay awake at night in pain.

They lived together in Sarah's basement along with Selena. Right through her teenage years, Selena shared a bed with Louise most nights. Wiggs slept across the room on a couch. They were a little family. Sarah, Louise, and Wiggs all took care of Selena together.

For someone with such a badly broken leg, Louise kept extremely busy. They were hustling harm reduction supplies, including clean needles and Narcan kits, when they had them. They also led overdose response trainings. "We knew all these people who injected drugs and were at so much risk," Louise says. "So not only was it good for us, it was good for everyone."

This drew the attention of police. The police hated them, and Louise especially. Greensboro's finest knew her on a first-name basis, having run into her more than a few times over the preceding decade. They didn't like that no matter how many times they arrested her, she never seemed to spend more than a night or two in jail. And now Louise's name and her harm reduction efforts were beginning to pop up on the local news. The authorities felt it was time to knock her down a peg.

Just after dawn on July 11, 2013, they made their move.

It was early, around 6:30 a.m. Sarah had already been awake for some time. She was sitting at her small desk, working on a computer by the house's back door. Louise, Wiggs, and Selena were all still asleep in the basement. Then their dog started barking, which made Sarah look up, toward the door. On the other side was a team of more than a dozen officers wearing full tactical gear including bulletproof vests and black face masks. It was a hit of total shock. They had automatic weapons drawn, dogs already sniffing around the yard, and a battering ram positioned to knock in Sarah's back door. She didn't know what else to do but let them in.

In the basement, Wiggs was the first to wake up on account of the commotion. He put the dog in a cage they had for him there, likely saving its life. "Then there were flashlights and assault rifles coming down the stairs." Officers shouted at all three of them to lie facedown on the ground. Louise's leg was still in an external fixator, immobilizing her. But Wiggs and 16-year-old Selena immediately complied. "I didn't have time to process what was going on," Wiggs says. "It was a full SWAT team on us."

With guns pointed at her, Louise painfully climbed the stairs. She, Wiggs, and Selena were handcuffed to chairs around the family's dining room table. The police didn't bother questioning Louise. She immediately made clear she wouldn't say a word and they didn't waste their time trying to make her. Wiggs was essentially ignored. It was Selena whom the cops went after. Two officers took her from the dining room to the living room and began questioning her. "Selena, don't you answer anything without me there," Louise shouted through the wall.

It was an odd line of questioning officers pushed on Selena. They tried to make her say something about injecting heroin with Louise. Selena had never done this and wouldn't have said so if she had. As this informal interrogation continued, officers carried boxes up from the basement. There were crates of clean syringes that Louise and Wiggs were distributing under the table for the North Carolina Harm Reduction Coalition (NCHRC), sharps containers full of used needles that they had collected in exchange, and boxes of ascorbic acid and other harm reduction supplies. There were no drugs. The cops found nothing that morning for which they could justify taking Louise back to the station.

"Here I am with all of these positive things going on," she says. "I'm running a syringe exchange, I'm going to all of these CDC meetings, I'm making a difference in the world. And yet I'm still getting arrested every other day. I've still got police running after me. I began to get very afraid. They were actively trying to put me away. I had a probation officer who said that. I really realized how vulnerable I was in every way. We were not safe. We were not safe from the police. Selena was not safe. They were even coming after Selena."

The police raid on Sarah's home was little more than a fishing expedition, but it came with a SWAT team bearing automatic weapons. Alex Vitale, in his book *The End of Policing*, describes how the war on terror has run into the war on drugs to contribute to this sort of dangerous aspect of overpolicing. He asserts: "The War on Drugs is the most damaging and ineffective form of policing facing us."[3]

Vitale describes the effects of such raids as "lifelong trauma." "If we do any kind of cost-benefit analysis, all we get are costs." Vitale explains that a "no-knock" warrant and similarly harsh tactics are felt beyond the individuals they target. "This is destabilizing for communities and this is not reducing the flow of drugs in any way," he says. "It sends this message: that the police are at war with a large segment of the population. And it sends this message: that there are these horrible threats looming on every corner. It creates an exaggerated sense of danger, which then is used to justify ever more powerful and invasive forms of policing."

That morning in July 2013, the police raid of Sarah's home didn't produce enough of anything to take Louise to jail. But it did yield one notable consequence. Before the raid, Sarah liked police officers. She had never broken a law in her life. She had never missed a Sunday at church. Sarah respected the police and supported their privileged position in society. She believed police were the good guys. "Now, she knows that everything that I've ever said about the police is true," Louise says. "That they have violated me in ways that criminals have not." Where once Sarah would have smiled and said hello to an officer she passed on the street, now they terrified her.

During the raid, she could only think: "Is this really the way we help people with an addiction?"

In addition to caring for her leg, endless doctors' appointments and rehabilitation sessions, running an underground syringe exchange, providing what structure she could to her teenage daughter (while her youngest remained with her paternal grandparents), attending court dates and regular meetings with her probation officer, and dodging police left and right—between all of that—Louise completed school, earning a master's degree in public health from the University of North Carolina at Greensboro. "I don't know how I did it," she says.

Serving as the NCHRC's syringe point person for Greensboro pulled Louise deeper into the world of harm reduction. The organization's new executive director, Robert Childs, paid Louise stipends for the work, and she began to feel some responsibility, which translated into purpose. Robert arranged for Louise to attend another drug policy conference, this one in Denver, Colorado. "And that's where everything sort of began to take off. That's where I met Shilo."

Shilo Jama comes from the streets of Seattle's University District, or U District. With slightly unkempt brown hair and usually wearing baggy clothes, Shilo looks a decade younger than his 41 years. He's noticeably kind, always checking on people, asking if they're okay, and offering to lend a hand. Shilo was homeless in the U District for years through the late 1990s after aging out of foster care. Then he became addicted to heroin and moved into abandoned buildings and wherever else he could find shelter from police. One night, in 1996, in one of those vacant homes, Shilo was shooting drugs with another street kid. The following morning, his friend didn't wake up. Shilo shook him and he didn't stir. "I became hysterical," Shilo says. He tried to revive him, performing mouth-to-mouth. But Shilo was likely hours too late. At some point during the night, his friend had overdosed quietly. Shilo had remained asleep, lying next to him close enough for their arms to touch. "It broke my heart," Shilo says. That morning, he gently carried the young man's body out of their hiding place and lay his friend down on a small patch of grass. "I didn't want him to die in shit," Shilo explains. "I didn't want to leave him in a squat."

Shilo didn't blame the drugs that killed his friend or the dealer who sold them to him. He didn't blame the parents that neither of them had had growing up. The only people for whom Shilo felt anger were the police. He explains it was the police who they had been hiding from when they crawled into that abandoned building the night before. If it weren't for that, if they hadn't had to hide, there might have been someone else around who could have noticed his friend's ragged breathing and stepped in to prevent his overdose from ending in his death. "If you are homeless and you're a drug user, you are targeted," Shilo says. "We have a drug war and police are the foot soldiers."

Shilo considered his friend's death an induction into the war on drugs. Before that night in 1996, he was collateral damage. After that morning, he was a rebel, determined to fight back.

At around the same time, Shilo met an older man named Bob Quinn who was already a veteran of America's struggle for harm reduction. Bob had started an illegal syringe exchange in Seattle in the late 1980s and now allowed Shilo to volunteer at the sanctioned exchange he ran. "He's one of the closest things I've ever had to a father figure," Shilo says. Bob introduced Shilo to the world of harm reduction and then to drug-user organizing. In 2007, the pair of them co-founded the People's Harm Reduction Alliance (PHRA), one of the first syringe exchange organizations in America that knowingly and deliberately employed active drug users in its harm reduction programs.

From there, the idea of forming Seattle's first drug-user union would come and go and start and stop, making it difficult to pin down where exactly it began. But Shilo gives credit to a group who called themselves Pirate Punk. They ran a little music venue and helped Seattle bands figure out how to tour. They also served as a pool of like-minded people who supported harm reduction and the organizing efforts that Shilo was increasingly excited about. A woman who everyone called Kourtne Kaoss, a bartender at an underground punk club, began volunteering with them. Then a guy named Gary Lee Smith, a former Black Panther, asked Bob if he could hand syringes out for them in Seattle's downtown core. Bob was thrilled. This would extend syringe access beyond the U District. Bob had stopped using drugs many years earlier but Shilo, Kourtne, and Gary all still dabbled. The three of them began meeting on their own in the basement of the U District's University Temple Methodist Church, and ideas about a drug-user union really started to percolate.

Previous attempts to herd Seattle users into an organized group had consisted of little more than Shilo and a couple of his friends. This group had strategic reach: Kourtne, Gary, and Shilo hailed from distinct neighborhoods in the city and had connections and organizing experience in each of those respective communities. Bob offered the trio what guidance he could and introduced them to the Industrial Workers of the World, an international labor organization better known by its nickname, the Wobblies. Founded in Chicago in 1905, this rough-and-tumble organization used a strength-in-numbers approach to lobby for policies that would benefit its members collectively. This is what Shilo, Kourtne, and Gary would try to do with Seattle's drug-user community, they decided. In 2009, they established the Seattle Drug Users Union.

Things were happening. Then Facebook put their plans on hold for a couple of weeks. An algorithm targeted, then shut down, their Seattle Drug Users Union page, instantly eliminating the small group's primary organizing tool. Shilo, Kourtne, Gary, and a handful of other activists discussed what to do. Should they continue with the name and abandon Facebook? As much as everyone claims to hate the social network, surviving in an organizing capacity without Facebook is tough these days. They would have to abandon the name, they reluctantly agreed. As they brainstormed a replacement, one of them floated an idea. Without the sort of city-specific name that Facebook had just deleted, they could leave room for an expansion beyond Seattle. "We could do a chapter-based system," Shilo realized. For the time being, their members all happened to reside in Seattle. But with their new name—the Urban Survivors Union, or USU for short—that could soon change. "We were the survivors of the drug war," Shilo says. "Not just in Seattle but in other cities, too. There were a lot of us."

It wasn't long before another survivor did find them. Down in San Francisco, a young man named Isaac Jackson had similarly tried to organize drug users there for some time. He and Shilo had met at a conference in Austin a couple of years earlier and the two of them had stayed in touch, checking in with one another on the phone every couple of weeks. Isaac found community in Shilo's efforts to unite drug users from different cities, but in San Francisco he felt alone. There was a group of drug-user activists in San Francisco at the time—the San Francisco Drug Users Union—but it was floundering and Isaac had had a falling out with some in the group. "I was really depressed," he says. "And then Shilo called me and he said, 'We could use you in our organization, the Urban Survivors Union. You could start a chapter in San Francisco.' And I said, 'Yeah, that's a way of doing it.'"

Now the USU was bigger than Seattle and looking to expand further when Shilo traveled to another conference in Denver, Colorado. There, he happened upon a woman in a wheelchair "who seemed really sad." It was Louise. "A couple of years earlier, that was me," Shilo thought to himself. He had been at a harm reduction conference in Miami, Florida, feeling lost and intimidated. Mona Bennett, the organizer who had taken Louise into the harm reduction world of Atlanta, found Shilo wandering the halls there and offered to show him around. "You're with me. Don't ever forget that," Mona told him. For Shilo, it was a beautiful moment that let him feel accepted and a part of something in a way he never had before. Now, a few years later at a similar conference in Denver, Shilo was on his way to a panel discussion with another drug-user organizer from Seattle, Reggie Thomas, when the pair of them bumped into Louise.

Louise told them that she was sad and confused. "She doesn't know whether or not she is a drug user, she doesn't know where she fits into this harm reduction stuff, she doesn't know where she fits in drug policy," Shilo says. "So me and Reggie, we said, 'Well, this is simple: you fit with us. Come on, you'll be with us. You'll never be alone. Drug users stick together.'"

Louise felt she had found her family. They embraced her and

Louise felt comfortable with them. After hearing about the USU expanding beyond Seattle, Louise asked Shilo if she could establish a third chapter, in Greensboro. "Of course!" he replied.

Louise had experience in harm reduction, a master's degree in public health, and now she was doing drug-user organizing. Slowly, she was forging a new identity and feeling empowered by a new purpose. At the same time, things were "beginning to go sideways." Back in Greensboro, Louise was depressed about her leg injury and the constant pain she felt. Once again, her cocaine and heroin use was getting heavy. Then another new man appeared in her life—an old friend, actually, whom she was looking at in new ways.

All the way back in 1993, when Louise was still a student at Grimsley High School, she met a boy named Don Jackson. He flirted with Louise but nothing ever came of it. "I dated one of his friends for a while, while he was running around following the Grateful Dead," Louise says. The two didn't spend a lot of time together through their teenage years. "But I'd always had a crush on Don," Louise adds. "He was sweet." Some 20 years later, in 2013, Don walked out of prison.

He doesn't talk about the time he spent inside. "Three years," is all Don says at the house he shares with Louise. "One thousand and 11 days." His entire demeanor changes, his constant joking and easy laugh fall silent. Don was never a hardened criminal. He was a Deadhead who followed the jam band around America, enjoying psychedelics and the music. But he was caught with a few ounces of coke, took the plea, and went away for three years. "Fucked," Don says.

Shortly after Don was released, a mutual friend asked Louise if they could all hang out. Before long, Louise and Don were inseparable. After so many relationships in which men had inflicted so much pain, Louise found a gentle soul who adored her. Don has remained at Louise's side ever since.

With school finally behind her and with a new sidekick in tow, Louise set to work establishing North Carolina's first drug-user union. Not everyone in Greensboro liked the idea. Officers with the Greensboro Police Department, for example, became a source of constant harassment. It seemed they were even more upset about Louise's new activist interests than they were about her well-known history with drugs.

But Louise, Don, and Wiggs persisted, and in the fall of 2014, they formally established the North Carolina Survivors Union (NCSU) as the Greensboro chapter of Shilo's Urban Survivors Union (USU). "We wrote our first grant, we got our first office. Now we're off and running," Louise says.

Well, soon they would be running. The USU's Greensboro chapter actually started a little slower than that. The big hurdle was finding a space of their own and the money to pay for it. A local HIV support group lent them a room for a while, but it was on the other side of town, where a group of drug users and budding activists just didn't fit in.

In addition to doing something for drug users as a group, these early organizing efforts were also about Louise attempting self-care. "I was trying to create a space for me to not fall apart. That's the truth. I wanted a group I could go to and talk about this shit. I wanted a space for me to find some reprieve from some of the struggle that I was having. I am not one of these people who believes that my substance use is not a problem. I do know it's been a problem and it does have the capacity to beat me up and destroy me. But what I really wanted was a place to have these discussions, like, 'I'm trying to slow down,' or 'I'm trying to do this.' Discussions that weren't just all or nothing."

Louise was creating a space where she could be herself, where she didn't have to hide her mental illness or the drugs she used to cope with it. But other people quickly found comfort in that space, too.

For Selena, Louise's harm reduction work was a source of pride. She and Louise fought like sisters, but Selena worshipped her mother. She understood that Louise was helping people, and doing it like a badass, ignoring the rules when the rules were wrong and refusing to let anything stop her. Selena wanted to be just like Louise.

She *was* just like Louise. Selena was barely a teenager when she was caught with cannabis and then arrested for shoplifting. It was obvious to Louise and Grandma Sarah that Selena was crying for attention. Thankfully, the family didn't have to struggle for years without a diagnosis, like they had with Louise. Selena had a visual processing disorder that made learning in the classroom difficult for her, doctors told them. "I tried everything," Sarah says. "Gymnastics and cheerleading and art classes and history camp and flag football." As with Louise, nothing helped. Selena felt alone in the world, misunderstood and alienated. The following year, she was diagnosed with bipolar disorder, just as Louise was when she was about the same age.

"She was affected by mental illness," Louise says. "Around the age of 13, life just came crashing in. Self-hatred, an inability to cope with massive feelings—that's huge. She struggled in a huge way, and so did I. And so I recognized it and saw it and wanted to spare her from that pain. But it was not something that I could do."

Selena resisted taking prescription medications. Again, as with Louise, nothing worked for her. She self-medicated with cannabis, alcohol, and prescription pills, and then, far too soon, Louise says, she started snorting heroin. While Louise and Wiggs ran harm reduction programs out of Sarah's basement, Selena was there with them whenever she could be. But her interest in opioids didn't come from Louise, who let Selena get away with a little pot but never heroin. "This was the height of the opioid epidemic," Louise says. "Everybody was using opioids and pills are expensive." Selena was one of countless Americans who turned to heroin. It was stronger and a fraction of the price of an Oxy pill, so why not?

Louise tried to get a handle on it early. "You know, why don't you go to rehab?" she asked Selena. "Not like a rehab that I've been to. Like a place that we pay for that's nice. You're not too far off-kilter. Why not?" Louise nudged her, offered love, and Selena agreed to give it a try.

10

Strange Dope on the Street

"This is when heroin stopped working," Jess says. "Heroin had always kept me safe, kept me from pain. And now I'm doing quadruple the amount I've ever done in my whole life, even at my very worst."

For more than a few years, Jess had sailed on an upward trend. She had cleaned up during her break from harm reduction in New Jersey. Eventually, she did start using again, but not problematically. In Boston, she was injecting drugs, but never to the point where she was staying up all night. She was never late for work at Cambridge Cares About AIDS. Jess had even earned a couple of promotions, and her work with drug users received attention from around the country. There were calls from journalists, who had begun to go to Jess for a unique perspective on the intensifying overdose crisis; invitations for speaking engagements presented her, a drug user, as an important voice in public health; and the harm reduction movement's social media world often buzzed with Jess's name. But recovery is seldom linear.

An opioid addiction is commonly characterized as a "chronic relapsing condition."[1] This means that a high probability of relapse is so intrinsically a component of the addiction that it is part of what defines it. Between 66 and 80 percent of people treated for a drug addiction will return to drug use within six months of exiting treatment.[2] "Relapse is a normal part of recovery," one paper reads.[3]

After Rachel Auspitz died, Jess abandoned her dream job at Cambridge Cares, lost her nice apartment in Boston, and moved into a depressing loft. There was a broken chair and an empty twin bed frame and that was it. The walls were painted brown and the paint was peeling. There was only one small window, and no matter what the weather was, it never seemed to let in any light. Jess slept on a thin mattress that was dropped directly on the floor, and for a while didn't even have a blanket. It was perfect, she thought. Jess called a dealer and went back to work burning through the last of her savings account. "I was pretty convinced that I would be dead by the time the year was out," she says. "And then Tom came."

Jess knew Tom Butler a little from her days shooting heroin on the streets of Northampton, back in the 1990s. "I used to call it 'Dante's circle of hell.' In the '90s, we all knew one another. We were the inner circle. Then there were the circles that moved out. Tom was in that second circle."

Tom had been through a lot since then, including struggling with heroin. In the early 2000s, he had worked as a nurse at a retirement home. A gentle person by nature, the work suited him and Tom was good at it, as long as he was high. But 'high' gradually became a state that was difficult to maintain. "I was in a spiral," he says. "I had warrants out all over the place. I knew it was coming to an end and so I was trying to kick before the inevitable came. I knew I was going to jail for at least a year. And I did. Within a couple of months, I was in jail." When he was released in 2008, Tom got sober, went on methadone, and stayed clean. "Methadone works for me," he says.

Jess and Tom hung out a few times in the early 2000s. They shared a dealer, both visited Tapestry Needle Exchange for supplies, and they bumped into each other because Northampton is a small town and they both used hard drugs. Nothing ever came of it. They drifted apart and didn't see each other for many years. Meanwhile, barely a couple of miles from where Jess was shooting her life away locked in a dark loft, a boy a few years younger than her named Mark Zuckerberg had developed a website called Facebook. Jess found it, and sent Tom a friend request. "Do you remember me?" she asked. "Yeah, of course I do," he messaged back.

With Jess in Boston and Tom in Northampton three hours away, their relationship remained online. Slowly, it grew flirtatious, but romantic as opposed to sexual. "I had come down with the [HIV] virus by then," Tom says. "So, at that point in my life, I never thought I'd date another person again." He was painting and shared photographs of his artwork on social media. Occasionally Jess would comment. Tom noticed and began clicking through to her profile more often. "You could see, through her pictures that she was posting, that something was wrong," he says. "I recognized it because I had been there."

One day, a year or so after they began messaging online, Tom decided it was time to reintroduce himself in the real world. Completely out of character, he spontaneously boarded a bus for Northampton. Tom found Jess in her loft drowning in drugs and misery and "kidnapped her," he says. It took a few days to convince Jess that her life was worth saving. Tom simply refused to leave and Jess was secretly grateful for the company.

One evening she was putting her laundry away when Tom noticed her lips losing color. "Jess, you're blue," Tom said to her. Deep in a nod, Jess replied softly with a joke. "Yeah, pretty sexy, right?" she said with a quiet laugh. "Breathe, Jess," Tom said. "You know what else is sexy? Breathing." They both let Jess's brush with death pass without making a big deal of it. But they also both knew that if Tom hadn't been there that night, Jess probably wouldn't be here today. "Look, I've got an apartment," Tom said to her the following morning. "You want to come back, detox? We can decide from there what to do." Jess bought one last half gram of heroin and then took the bus home to Northampton with Tom.

On their first morning together in Tom's tiny apartment, he gave Jess a high dose of methadone and stayed in bed with her watching movies. "It was the first normal day I'd had in nine months,"

Jess says. "We ended up living together in that small space for three years."

It was a period of beautiful calm. "Jess started doing NA," Tom says. "I went to NA with her. We went most nights. That's what we would do. She had to kick [get through withdrawal] and everything, and adjust to living without dope, which isn't easy. We watched a lot of TV."

In March 2012, they were married. "We were head over heels," Tom says. "When you can live in a tiny room like that with somebody and never fight . . . he adds, trailing off. It was just the two of them at their wedding. Jess ditched her usual goth uniform for a peach-colored dress. A justice of the peace pronounced them husband and wife as they stood surrounded by flowers and the glass atrium of the Botanic Garden of Smith College. "It was really, really cute," Jess says.

Later that year, Jess returned to where she got her start in harm reduction: Tapestry Needle Exchange. By this time, she was something of a small celebrity in the drug policy world. The national harm reduction community looked to the user-employment program that she had pioneered at Cambridge Cares as a model. And while Jess didn't make a lot of new friends outing herself as an active drug user at the Austin conference, it did make her a few new friends. It also sparked an overdue debate that continues within the harm reduction community today.

Jess knew the folks at Tapestry from the days she volunteered there as a teen. She figured her old colleagues would jump at the chance to hire her. But they didn't. Jess was volunteering at Tapestry and management promised her a job as soon as one opened up, but, week after week, it was the same story: "Any day now, we'll have a position for you." But they never did. Finally, Tapestry told Jess they couldn't hire her.

"You can volunteer up to 40 hours a week," the organization's program manager told her. "But we can't hire you because you don't have a driver's license." Jess didn't have a driver's license—this was true. She's epileptic and therefore has never had one. But a driver's license was never a requirement to work at Tapestry before.

"That's when I realized how much me outing myself as a drug user had affected my future in harm reduction," Jess says. It was the speech that she gave in Austin. Tapestry, despite its stated dedication to harm reduction, would not hire someone who was known to use drugs. And if Tapestry wouldn't hire her, Jess knew no other organization would even consider it. "A harm reduction program won't even hire me as a health educator? I've been a program manager!"

Like so many people who use drugs, Jess could no longer find meaningful employment. An incredible one in four American adults has some sort of a criminal record (not necessarily for an arrest or time in prison; many types of background checks also search for apprehensions where a formal arrest did not occur).[4] Furthermore, an estimated 87 percent of large companies run background checks on a random selection of job applicants and 69 percent run them on every applicant.[5] If a white person attending a job interview admits to having a criminal record, their chance of receiving a callback is just 17 percent; for a Black applicant who concedes to having a record, it is only 5 percent.[6] This sort of systemic rejection leads many to break the law. One paper describes an unemployed criminal's odds of recidivism as "almost inevitable."[7] Termed "perpetual punishment" or "forever punishment," this lifetime ban from the legitimate economy does not prevent crime, but rather is highly effective at turning a mistake into a career criminal.[8]

After Tapestry's rejection, Jess felt utterly alone. "I cannot explain to you how badly I was kicked to the ground," she says. "But I picked myself up."

Still looking to return to her roots, Jess operated as a one-woman underground needle exchange. Among every population of intra-venous drug users, there will always be a certain number of people who will never access services via a government-funded health care program or anything that resembles one. Maybe they can't risk a friend or co-worker spotting them visiting a needle exchange; may-be in the past a doctor treated them poorly enough to create a life-time phobia of government systems; or maybe they are simply not comfortable with anyone knowing that they use injection drugs. Whatever the reason—and there are many good ones—there will always be people who can benefit from harm reduction programs but who will never access them on their own. And now, working outside the system that had rejected her, Jess knew how to connect with this group. She tapped into America's underground harm reduction community and secured a semiconsistent supply of clean syringes and other supplies And then she got to work.

Most of this guerrilla operation ran out of the back of a Northamp-ton pet store where Jess was employed at the time. Her responsibili-ties there gave her plenty of hours without a lot of humans around to notice the bags of needles and naloxone that she was running out the back door. At this point in her career, Jess would have preferred to be working for a legitimate program (or even running one), but she enjoyed the grassroots feel of underground needle exchange. It was hands-on and at the end of the day, Jess felt like she was accom-plishing something. "I'm counseling people in the back, running syringes out of there. It was nuts. I ran so much Narcan out of that place."

It was older users who first noticed something was different. "What the hell is going on with this?" they would ask Jess. The dope looked the same. It usually came as a white powder, sometimes with a gray or brown tint to it, chopped fine, same as always. It also served its purpose. The dope eliminated the pain and anxiety of withdrawal. But this new stuff didn't do much more than that. It also didn't last very long. Within four or three or even as few as two hours, you were beginning to itch for more. It also often lacked the calm euphoria that comes with heroin. This dope came on strong, even putting its user straight into a nod. But the nod never felt like much. It just put you to sleep. It didn't "hug" you. It didn't have that "warm blanket" feel that so many people use to describe heroin's effect. Something was different.

Next Jess started hearing strange reports from lower-level dealers. These guys—users who mostly sold drugs just to maintain their own addictions—were saying that all of a sudden, their suppliers were selling them dope at half the price it cost just a month earlier. Grateful for the break, nobody was asking questions. Purchased wholesale, this stuff came at a huge discount, and then you could sell it by the point or by the gram for the same price you always had. The profit margin was ridiculous. And users at the end of the line weren't complaining, or not much, anyway. Not yet. Nobody was going to mess with a good thing, or a thing that was good enough.

Jess wasn't doing a lot of heroin around this time but she had a cell phone number that was known to practically everyone with a drug habit who lived within a 50-mile radius. At the pet store, she constantly received calls for syringes and other supplies. Jess was also making another attempt at drug-user organizing. "We were meeting wherever we could. There would be five or six people. We would meet at the library, we would meet at the coffee shop." At these informal gatherings, younger users shared concerns similar to what Jess had first heard from the older veterans. There was strange dope on the street. Really sleepy stuff that left you numb but didn't feel like much of anything else.

Still occasionally volunteering at Tapestry, Jess told the staff there that something was going on. "Can you put the word out?" she asked. "Something is wrong with these bags." But Tapestry increasingly had a bit of a corporate feel. Gone were the days when management allowed the exchange's back room to operate as a clubhouse for 20-something heroin addicts. The fun photographs, postcards, and messages from transient youth had long disappeared from the drop-in's bulletin boards. Jess couldn't get anyone interested in the warnings she shared. Meanwhile, things continued to get weird. "I just shot cocaine and fell asleep," Jess told Tom one night after waking. Then an overdose hit close to them.

Marianne and Michael were an older couple that Jess and Tom had known for years. Michael was a close friend of Tom's from the 1990s, when they were both addicted to heroin. The couple had gotten their habits under control and now only used opioids once every few weeks or so. They did not overdose. They just weren't those types of users. They were older, experienced, and cautious, always going slow and starting with tester shots. Then Michael woke up on the couch one morning, called Marianne's name, and she didn't answer. He found her on the bathroom floor unconscious. Paramedics revived her but not soon enough: Marianne was brain dead and taken off life support shortly after. A couple of nights later, Michael tried to kill himself. In one go, he injected the six remaining bags of heroin that he and Marianne had planned to use together that weekend. Miraculously, he survived. But that only made the whole thing more confusing. Marianne did one bag and was gone forever. Michael did six and survived to spend his life without her.

Drugs purchased on the black market are often inconsistent, but this was something else. "I wonder if it was fentanyl," Michael said to Jess. She had heard of the drug before. She knew it was a synthetic opioid that was mostly used in hospitals, similar to heroin but seldom found on the street. "Fentanyl?" she wondered.

A month or so later, Jess texted a friend named Joe. "What are you, dead?" her message read. They were supposed to hang out that afternoon and Joe never showed. Jess was annoyed, hence the "Are you dead?" text. Later, she heard that Joe had passed away. "He had been in his room dead for three days," Jess says.

One of the scariest elements of this wave of overdoses through 2013 was that nobody knew what was causing it, Tom and Jess say. There were only theories and rumors. The unknown was terrifying.

"We lost a lot of people in those couple of years, at the beginning of it," Tom says.

It happens too often, but it is always a crushing blow when someone you know dies of a drug overdose. "There's always a memorial," Jess says. "When Matty died, when Pauly died, they had memorials. Now, within a couple of months, people were just dropping. It was like, 'Do we do a monthly memorial?'"

Outside of America's official health care establishment, there exists a national group called Naloxone Overdose Prevention Education, or NOPE for short. It's a small group, consisting of regional harm reduction leaders like Jess, Louise, the National Harm Reduction Coalition's overdose response specialist Eliza Wheeler, and Dan Bigg, for example. They maintain a listserv and meet on regular conference calls. They share information from the ground and coordinate the underground distribution of harm reduction supplies to states where syringe exchange is still illegal. On one of these calls in late 2013, Jess tried to sound an alarm.

"I think this is fentanyl," Jess told them. "People in their 50s and 60s who have been doing dope forever, they're telling me, 'Look, we think this is fentanyl. We know what it is. It wears off quickly. Gives you a quick rush and then it's gone.'"

Similar reports came in from Pennsylvania and Ohio. "Look, there is fentanyl here in Massachusetts," Jess said on one of the NOPE calls. "We are going to start seeing a lot of deaths." Most members on the call remained silent. A couple said they wanted confirmation via laboratory testing. Dan Bigg spoke up in support of the urgency that Jess expressed and said he would put a shipment of naloxone in the mail for her. Then the group scheduled another conference call to discuss the matter further in a couple of weeks.

"How many lives could we have saved?" Jess asks. "I think back and I ask, 'How many deaths could we have prevented, had they just listened to us?'"

11

Narco Feminism

In the summer of 2018, journalists noticed something strange happening in Mexico. "Opium Poppy Growers See Price Drop, Turn to Marijuana," reads one headline. It didn't make sense. Opium is the organic precursor of heroin, and since when is cannabis worth more than heroin? Just a few years earlier, a kilogram of opium paste purchased in the hills of Guerrero state went for 20,000 to 25,000 pesos (US$1,000 to $1,250). Now, the same amount was barely worth 5,000 pesos ($250). "Prices for opium paste—which oozes from the bulbs of poppies after they're cut—have fallen so low they don't even pay for the cost of planting, fertilizing, irrigating, weeding and harvesting the raw material for heroin," the article reads.[1]

By the spring of 2019, Mexican cartels were abandoning poppies and heroin for chemicals and fentanyl. They had watched companies in China manufacture the drug out in the open, sell it to Americans via the internet, and make a lot of money.[2] Now, while U.S. authorities pressured China to crack down on illicit fentanyl manufacturers there, criminal organizations based in Mexico, including the Sinaloa Cartel and the Cártel de Jalisco Nueva Generación, took note and shifted operations from heroin to fentanyl, thus pushing many of the country's poppy farmers out of business. Whereas fentanyl from China came into America in drips, the Mexican cartels would open the floodgates.[3]

The same year, the *New York Times* revealed another aspect of the same story, this one unfolding some 2,000 miles northeast of the Mexican border, in Maryland. Heroin was disappearing from the Eastern Seaboard. Regions where heroin had only recently become

widely available—rural Appalachia and parts of the Midwest—
were already seeing the drug replaced by one even more potent:
fentanyl. Focusing on Baltimore, the paper explained the deadly
consequences. Working professionals who had survived heroin
addictions for decades were overdosing on fentanyl and dying in
shocking numbers.[4]

In 2016, a drug overdose became the most common cause of
death in America for people under the age of 50.[5] That year, 63,600
people died after taking drugs. In 2017, the number increased to
70,200.[6]

The greatest drug crisis the country has ever faced had transitioned from legitimate companies and prescription painkillers to
international drug cartels and an illicit opioid so potent that it can
kill a human with volumes as small as a few grains of sand.[7] But
why now? Licit fentanyl was approved for use in a medical setting
in the early 1970s. Why was it not until the 2010s that it became
widely available on the black market?

A phenomenon called the "iron law of prohibition" says that the
rise of fentanyl was inevitable. It states that a substance's classifica-
tion as illegal will not make that substance any less available, but
rather will lead to a wider availability of a more potent formulation.[8]
As authorities intensify enforcement, groups selling illicit drugs
work harder to maintain the secrecy of their drug-dealing operations. One of the most effective ways they can do that is by making
their products smaller and therefore more difficult to detect. And to
make a drug smaller, you need it in a more potent form. Al Capone
didn't get rich selling beer; he dealt whiskey. Likewise, compared
to heroin, fentanyl is easier and cheaper to produce, is less risky to
transport, and delivers a more potent high. Explained by the iron
law of prohibition, fentanyl is a product of the drug war.*

---

* There is a plausible theory that if opium were legalized, many heroin users would gladly transition to that weaker opioid, the same way that today,
people living in regions of the country where all that's left is fentanyl say that
despite fentanyl's relative strength, all they want is heroin.

Beyond that, the timing of a drug's popularity is often a tricky thing to pin down. Ecstasy (MDMA) was the thing to do in the 1990s, crystal meth was everywhere through the 2000s, and benzodiazepines (Xanax and Valium) took off in the 2010s. Acid (LSD) has become very hard to find and Quaaludes have completely disappeared. Drug scenes are fluid. Ben Westhoff, author of *Fentanyl, Inc.: How Rogue Chemists Are Creating the Deadliest Wave of the Opioid Epidemic*, says he has a few guesses as to why fentanyl hit the streets when it did. "It was only in recent years that chemists developed a production method that made fentanyl much easier to synthesize," he says. "It was a game-changer." Whereas the Janssen Method, used to produce fentanyl since the 1960s, requires an advanced level of chemistry, the simpler Siegfried Method appeared in the 2000s and, all of a sudden, this very powerful opioid was much easier to cook.[9] Other factors include the widespread adoption of the internet, easier access to the dark web (sections of the internet that cannot be accessed with a standard browser such as Chrome), and improved international shipping. Thanks to technology, one can order fentanyl without leaving the couch.

Thus, the heroin that had gradually replaced prescription painkillers as Americans' drug of choice was supplanted by an even deadlier substance. The third wave of the opioid epidemic had arrived.

Why would drug dealers risk killing their customers? The answer is simple economics.

In Mexico, it is a lot of work to grow opium, manufacture the raw substance into heroin, and traffic the narcotic across the border into the United States.* It is labor intensive, high risk, and expensive. First, one needs to employ farmers to maintain a poppy field, which

---

* An estimated 84 percent of the world's opium is grown in Afghanistan, according to the United Nations, while Myanmar accounts for 7 percent and Mexico for 6 percent. However, the vast majority of North America's opium (in the form of heroin) originates in Mexico.

is a large piece of land that's tough to keep hidden from authorities. Then one has to pay laborers to harvest the crop and chemists to process the poppy plant's opium into heroin. Finally, one needs to establish a vast network of smugglers who can securely transport the drug over hundreds of miles and across a border that is increasingly militarized.

Fentanyl is easier.

Fentanyl is a synthetic drug, meaning it is produced from chemicals in a laboratory. Instead of growing a field of poppies, one can find a good recipe for fentanyl on the dark web and purchase large amounts of precursor chemicals from China. Or, for a little more money, you can simply order the finished product. The risks are statistically minimal. Chemists with barely more than a high-school education can cook fentanyl in rudimentary laboratories invisible to authorities. The drug is so potent that tiny amounts can be mixed into large volumes of cutting agents (such as talcum powder and caffeine) to create many doses that, despite the minuscule amount of fentanyl each dose contains, can still get people very high. Instead of taking huge risks to smuggle large volumes of heroin over the border, producers can ship fentanyl into America in envelopes using the country's own U.S. Postal Service.

Thus, compared to heroin, fentanyl is easier to produce, less of a hassle to transport, significantly less risky at every step of the way, and almost unfathomably more profitable.

The *New York Times* made comparable calculations for heroin and fentanyl and found that a kilogram (2.2 pounds) of heroin can be purchased in a source country such as Colombia for $6,000 and then sold wholesale in America for $80,000; meanwhile, a kilogram of fentanyl can be purchased from a manufacturer in China for $5,000 and then mixed with cutting agents to create enough doses for $1.6 million in profit on the street.[10] The *Philadelphia Enquirer* did the math a little differently but arrived at a similarly astounding profit margin: One kilogram of heroin can be purchased for between $50,000 to $80,000 in America and then diluted and resold for about $500,000 profit, while a kilogram of fentanyl that goes for roughly $55,000 in America can be broken up and resold for a profit of as much as $5 million.[11] Why do drug dealers want to kill their customers? They don't. But losing a few customers or even tens of thousands of customers to overdose deaths—which the cartels do now lose in the United States every year—is not going to result in an overall customer base diminished by any meaningful measure. The difference in profit margin between heroin and fentanyl is not a matter of one or two zeros, but a whole string of them. The cartels can continue killing tens of thousands of customers every year via overdose deaths and their profits will remain greater than ever. As a matter of cold economics, fentanyl makes perfect sense. If you're a drug dealer who hasn't switched from heroin to fentanyl, the question isn't "Why?" It's "Why not?"

And while fentanyl is dangerous, it is not as dangerous as authorities lead the general public to believe. Fentanyl is a lot stronger than heroin and can quickly bring on an overdose. But one can use fentanyl recreationally without dying; indeed, with fentanyl now having almost fully supplanted heroin across large swaths of America, many thousands of people addicted to opioids do exactly that every day. The false belief that fentanyl kills anything it touches primarily stems from police. A few examples include Orlando first responders claiming colleagues were "recovering" after experiencing "fentanyl exposure" during a traffic stop,[12] a Columbus police officer allegedly losing consciousness upon "coming into contact" with fentanyl while apprehending a shoplifter,[13] and a Canadian police department evacuating an entire station in response to a "suspected fentanyl contamination."[14] Other reports include photographs and video of authorities responding to instances of fentanyl "exposure" wearing full hazmat suits like one sees in movies such as *Outbreak* or *World War Z*.[15]

Illicit fentanyl is not so deadly that simply touching it can kill you. We know this because every day thousands of Americans intentionally put the drug up their noses or inject it straight into their veins. A pair of harm reduction advocates named Chad Sabora and Sarah Sottile tried to put this urban myth to bed in July 2018. The two shared a video on Facebook doing what so many police departments have told journalists would kill them. They took a powdery substance in their hands, displayed it testing positive for fentanyl, and then placed the drug against Sabora's skin. Of course, nothing happened. Forget dying—neither of the two became impaired in any way. Contrary to police reports, illicit fentanyl cannot enter the body via contact with one's skin.[16] It's impossible. In November 2017, the fact-checking website Snopes even devoted an article to the fentanyl-kills-by-touch myth. "False," it concludes.[17] Yet authorities continue to warn that fentanyl "exposure" puts officers and even the general public at risk.

That said, the drug is strong and does put users at a greater risk of overdose than if they were using heroin. In addition to fentanyl's potency resulting in an abundance of overdose deaths, there is another drawback to the drug. The synthetic opioid, which is used in American hospitals as a legitimate painkiller every day, feels a lot like heroin but not exactly like heroin. Many users say it lacks the "warmth" or "hug" that makes heroin so appealing, but this aspect of the shift in the opioid supply is never discussed in newspapers, likely because the only people who would care are drug users. But what this means is, if someone is using heroin to self-medicate the wounds of childhood trauma, like Jess, or seeking comfort in a world for which their mind is simply too sensitive, like Louise, fentanyl will not do for you what heroin has. With fentanyl, there's no hug. But if you're addicted to opioids, it's increasingly all that's left.

Against this backdrop of a more terrible opioid epidemic, Jess was looking for a partner in crime. She kept hearing the name "Louise

Vincent" and stories of the work Louise was doing down in North Carolina. Meanwhile, Louise had similarly heard of Jess and was thinking of her as something of a possible mentor. More than once, both noticed they were on the same conference calls as one another, but they never spoke directly. Robert Childs, executive director of the North Carolina Harm Reduction Coalition, repeatedly tried to bring Jess to the organization's office in Greensboro, hoping she would share her experience doing underground exchange. And Urban Survivors Union founder Shilo Jama, now a mutual friend of Jess and Louise, had tried to put the two of them in a room together on several occasions. From the instant he met Jess, Shilo thought the world of her and would often hold Jess up as a shining example of drug-user activism. And because Louise was a woman using drugs and one on a similar path as Jess, perhaps just a few feet behind, Shilo repeatedly encouraged Louise to get in touch with her. Similarly, he was telling Jess that she needed to travel to North Carolina to see what the Urban Survivors Union's rising star was doing with harm reduction in a jurisdiction where authorities remained overtly hostile to it. But Shilo similarly failed to make it happen. There was always a scheduling conflict or one of them was coming when the other was going. A meeting of the two of them felt inevitable, but for years it somehow never happened.

By this time, Louise was chasing Jess outright, sending her emails explaining that Shilo kept saying they had to meet. But Jess never replied. She was avoiding Louise, worried she would be a disappointment. She admits this was internalized stigma. The two of them even attended several of the same conferences during this period, but still never spoke. Finally, at a conference in Baltimore in 2014, Shilo brought the two of them face to face. The first meeting was a very quick one, in a hotel corridor between conference sessions. "You're Louise Vincent," Jess exclaimed. "You're Jess Tilley," Louise replied excitedly. They barely had time to say more than hello and exchange numbers. But there were sparks.

From there, Jess recalls ideas flying back and forth at a rapid-fire pace. "It was like we already knew each other," she says. "I somehow ended up in her hotel room and we just instantly started talking about what we needed to do and how we were going to do it. And from that moment, we took off like wildfire." Louise and Jess talked for days, putting off sleep for fear of losing any more time. They decided they wanted to take drug-user organizing national, far beyond the couple of cities that Shilo had signed up to the USU, and that it was crucial that women lead this larger movement.

"The voice of women, especially women drug users—women who actively use drugs—has always been stifled and shamed," Jess says. "Our own narrative has been taken from us. We are not allowed to tell our own authentic story. We have never been allowed to talk, we've never been listened to, we've never been heard. We've been shunned, shamed, and shut down."

Louise adds that the hatred that society holds against women who use drugs gradually becomes deeply ingrained in women's perceptions of themselves. "I've never even thought of myself as a woman," she explains. "I've only been able to identify as these other things. So it's like I've never had a space where I was even able to live in my own womanhood. It's strange. It's this idea of being invisible and exploited at the same time. It is a really strange space, to be a woman drug user and, certainly, one with some education and some credentials who still is not seen as anything more than just a drug user."

Louise also describes this need for a feminist leadership model in more tangible ways—as a matter of safety and security, for example. If you're a woman who uses drugs, and especially if you're a woman who uses drugs who also has a child, in the event of an emergency, "you cannot call 911," Louise emphasizes. That option—that safety net that so many take for granted—does not exist for a mother who uses drugs. "I've always had way too much dope everywhere for that to ever be okay," Louise says with a small laugh. "That is where I learned a stupid-powerful lesson: I cannot be safe. . . . These [police] are not the fucking people to call when I need help."

For women who use drugs, police are a source of danger. One study of women passing through drug courts in St. Louis found fully a quarter had experienced sexual misconduct at the hands of a police officer.[18] It's been well established that police officers can exploit a woman's drug use to inflict harassment and that, aware of possible imprisonment, women refrain from seeking help for abuse.[19] The threat of an arrest for drugs leads drug-using women to decide against reporting many crimes, including property theft, spousal abuse, and offenses a romantic partner or relative inflicts on their children.[20]

Louise emphasizes how this break from societal norms can shake a drug-using woman's faith in the entirety of the systems in which we live. From childhood, we are taught that a police officer should stand as a source of security, she says. But for a woman using drugs, police are a point of intense fear. "To this day, they can stop me in my fucking tracks. I don't think I'm really scared of anything else. . . . I see them as enemies. They have misused their power."

Jess remembers understanding something similar from her early days at Tapestry Needle Exchange, realizing that the needs of women who use drugs are very different and usually significantly more complicated than those of men. There's a power dynamic that makes it easy for men to force women into sexual favors, into exchanging sex for drugs, and into sex work that raises money for drugs that women are then forced to turn over to the men injecting them. "That's a lot of power," Jess says. She would connect women who didn't have their own drug supply with her dealer. "When I think about my first attempts at activism, the most important things were the little things I did. Connecting a woman with a dealer, that was one of them.

She and Louise shared a lifetime of experiences and observations with one another in Baltimore. One issue they returned to repeatedly was the uncertainty inherent in a drug supply that remains illegal. For this conference and every conference, they flew into a city where they had no preexisting relationships with the local dealers, were not accustomed to the drugs, and usually had no clue of their potency or what they were cut with. So many unknowns created situations that were dangerous and downright terrifying. "The overdoses we see at conferences are tangible evidence of how horrible this is," Jess said.

Louise shared an experience she had in Greensboro, where she did know a little bit about the city's drugs. Don had to take her to the hospital because of side effects brought on by what they determined was a bad cutting agent someone up the chain had used to dilute their cocaine. "This is the drug war," Jess exclaimed on hearing the story. As long as drugs are illegal, they are bought and sold outside the reach of government regulations. This means there is no ability to implement quality control mechanisms like those that ensure that when you walk into a liquor store and purchase a bottle of gin, gin is what you get. If drugs like cocaine and heroin were legal, regulators could insist on their purities and enforce standards of consistency. That would eliminate one of the primary factors driving overdose deaths, the pair agreed. "It's not fentanyl that's killing us," Louise said. "It's the drug war."

Things moved slowly at first. From Baltimore, their excitement continued on regular phone calls. They spoke every week or so and then almost every night.

There were a couple of earlier attempts to form a national drug-user union—notably, in October 2013, at a conference in Denver, Colorado.

Shilo was one of the organizers who brought that meeting together. "There were five drug-user unions at the time," he begins. The Urban Survivors Union, which was making its debut as a multi-chapter organization with representatives attending from Seattle,

San Francisco, and Greensboro; VOCAL-NY, a well-established grassroots organization where drug users had organized since 1999; Users United, a smaller group of New York drug users; the San Francisco Drug Users Union; and Jess's New England Users Union, which didn't attend the meeting but was represented there by Jess calling in via phone. "And we all sat together and we talked this out," Shilo says. "There were cultural differences and there were different ideas about what a national user union should and should not be. But we talked and this became the United States Alliance of Drug User Unions, USADUU."

Robert Suarez, another of the event's organizers, is a drug-user activist based in the Bronx who got his start with VOCAL-NY. He says the two locations that are most important to his harm reduction story are the rocks beneath the George Washington Bridge, where he once spent years smoking crack, and Washington Heights Corner Project, the first needle exchange in which Robert set foot. "I was ready to walk off those rocks, into the river," he says. "And that's when, instead, I walked into the Corner Project." Ever since, Robert has worked to unite drug users into a larger movement. Regarding the Denver summit, he says it was the first time that the country's user unions really tried to come together. "We moved forward as five drug-user unions from around the country," Robert says. "That's where we actually hashed out the name and came up with a mission statement."

A 2014 documentary called *We Are the People* captures what happened at that gathering in Denver. "It's going to be up to us to make changes," Shilo says in the film. Most speakers in the documentary mount a shared argument: that the war on drugs does more harm than good, translating into stigma wherein mainstream society views people who use drugs as something less than human and thus treats them as such.

From there, attendees share how they hope the creation of a national union will help them fight back against that stigma. "We're locked up, we're locked out of health care, housing, education, and employment, locked into poverty, and recycled back into prison," Louie Jones, a co-founder of Users United, says in the film. "What we want to do . . . as former and current users is organize in a way to raise consciousness and education." The Chicago Recovery Alliance's Dan Bigg facilitated the Denver convention. "There was a revolutionary tone in that meeting," he says in the film.

Discussions around the USADUU continued on conference calls and online, but it didn't last long as a formal organization. Shilo concedes mistakes were made. People's egos got in the way. There was a general lack of communication and too much of an emphasis on the organization's structure and protocols, which came at the expense of actually getting anything done. Robert says it simply "fizzled out." "The Urban Survivors Union already existed, but now what we did was take everything that we had gained [in Denver] and all of that momentum from the USADUU and put it into the USU."

Despite Robert's positivity, the USADUU's failure set back the nationalization of the movement by several years. What else went wrong? There were too many men, Jess says. Too many men jostling for control and recognition and that hampered cooperation. "The voice of drug users had been dominated by white men for so long," she emphasizes. "We'd get together, we'd set up a conference call, get it going, and then, within a month or two, it always just died out. So I was disillusioned. But I'd finally started taking Louise's calls and we began talking about a feminist-led, team-based approach."

Louise thinks it was their shared emphasis on feminism that finally convinced Jess to dedicate time to a national organizing effort. "She was frustrated with all of the ego bullshit in the movement," Louise says. Late one night on the phone, Louise told Jess that she really admired her work as an activist. "What are you making?" she asked, referring to money. Jess, somewhat sheepishly, replied that her years of harm reduction experience hadn't translated into a steady paycheck, and that she wasn't making anything. "I'm working at a pet store," Jess said. "What? Oh, hell no," Louise replied. "We're going to get you some money." Extraordinarily proficient at grant writing and scrounging together cash, Louise began sending Jess small contracts that helped pay the rent. It was mostly for work that Jess was already doing for free and so greatly appreciated. Jess was impressed and was quickly convinced that Louise was serious.

"We were both sort of feeling each other out," Louise says. "Women in drug-using circles can be pretty fucking vicious. And so I think there was a lot of feeling out what this was. And getting close to people and being close to people is hard. I don't have a lot of close friends. You lose so many people in this shit. It's easy to stay pretty distant."

Jess likewise says their partnership was slow to start. But once she decided she was in, she was in. "We've really got to throw something together," the two of them agreed.

By this time, the Urban Survivors Union had gained some structure. It had official members who elected a board of directors, and the board appointed a board president, treasurer, and an executive director. In 2015, they selected Louise to fill that top position. The organization was still just three chapters: Seattle, San Francisco, and Greensboro, plus Jess's New England Users Union, which has always been an unofficial affiliate. But they were beginning to call it a national organization and Louise was selected to lead their efforts.

In forming a national drug-user union, both Louise and Jess felt it was crucial that they break from past leadership hierarchies and avoid the egos and potential abuses that can hinder the work of people in positions of power. They were acutely aware that when no one has listened to you your whole life, when your opinion has always been discounted or dismissed outright—the reality for so many people who use drugs—finding oneself with decision-making

authority at the head of a national organization can quickly com-
promise a person's morals. Louise didn't want to catch herself
directing funding and contracts only to friends or saving all the
conference invitations for herself.

To this end, she convened with Jess and together they convinced
the USU's membership to let the pair of them lead the organization side by side, making them co-directors. "We realized we would
have more power as women in a partnership sort of role," Louise
says. They developed a team-based, feminist-led leadership structure. The two of them would function as one, making decisions
together, and also lean heavily on drug-user-organizing veterans
like Shilo, Robert, and Becki Brooks, an old friend of Jess's from
North Bend, Oregon, who was spending time with Louise. Shilo
brought street knowledge from the period he had spent homeless in Seattle, Robert helped the group see through the eyes of a
Black man who used drugs and shared his years of experience with
grassroots activism in New York, and Becki was a proud feminist
who served as a wise and loving mentor (and was also a ton of fun).
"Team-based, feminist-led," Jess says. "This was really important."

They were determined to learn from the mistakes of past
attempts to unify drug users and avoid the pitfalls that sunk previous attempts at national organizing.

Louise, especially, leaned heavily on this flattened leadership
structure. She was struggling with her new reality as someone who
was physically disabled, and her injured leg added to the insecuri-
ties she felt from the stigma that was inflicted on her as a drug-using
woman. She often felt weak, and working alongside Jess, Shilo, Robert, and Becki gave her strength. But, while she doesn't always realize it, Louise has a will that can move mountains. "Every time we
meet at a conference, they're talking about setting up the structure
of a union. This is the whole problem that I recognize," Louise says.
"They come together, they talk about how we're going to create a
constitution. And that is where everybody gets into a fight: How are

we going to set this up? What is this going to look like? All of this really tedious junk. That's what happened in Denver. And over and over again."

Jess had also grown cynical. "We were stuck talking about talking about doing something," she says, "not having the bandwidth or the people on the ground to actually do the work."

Louise came up with what they hoped was a solution. Instead of focusing on internal details—arguing over the minutia of decision-making protocols and hierarchical infrastructure—they were going to first get something done. Louise and Jess working as co-directors lent their decisions a degree of democratic legitimacy. "Now we needed to have an action," Louise says. "We needed to have a campaign; we needed to do something that would be successful, so that people could rally around that success and feel good about drug users, sex workers, and our ability to organize." Jess liked this new direction a lot. "This is where I give Louise so much credit," she says. "I was burned out, having tried to do this for years. Then Louise actually did something. She blew it up. She took it and ran with it."

The pair connected with Becki and found something that worked: regular phone calls. Years earlier, Becki had worked with the International Network of People Who Use Drugs (INPUD) when they had joined users together from across Europe. The trio decided they could emulate what worked for INPUD and open their regular calls to others who were interested. There already existed a number of cross-country conference calls convened by different harm reduction groups—the Naloxone Overdose Prevention Education call on which Jess had tried to sound the alarm for fentanyl, for example—but this call would be the first national meeting place specifically for people who use drugs. The calls were set at regular times and served as a sort of glue to hold their national efforts together in lieu of all the bureaucratic details that had stalled previous efforts.

"Fuck the structure," Louise said on a call with Jess and Becki.

"We don't need structure to organize a campaign. The structure is the call. If you're part of the call, you're part of the USU."

This worked, although there was some pushback from older members of the movement who felt it was necessary to first establish mechanisms for organizational accountability and define clear goals. But the trio of women powered through it. "It starts off with just a couple of people on the phone, just drug users talking," Louise says. They invited experts to lead discussions about methadone maintenance, for example, or how to set up an underground syringe exchange. It was like a phone-in class in harm reduction. Word spread and a couple more people showed up. The calls grew in size from Louise, Jess, and Becki to five or six people, and then to nine or ten. "We've started talking to drug users from around the country and we're finding out what's going on," Louise says. The next thing they knew, people were asking how they could set up USU chapters in their hometowns like the groups that Shilo, Jess, and Louise had organized in Seattle, Northampton, and Greensboro.

People's willingness to join these early calls also likely had something to do with a growing state of crisis within America's drug-user communities. By 2016, everyone knew the word "fentanyl" and that the synthetic drug was killing members of their community at a growing rate. "People were dying, so it was in the middle of this really intense time," Louise says. "That mattered."

The regular organizing calls served to unite a growing interest in the movement. "All of a sudden, you have a table that drug users can sit around," Shilo says. "Louise and the Urban Survivors Union developed that call. People don't realize how significant that was."

"So we started with one conference call," Jess says. "That turned into two calls, then three calls, and more people started joining." Louise and Jess served as co-facilitators. People dialed in and, once everyone had introduced themselves, they took the group through the topic or items of the day. One call was dedicated to collecting complaints about each member's local police department, another hosted a guest presenter that offered tips on grant writing.

A loose consensus emerged around the issues that people wanted the USU to prioritize. Every state government in America needed to permit syringe exchange and fund those operations like they do any health program. While most people on these early calls happened to live in jurisdictions where syringe exchange was allowed, they decided that all members still needed to make this a priority and push for the legalization of syringe exchange wherever it remained prohibited.

At the federal level, the USU would fight to reform arduous and stigmatizing regulations around methadone. It was needlessly difficult for health professionals to open a methadone clinic, and that created a shortage of clinics, forcing many patients into long daily commutes. The science said that methadone as a form of medication-assisted treatment was the most effective tool available for managing a chronic addiction to opioids.[21] Regulators needed to follow the science and make methadone more widely available.

Third, USU members wanted an end to the war on drugs. Police harassment needed to stop. They would demand the repeal of laws criminalizing drug possession and fight for the immediate release of people who were already in prison for nonviolent drug crimes. Decriminalizing drugs would change everything. It was the criminalization of drugs that created stigma—stigma that discouraged drug users from seeking help for an addiction, lest friends and family learn of their problem, and stigma that pushed people who use drugs into the shadows, leading them to hide their drug use in basements and back alleys, where there is no one to respond in the event of an overdose.

A push to end the drug war was the objective that received more time on USU calls than any other. Most people tuning in had served time in jail or prison for drug-related offenses, and the drug war's roots, history, and impacts were frequent topics of discussion.

———

America's problem of mass incarceration is bigger than the war on drugs, but without prohibition and the drug war, it is unlikely that mass incarceration would have reached the scale it has today. The war on drugs began under the administration of President Richard Nixon in 1971. "America's public enemy number one, in the United States, is drug abuse," Nixon said at a press conference that year. "In order to fight and defeat this enemy, it is necessary to wage a new, all-out offensive. I've asked the Congress to provide the legislative authority and the funds to fuel this kind of an offensive."[22] For the duration of Nixon's administration and the subsequent half century, Congress obliged and devoted billions to the fight against drugs.

Or so we were told. In 2016, Nixon's counsel and assistant to the president for domestic affairs, John Ehrlichman, admitted that the war on drugs was never actually about the drugs themselves.

"The Nixon campaign in 1968, and the Nixon White House after that, had two enemies: the antiwar left and Black people," he told *Harper's Magazine*. "We knew we couldn't make it illegal to be either against the war or Black, but by getting the public to associate the hippies with marijuana and Blacks with heroin, and then criminalizing both heavily, we could disrupt those communities. We could arrest their leaders, raid their homes, break up their meetings, and vilify them night after night on the evening news. Did we know we were lying about the drugs? Of course we did."[23]

Disrupting those communities caused the country's prisons and jails to fill up. From 1971 to 1980, the number of inmates in U.S. state and federal prisons increased from roughly 200,000 to 329,000.[24] President Ronald Reagan inherited Nixon's drug war in 1981. He doubled down on its tactics and significantly intensified the rate at which people were sent to prison for drug crimes. From 1981 to 1990, the country's prison population grew from 369,000 inmates to 771,243.[25] Subsequent politicians—Republican and Democrat—continued this trend, each one seeking to adopt a "tough on crime" approach that was tougher than their opponents'.

By 2009, the peak year for the U.S. prison population before a slow decline began under President Barack Obama, there were 1,614,000 people in America sitting behind bars.[26] That marks a 700 percent increase from the early 1970s to the late 2000s. The reason this occurred is the war on drugs.[27] From 1980 to 1996, the incarceration rate for drug crimes increased from 15 inmates per 100,000 to 148, a 10-fold increase.[28] Left out of these statistics are people sent to prison for violent crimes—another category of the incarcerated that skyrocketed during this period—and a significant portion of violent crimes occur because of drugs or, more specifically, because drugs are illegal.[29]

As Ehrlichman admitted, these related problems of the drug war and mass incarceration did not impact all groups evenly—they were not intended to. From its outset, the war's primary target—buried in coded language for the public but stated bluntly behind closed doors—was communities of color. By this measure, Nixon could declare victory. Black people comprise about 13 percent of the U.S. population, and study after study has shown they both use and sell illicit narcotics at rates roughly even with whites.[30] Yet in 2015, Black people accounted for nearly a third of people arrested for drug-law offenses and 40 percent of those incarcerated for drug crimes.[31] The United States imprisons a larger percentage of its Black population than South Africa did with the judicial system it used to implement apartheid.[32] In some cities, more than half of young adult Black men are under the control of the state, either in prison, in jail, or on parole.[33] Michelle Alexander's seminal work, *The New Jim Crow: Mass Incarceration in the Age of Colorblindness*, describes how those individuals who manage to escape this carceral archipelago exit as permanent second-class citizens, legally discriminated against in terms of housing, employment, education, and public benefits. They are locked out of the legitimate economy and virtually exiled from mainstream society. It amounts to nothing less than a "new racial caste system," Alexander concludes.[34] Fifty years after Nixon's declaration, drug use remains as prevalent as ever and overdose deaths are at an all-time high. But as a means of control, the war on drugs can be considered a resounding success.

On USU conference calls, members talked through these issues at length. At one point, they joked they had not established a drug-user union but rather the country's first national history class.

The fourth and final issue that USU members rallied around was the overdose crisis. Everyone agreed that people were not dying because they did drugs; they were dying because they did not know what was in their drugs. If illicit narcotics were legalized and regulated—perhaps similar to how alcohol is today or through a more medicalized model—dealers wouldn't have the opportunity to mix fentanyl into the substances people used. Overdoses might still happen, but in far, far fewer numbers, and with significantly fewer deaths.

On these early national calls, Louise and Jess also led brainstorming sessions for political actions and projects that could improve the lives of people who use drugs in the short term. One early idea was a takeover of the National Mall in Washington, DC. People wanted to erect a field of crosses there representing the more than 65,000 people who at the time were dying every year due to drug overdoses. That one never went anywhere, or at least it hasn't yet, but the group was growing in ambition. "That's when people from all across the nation started reaching out to us," Jess says. People began to ask, 'How do we do a union?'"

12
Blow the System Up

Despite her success with the Urban Survivors Union, Louise was miserable. She was still in a wheelchair with a broken leg that stubbornly refused to heal more than a year after the unexplained hit-and-run outside Jimmy's place on the outskirts of Greensboro. She couldn't move around on her own, and Wiggs continued to care for his best friend with absolute dedication. This was a huge help, but Louise had developed an infection and it was making her sick. In discussions with doctors, the word "amputation" had come up, but Louise refused to even acknowledge the idea. "I tried convincing her early on," Wiggs says, "but she wasn't going to hear it."

Louise maintained a hectic schedule that didn't leave her much time to care for herself. While the police didn't find anything with their early-morning raid at her mother's home, they continued to harass Louise and stop her whenever they caught her out in public. Eventually, Louise picked up a possession charge that left her on probation for a time. She still couldn't find a doctor who would prescribe her adequate pain medication, so, even with the added risks of probation combined with sustained police harassment, she was using heroin several times each day. Meanwhile, Louise's daughter Selena was struggling with her recent bipolar diagnosis and getting into trouble at school. With Wiggs and Don with her in Greensboro and Jess on the phone from Northampton, Louise was also more involved in harm reduction and drug-user organizing, operating as the region's primary underground syringe exchange. She could have prioritized her health, but putting herself first was never Louise's strong suit, even when it approached a matter of life or death.

She could not bring herself to comprehend the reality of the situation. "People were talking about amputation and I was not okay with that. I couldn't accept that I was not going to be me anymore."

For months she struggled with her external fixator, and then for many more months endured endless doctors' appointments and nurses' visits—interactions that, with her intense fear of the health care system, each came with mental anguish. Finally, after being told that the infection was putting her life at risk, Louise conceded the inevitable. She was going to lose her right leg.

Louise felt shame at the prospect of becoming permanently physically disabled, as misplaced as she knew it was, and this feeling was compounded by judgments people made about her for using drugs. "People assumed that I had shot up in my leg or done something wrong, which was not the case," she explains. Louise believes she lost her leg as a result of receiving substandard care for her injury because of the ways doctors and the entire medical establishment viewed her for using drugs.

She can't bring herself to discuss the amputation, but her mother recounts how Louise felt she never received proper care. Her doctors were reluctant to even try to rebuild her ankle. "Nobody in Greensboro thought it was worth trying," Sarah says. "If she had followed absolute directions and done exactly as doctors wanted a compliant patient to do, maybe it would have healed. *Maybe*. But it didn't heal. Whatever was being proposed was going to be long, drawn out, and was going to require perfect compliance in every direction. Through it all, the doctors told her, No, we can't give you painkillers. You're an addict."

This didn't just leave Louise in pain. It was much more detrimental than that. A lack of legal pain medication forced Louise to find alternatives on the black market. That required money, which required a hustle. So Louise wasn't driven back only to heroin, but also to the constant hassles that come with finding and paying for heroin. Such a lifestyle is not conducive to a long and complicated recovery of a severely broken leg.

After the amputation, Louise fell into a deep depression. A total black hole. "The amputation, I tried to avoid. I kept my leg much longer than I should have," Louise says. "They were telling me, 'If you cut your leg off, this is going to get better.' But the idea of it was too much. . . . And nobody can talk about it. Amputation is not one of the things that we are taught how to discuss. Nobody knows how to be there for you. So I was angry."

Discharged from the hospital, Louise, Don, and Wiggs, most nights, moved back into the little house that Sarah had purchased for Louise when Selena was born. The guys cared for Louise as best they could, but she barely allowed them to keep her alive. Louise tried to convince Don to leave her. "The self-hatred I experienced was overwhelming," she says. Louise didn't want their care. "That accident is a dark piece of my life. I did not think that I was going to come back from that." Months passed while Louise lay in bed injecting heroin. "It was an overwhelming despair," she says.

Louise would occasionally leave the house, but these outings often only made her feel worse. "Everything changes when you're disabled. Your sexuality is gone. The day I got my prosthetic and you could tell I didn't have a leg, I saw it happen that day. I was at the store and the banter between me and other men and women changed. It's so weird," she explains. "And you are aware of it. People look to the ground. People don't look at you. People talk loud to you like you're slow and can't understand or something."

Her depression worsened. "At one point, I tried to sit Selena down and explain to her why I needed to kill myself," Louise says, openly shedding tears. "I didn't want her to be upset about it. She needed to understand that this just needed to happen. I absolutely wanted to die, in every way."

Louise took heroin to keep herself alive, to dull her pain enough to a point where she could bear it. "I am truly scared of that space in my mind. That was the darkest, fucking most horrific, loneliest place I had ever bottomed out at. And I didn't know how to get out of there and it was eating me whole. It was an overwhelming despair and devastation."

A few months after Louise lost her leg, Selena was still having problems at school and more than once had gotten into trouble with police. She was caught shoplifting and given a severe warning for possessing marijuana. It was more than enough to keep everyone very worried.

While police never found hard drugs on her, Sarah and Louise knew she was using them. And not just any hard drug—heroin. Eventually, Selena agreed to go to a treatment facility. And she went willingly, with Louise tactfully nudging her there as opposed to forcing the issue. That's where Selena was now, at a facility on the other side of the country, in Culver City, California. So Sarah figured Selena was safe and sound in treatment, and was feeling a little better about her granddaughter's troubles. But when her phone rang at a little after four in the morning on March 13, 2016, Sarah knew that something was wrong.

Louise hates falling asleep. She hates sleep itself. "Sleeping is dangerous," she explains. When Louise was with Brice, he would wake her up with physical abuse, sometimes throwing Louise's petite body across the room.

"So many mornings, I wake up in just pure panic. It's PTSD. That's just the way I wake up. I never wake up peacefully and just sort of go on about my day. And then you add dope sickness to that equation. All of these different things have happened to me after I've fallen asleep. It affects me to this day, even when I'm safe. So many mornings, I wake up in just a pure fucking panic."

The March morning that Sarah received such an early phone call, Louise was asleep in bed with Don. They both awoke to a loud and relentless banging. It was still before 5 a.m. The knocking continued and Louise quickly got out of bed.

She opened the front door to her mother standing there. "Selena's dead," Sarah gently told her. Across the country, Louise's daughter was found unresponsive and later confirmed the victim of an opioid overdose.

Louise screamed. "What? She's dead? She can't be dead. She's dead? We've got to be able to do something. She can't be dead." Louise collapsed onto the floor, howling. She peed herself. As she lay there, Don tried to console her. Louise wept.

Selena had been Louise's daughter, sister, and best friend. Louise loved her more than anything. She was supposed to have been getting better—she had even agreed to go to rehab. At just 19, there was still plenty of time to turn things around. She was in a treatment facility when she overdosed. Why hadn't somebody saved her? Louise lay in a ball on the floor and sobbed. Sarah didn't know what to do. Louise was screaming at her, releasing her anguish on whoever had delivered the news. After a few minutes, Sarah, equally devastated and feeling helpless, left Louise with Don.

Sarah worried that Louise wouldn't survive. The concern was not that Louise would kill herself, although that was a possibility. It was that Louise would die of heartache. She wouldn't eat. She couldn't even think. Sarah worried she would simply stop living. And there was so little she could do to help her.

For no reason, Louise was furious with her. "I needed somebody to be angry with. Sadness isn't good enough. You need fury and rage. So I wasn't nice. It wasn't like I was crying and there was a sweet, sensitive moment between all of us. There was only terror and fury. That's how that day exists for me. I wasn't talking. Don answered the phone. I couldn't take calls. There was just too much stimulation. I felt like I was being hit with lightning. There was too much energy—disbelief, shock, and horror.

"In that moment, I had to have drugs. I think I would have died without them. I could almost see myself spontaneously combusting, with that kind of energy. For so long, it was just me screaming and crying. It's a realization that you have over and over and over again. You fall asleep and you wake up and again, you realize that it's all true. It's the most horrific nightmare. It's ongoing because it is something that your brain doesn't want to wrap around. I just wanted drugs."

In the months following Selena's passing, Louise did not inject heroin to party, spur creativity, or relax. She used the drug to soften her pain, if only for a moment. In the minutes after a dose of heroin, as she felt each shot's initial warm blanket wrap around her, Louise felt okay. Perhaps not okay—it's difficult to describe heroin's feeling of comfort—but somewhat content. Not like everything was all right—nothing could cure this pain—but, simply, that this was the way things were. "Using was not the worst thing that I could do," Louise says. "It was the thing that I needed to do to save my life."

Don called a dealer they had known for years named Sleepy, but Sleepy wouldn't deliver to them. He had just lost his mother to an overdose and was scared that Louise would try to kill herself. Instead, Sleepy came over and held Louise's hand, still refusing to give her drugs. "I just can't do that for you right now," he said.

Don called another dealer, named Pure. Louise tried to speak with him but she was hysterical, making no sense. Don took the phone back and arranged a meet. They didn't have any money but Pure didn't care. He gave Louise whatever she asked for. "He came and checked on me. These guys aren't just dealers. I've known some of them for 20 years."

Weeks passed. Don waited on Louise hand and foot, but there was little he could do other than try to keep her fed, just try to keep her alive. "You go to sleep and you wake up and you think, maybe it's different. It's not different," Louise says. "I dream a lot when I'm upset. So there was really intense confusion in my dreams. All of it just felt fucking numb." Months passed.

How did Selena die of an overdose inside a facility that treated people for addictions to drugs? Years later, Louise and Sarah reached an out-of-court settlement with the recovery home that was caring for Selena when she died. This facility did not stock or even allow the overdose-reversal drug naloxone on its premises. If it had, there is a good chance that Selena Vincent would still be alive today.

Naloxone has no adverse side effects and has not required a prescription in California since 2015. The reason this recovery center did not keep naloxone was that its operators believed that doing so would be "enabling." They worried it would send a mixed message, in some way promoting drug use among the population that was there to stop using drugs.

Prescriptions for intramuscular naloxone and its brand-name equivalent, nasal Narcan, increased 800 percent from 2015 to 2017.[1] And yet many recovery homes do not make naloxone available. In the United States, recovery homes remain unregulated in most jurisdictions, which makes it difficult for researchers to know what's going on inside. A recent initiative by the Clinton Foundation, however, reveals the scale of the problem. In August 2020, the recovery activist and former Obama White House staffer Ryan Hampton partnered with the Clinton Foundation to begin equipping some 500 recovery homes in five states with 155,000 doses of the lifesaving medication. "I've lost well over two dozen friends to preventable drug overdoses," Hampton told *USA Today.* "Many of them in sober home living facilities that should have had naloxone and correct overdose response measures."[2] Hampton, himself in recovery, was inspired by the loss of a friend who, like Selena, died in a recovery home that refused to stock naloxone.

Selena's recovery home did not keep naloxone because of stigma, because America's war-on-drugs ideology says that anything that might make drug use safer in any way is wrong and should be outlawed.

"Drug policy killed my daughter," Louise says. "Everywhere I look, there's pain and horror because of those kinds of fucked up decisions that we as Americans have made. Something I hear people say all the time is, 'We've got to work within the system.' No, we don't. We need to blow the system up. Because it was that system that killed my daughter."

Later that year, Louise, Don, Wiggs, and Sarah created something out of their pain. They called August 11, 2016, "Selena Lives Overdose Awareness Day," and held a memorial and mini harm reduction conference in Greensboro. Shilo traveled from Seattle for the event. He brought a large photograph of Selena that was signed by every member of the Urban Survivors Union. Throughout the day, there were drug policy experts who had traveled from out of town and spoke on a variety of topics. Shilo called the event "Harm Reduction 101." He brought USU members from both Seattle and San Francisco with him, and so it was a family affair and a great opportunity for everyone to get to know one another. But it was also a ton of work. "I had never really thrown any sort of event, so I didn't know what was involved, and it about killed me," Louise says. "But it was a nice coming-out party for the USU."

The day marked a turning point for Louise. It reminded her of the purpose she had found in harm reduction and allowed her to begin to pull herself out of depression. After her leg was amputated, she was secretly consumed by thoughts of suicide. The utter hopelessness she felt frightened her. Now, months after Selena passed away, the shock was beginning to wear off but only to be replaced by those same feelings of total darkness. So, a while after Selena died, Louise went on what she calls a "work binge," in order to stave off those dark feelings.

She was still grieving, but there was work to do, she decided. Selena was one of roughly 64,000 people across America that died of an overdose in 2016. Louise was going to do something about that.

13

Harm Reduction Works

The Urban Survivors Union's weekly calls helped Jess feel like she was part of something and alleviated her depression. But she was still badly stung by Tapestry's tacit rejection. "I'm feeling, like, 'A harm reduction program won't even hire me to be a health educator?'" she says. Then she caught the attention of a soft-spoken man named Albie Park.

In addition to Jess's national profile within the harm reduction movement, she'd kept busy at a regional level, speaking on panels, organizing protests throughout New England, and giving interviews to local media. One of her quotes really stuck with Albie: "People always think recovery is either you're completely abstinent or you're in full chaotic use, and there is a world in between," Jess told an NPR affiliate.[1] Albie thought they might have a lot in common.

Albie is a veteran of the HIV/AIDS crisis of the 1980s and 1990s, from an entire generation of gay men whom catastrophe forced into activism. He believes harm reduction advocates can learn from that struggle. "There are all these people in their 50s, and 60s, some older, who lived through the apocalypse. We [gay men] have already done this," Albie says, comparing the HIV/AIDS crisis to today's drug overdose epidemic. "We know what happens. We were broken by it, we were healed by it. We were every-which-wayed by it. And now there are all these younger people who are saying, 'What do we do? What does this mean?' And we're here and we've already lived through it. Having lived through an apocalypse already, what gay men have to teach is resilience."

The worst year for AIDS-related deaths in America was 1995, when about 51,400 people succumbed to health complications associated with the virus.[2] During October 2020, the most recent period for which data are available and also the worst year of the overdose crisis thus far, a projected 93,300 people in America died after taking drugs.[3] Through the first of these two crises, Albie learned about activism and also about loss, grief, and love.

Albie spent his formative years in San Francisco. When he met his first husband, Randy, there, the man revealed he was sick with HIV. But Albie decided that the risk of losing Randy to the virus in the future was worth the time they could spend together in the present. The two of them fell in love and shared something very special for several years. Eventually, however, in 2011, Randy succumbed to the disease. The two had just gotten out of bed for the day when Randy collapsed. Albie never forgave himself for failing to catch him before his body roughly hit the ground. He was pronounced dead later that day.

Albie was 35 and spent the next several years crippled by depression. "Sometimes I couldn't move," he says. "But eventually, I had to pull myself out of it. So I have a very strong sort of affinity for grief and helping people through that process."

Emerging from depression, Albie realized he needed an income and began looking for work in the field of addiction treatment services. A friend with an organization called the Stimulant Treatment Outpatient Program, an addiction treatment center that utilized the 12 steps, hired him as a part-time counselor. "How can you tell when a drug addict is lying?" a colleague asked him on his first day. "Their lips are moving."

Another friend offered Albie a similar position at a nonprofit called the Stonewall Project, a treatment center that spurned the 12 steps in favor of harm reduction philosophies. "I was going from this hard-core abstinence-based program in the morning to this hard-core harm reduction program in the afternoon. It was like, compare and contrast."

For the next 13 years, Albie lived in San Francisco and worked for Stonewall. He met his second husband, John Chambers. They moved to Mexico together, then Germany, and then, in 2014, to Northampton, Massachusetts. "And what happened was, I started hearing the name Jess Tilley," Albie says. A few months later, Albie and Jess were both in attendance at a western Massachusetts meeting about overdose deaths and decided to carpool together. Albie says Jess was frustrated. She was an expert in harm reduction with years in the field, but she couldn't translate that experience into a steady paycheck.

Albie picked Jess up off the ground. You need to put your name out there as a consultant, he told her. They formed a nonprofit organization called HRH413, short for Harm Reduction Hedgehogs, an inside joke referencing Jess's two favorite things and the area code for western Massachusetts. Next, the pair secured a two-year grant from a large nonprofit called AIDS United and began to figure out how their skills complemented one another's. Albie recognized that his strength was running logistics so he positioned himself behind Jess. They put to work her two decades of experience both as a drug user and as a pioneer of grassroots harm reduction. Jess was booked for speaking engagements, sat on panels, and accepted positions on the occasional task force such as Cambridge's Overdose Prevention Education Network. She ensured that a voice for drug users was incorporated into policies, programs, and services aimed at people who use drugs. The pair also hosted trainings in naloxone and overdose response for nonprofit organizations working with the homeless and other marginalized populations, and expanded Jess's long-standing underground network distributing syringes, naloxone, and fentanyl test strips. "We took on the people that didn't want to go to Tapestry," Albie says. "Because there are people who will just never step into a brick-and-mortar needle exchange—people for whom, for whatever reason, that will just never work."

The arrival of fentanyl and a sharp rise in overdose deaths put the words "harm reduction" on more people's radars. All of a sudden, right-leaning jurisdictions such as Florida and West Virginia were talking about needle exchange. Jess and Albie capitalized on the country's newfound interest. They combined Albie's experience as an addictions-focused therapist with Jess's expertise in on-the-ground service provision. "And things start happening," Jess says.

In 2018, Albie was at a recovery conference in Las Vegas. Jess was supposed to attend with him but her cat died and she couldn't bring herself to travel. She was depressed and easily overwhelmed. In the conference's first session, Albie found himself bored and alone. The lecturer's focus was on stuff so basic that Albie not only knew it but had practiced it for 20 years. Toward the end of the session, he posed a question to the room: "What I am curious about is whether or not recovery can stop pathologizing and condemning the use of drugs, because what happens is that that doesn't only condemn drugs, it rolls over right onto the people who use drugs. So, I'm curious, is it possible? Can recovery stop pathologizing the use of drugs?"

There were murmurs, but no one really answered Albie's question. But a few minutes later, as people left the room, one of the session's speakers came over to him. "You know, my journey is changing, from total abstinence to having some wine now and then," she said. "And my life is not falling apart. But I have nowhere to take this. And I would be so much happier if I didn't have to lie in AA meetings about what I'm doing."

The conversation reminded Albie of a paper he had written in grad school: a description of a theoretical model for addictions support. When Albie returned to Northampton, he dug up the essay and shared it with Jess. She was blown away and went to work with him shaping the ideas there into a real-world program.

Albie and Jess's new model for a support group took the best components of 12-step and abstinence-based recovery groups, stripped the parts they felt were counterproductive, lost the spiritual stuff, and filled in the holes with a harm reduction philosophy that emphasizes acceptance, love, and, perhaps above all, reality. They gave it the simple title of Harm Reduction Works (HRW).

Originally, each meeting following their model began with a reading from a book. Albie and Jess usually used a couple of pages from Jeannie Little and Patt Denning's *Over the Influence: The Harm Reduction Guide to Controlling Your Drug and Alcohol Use*, a pivotal text published in 2003 that helped open the door for harm-reduction-based alternatives to 12-step programs. But that was really little more than a stated reason for being there. The real draw for participants was the group; it was community.

HRW meetings are structured because structure is important. They begin with a reading and end with a reading, and in the middle is a topic of the day and time for people to share. The skeleton will therefore feel familiar to the millions who have attended Narcotics Anonymous (NA) or Alcoholics Anonymous (AA). But from there, HRW departs from NA in ways that some 12-steppers will disapprove of while others will find refreshing.

While most NA groups forbid attendees from offering advice to one another or addressing an individual as opposed to the group—"crosstalk," in NA parlance—HRW meetings place feedback and discussion at the center of their meetings. Anyone sharing does, however, have the option to ask that the group only listen. In addition, HRW lacks NA's sponsorship structure. After attending a few NA meetings, one is expected to select another member who has more time sober to act as a mentor. Sponsors make themselves available for daily phone calls and guide their sponsee through the 12 steps. NA sponsors serve as an invaluable lifeline for many people new to sobriety and the system produces friendships that last a lifetime. However, there are pitfalls that come with the sort of power that sponsorship gives one NA member over another. There's no screening process for sponsors—anyone can become one—and not everyone is a good person. Some sponsors don't build you up, they drag you down. Other sponsors use sponsees to feed their egos, controlling their entire lives with an insistence that they always know best. It's an intense relationship that keeps the sponsee in a highly vulnerable position. HRW had no interest in this sort of power dynamic. Jess and Albie wanted to empower people, not force them to admit they were powerless.

The most notable aspect of HRW, setting it apart not just from NA but from the vast majority of recovery support groups—including SMART Recovery, Secular Organizations for Sobriety, and Celebrate Recovery, for example—is that HRW has no requirement for abstinence. Attendees can express a desire for abstinence or share that they're actually not interested in abstinence at all. Maybe they want to transition from injecting drugs to smoking them, or maybe they want to stop sharing needles and instead begin visiting a syringe exchange. Perhaps they are considering giving methadone a try. Or maybe a participant is simply looking for a shoulder to lean on.

"What 12-step has is a redemption-story machine with that classic story arc," Albie says. "HRW is just your life. There's no demarcation point around abstinence. It's not that clean. HRW makes room for things to be a little bit messy. It makes room for people to figure shit out. It was conceived for the person who is saying, 'I don't know what's going on, I don't know what's happening, but I know I have to do something.'"

People are allowed to attend HRW meetings when they're high—something that is definitely frowned upon by support groups that insist on abstinence. In addition, while many NA groups reject medication-assisted treatments (MAT) such as methadone or buprenorphine (brand name Suboxone), or even view the availability of naloxone as enabling, HRW fully welcomes people on MAT and often distributes Narcan and syringes in the same rooms where participants discuss aspirations for abstinence.

In fact, there's virtually nothing that prohibits someone from attending an HRW meeting. Support is unconditional, totally indiscriminate of where someone stands in their recovery or drug use. At an HRW meeting in Northampton during the fall of 2019, a couple of teenage runaways who were intoxicated (just enough to keep themselves level) sat alongside a pair of parents who had lost their 20-something daughter to an overdose the year before. There was also a paramedic who struggled with an opioid addiction next to a young aspiring writer who used drugs recreationally. Everyone got along well, sharing diverse experiences and equally varied insight.

Cara Moser was one of the parents there that night who had lost her child to an overdose. Her daughter's name was Eliza. "It was a mix of trauma and mental illness and substance use," Cara says. "She just ended up being one of those kids. She was experimenting and then she was trying to escape her pain. And then I lost my baby." Since Cara first learned about her daughter's addiction to heroin, the two of them agreed that they would speak openly about it and help reduce the stigma that prevents so many from asking for help. "We couldn't just separate ourselves from other people's suffering," Cara says. "At HRW, I can share my experiences as a parent. It just seems to me it's like a really safe place to be open and honest." Cara doesn't seem to mind sitting next to people who use drugs. "I think people get stuck on their anger," she says. Cara says HRW gives parents a place to explore those feelings. "I wish there had been an HRW meeting before Eliza died. It may have helped save her life. Really. She would have gone to these meetings with me and held my hand."

Albie and Jess have brainstormed how these groups should track participants' progress in recovery. HRW declines to count participants' "clean time" the way that NA and AA do. There are no keychains for days abstinent and therefore none of the shame or stigma that abstinence-only groups can inflict on members who slip. For many people, a count of days clean is a helpful motivator. You don't want to start your count over and you don't want to let the group down by starting over; you think about those things when you feel like using drugs and that helps you avoid relapse. But, in practice, NA's emphasis on a black-and-white number for days without drugs can backfire. If an NA member who previously struggled with cocaine remains abstinent for two years and then has a glass of wine, the count of their days sober is reset to zero. So why not go all in and indulge with a night of blow?

Jess has firsthand experience with that sort of relapse. She wanted to incorporate something into HRW that could help others avoid it. Instead of counting days "clean," she and Albie thought HRW participants could track the amount of time that's passed since they made a decision to stop using drugs or to use fewer drugs. The count wouldn't reset when they slipped. Occasional drug use wouldn't qualify as a full-blown relapse. Therefore, one rationale for returning to problematic drug use would be removed.

Another idea Jess and Albie had was for HRW to count the percentage of days that someone has abstained from drugs since the date they made the decision to try to stop using. For example, if a meth user set in motion a New Year's resolution on January 1, used twice that month, four times in February, twice in March, and then attended an HRW meeting on March 31, they could report that, despite using drugs eight times since beginning their recovery journey three months earlier, their progress to date was counted as 91 percent drug free.

"Every week, I have no idea where anybody's been; I have no idea what anybody's been through," Albie says.

He and Jess have refined the group's structure over time, but Albie stresses that there's really not much to it. "In the end, this was conceived to be skeletal so that other communities can put whatever is important from their communities on top of it."

HRW remains in a startup phase and so far no data exist on how this specific harm reduction model might assist people with recovery or otherwise improve health outcomes. But Rize, a nonprofit working to reduce overdose deaths, has commissioned a small team of addiction researchers to evaluate groups incorporating harm reduction into recovery, and one of the initiatives they're investigating is HRH413's Harm Reduction Works support network.

A medical anthropologist and assistant professor at Elon University in North Carolina named Jennifer Carroll is a member of the research team. She believes there truly is a need for alternatives to 12-step and abstinence-only models. "If there is someone who is interested in 12-step, they absolutely deserve and need to have access to that tool," Carroll says. "The challenge comes when people are shuffled into 12-step programs when that is an inappropriate form of care." For example, if someone is coming into a support group after being abused, a recovery platform that requires them to acknowledge their powerlessness could cause them substantially more harm. What is clear is that 12-step recovery groups don't work for everyone.[4]

Carroll's experience is that there is an obvious appetite for new models and philosophies for recovery. "My inbox blows up a lot with people who want a neutral source of advice. 'This is happening with my nephew'; 'This is going on with my husband'; 'Do you have any thoughts or do you know anyone in this area?' And frequently, those requests are for any suggestion I can make about support groups or mutual-aid groups that are not 12-step oriented."

Roughly two years after Albie and Jess first formulated the Harm Reduction Works model, it's in use in more than a dozen cities across the United States. At its core, HRW is a place where people with something in common—an addiction or experience with someone using drugs—can be together. And, if they are ready for it, they can find support to stop using drugs or to use fewer drugs less often. Or not. Regardless, the group is there for them.

Jess recalls a favorite moment from one of HRW's early meetings. A middle-aged woman sat attentively as the group positioned in a circle went around introducing themselves. As it neared her turn, a smile grew. "My name is Stephanie and I am so grateful to finally be at a meeting where I don't have to tell you that I'm an alcoholic," she said. "Because I am so much more than that."

14

Light Up the Night

In June 2018, Louise was back in the hospital. Even after her leg was amputated, its stubborn infection remained. "I had a little spot on my knee. I went to the doctor. He said, 'Don't worry about it.' So I didn't. And then I had to deal with the police."

The North Carolina Survivors Union (NCSU) was developing into a real organization. It had recently hired one woman to sometimes replace Don at the front desk of the needle exchange and then had hired a second to help with administrative tasks. Don's brother, Derek Jackson, was also hanging around the exchange. A quiet guy and initially hesitant to involve himself in activism, he began helping with education and communications materials. The grant money was limited and only allowed for part-time hires, but Louise was a boss. The NCSU had also just moved into a new space on Grove Street. It was a "rough" neighborhood long before Louise and Don set up a syringe exchange there. That was why they picked it. There's a convenience store on the corner that sells 40-cent packets of noodles and loose cigarettes and a furniture store across from it that never has any customers in it. The rest of the block is boarded up and vacant. A few teenagers and 20-somethings hang around, selling drugs and playing music to fend off boredom. It's not really dangerous—the kids on the corner are friendly enough after they've seen you around a couple of times—but it's an obvious spot to hit if you're looking for drugs. Despite it having been that way for years prior to the exchange arriving, Greensboro police acted like Louise was bringing down the neighborhood. They told her they would eventually bust the USU for the drugs she honestly was no longer selling.

This was nothing but naked police harassment. The Grove Street needle exchange was a pretty quiet operation. When someone wandered in, Louise and Don helped them with condoms, syringes, and other harm reduction supplies, and answered any questions they might have as best they could. The drop-in offered plenty of educational materials on HIV, hepatitis C, safe sex, family planning, and, of course, healthier drug-use practices. It also served as a meeting place for a couple of groups, one for women and another the NCSU's regular weekly group, named "Any Positive Change," a low-barrier, anything-goes support network where people who used drugs could talk about their use in a nonjudgmental space, where no one would push them toward abstinence if that wasn't what they were there to talk about. There were a few comfy couches near the front door where people could just hang out. It was a tranquil refuge; a casual drop-in for drug users where they could simply take a minute away from police harassment, the daily grind, an abusive boyfriend, or whatever else from which they needed a break.

Cops raided the place one morning and Louise took it unusually hard. By this time, the grants that she had secured for the USU's North Carolina chapter were adding up to real money—not a lot but enough for Louise to feel responsible for the few people she now employed. And so she and Don had made a decision to stop dealing drugs. In the past, they had only sold enough to cover their habits and had kept their circle of customers small, but even that had stopped several years back. People would call them all the time but Louise would no longer even serve as a go-between—there was too much at stake. Even if she was only accused of selling drugs, if the accusation held any credibility at all, it would jeopardize everything that they were trying to do with harm reduction in North Carolina and with the USU across the United States. "It would have ended everything," Louise says. "So we had finished with all of that." So, when police raided the USU exchange, it stressed her out. A lot. They were no longer selling, but drugs were sometimes still around for personal consumption.

In the end, the police left empty-handed. But the raid scared Louise and Don. Louise felt that anxiety deeply. Psychological stress can manifest itself physically, suppressing the immune system and raising the risk of viral infections and other health problems.[1] For Louise, this was a lifelong pattern. After the raid, the spot on her knee got worse and a fever came on. By the end of the day, her temperature was 102°F. "If I can't manage my emotions, they will kill me," Louise laments.

Eventually, doctors said they had no choice but to proceed with a second amputation, this time above the knee. This was a brutal diagnosis. With an amputation below the knee, one can learn to walk again with a prosthetic that's relatively simple and easy to master. An amputation above the knee is a more complicated problem. Prosthetics that include an artificial joint are heavier and require a much longer learning curve. Louise simply did not want this second amputation to happen. Furthermore, she felt it would have been unnecessary if it weren't for the intense stress brought on by police harassment. Finally, she accepted that she had to go through with it.

The day of the operation, her hospital room was crowded with people and buzzing with activity. Her daughter Summer was there, lending support alongside her grandmother on Tommy's side. NCSU members came and went and activists from other nonprofit organizations waited for Louise's attention. Every so often, a nurse or doctor paid a quick visit. In the middle of it all, Louise was on a call with Jess and other harm-reduction activists from across the country. They were making early preparations for the National Harm Reduction Coalition's 2018 conference scheduled for New Orleans later in the year. At the same time, Louise had a laptop

open in front of her and furiously drafted emails about the conference and a demonstration the USU intended to hold there.

Her spirits were high and her work kept her mind off her leg.
Eventually, however, the reality of the situation sunk in. Doctors
were about to take another piece of her. As she was wheeled toward
the operating room, Louise cried openly and screamed, "I don't
want to do this."

A couple of months later, in August 2018, America's harm reduction movement lost its "godfather," as Dan Bigg was often called. He
overdosed at his home on a combination of substances, including
fentanyl.[2] Dan died because he broke the number-one rule of hard
drugs: never use alone.

Dan was a harm reduction pioneer who had helped establish the
country's first underground networks for syringe and naloxone
distribution. In addition, on a personal level for Louise and Jess,
he supplied them both with Narcan, needles, and, more recently,
fentanyl test strips. The two were devastated by the loss of Dan.
"Broken," Jess says.

One coroner's review found that of 872 overdose deaths that
occurred in 2016 and early 2017, 69 percent of the deceased used
the drugs that killed them in isolation.[3] Another study reported
that only 15 percent of fatal overdoses happened in a public space,
while 75 percent occurred in a person's home, the most common
location for someone to use alone.[4]

The same month that Dan passed away, the New York Times com-
piled data from across the nation to give the first estimate for the
total number of overdose deaths in 2017. The figure was astounding:
72,000, a record at the time.* By comparison, through the 1990s,

---

* The National Institute on Drug Abuse later confirmed the New York Times'
number and then revised it to the slightly lower official tally of 70,237 deaths
in 2017—still a record then.

America saw a rough annual average of 15,000 fatal overdoses each year.

Dan Bigg is the best-known name that America's harm reduction movement has lost to the overdose epidemic. But there are many others. In October 2018, the Urban Survivors Union planned to mourn, celebrate, and work to avenge those deaths.

At the National Harm Reduction Coalition's meeting in New Orleans, drug users would host a demonstration, offering people an outlet for the grief and anger they felt on account of so many overdose deaths. The plan was for a silent march with candles from the conference hotel to the New Orleans waterfront, where the group would end the night with a vigil for the victims of the overdose crisis. Well aware of how important it would be for conference attendees, Louise and Jess placed an immense amount of pressure on themselves to bring it all together. They were determined and fully capable. But then it seemed like everything that could go wrong, did go wrong.

There was simply too much for too few people to do. An unsustainable number of tasks and responsibilities had piled up at their feet. The conference took place at the Marriott Hotel on Canal Street, and Jess was half walking, half running through the lobby when a young woman stopped her in her tracks. "You're Jess Tilley," the woman said with glee. "You have no idea how much I've wanted to meet you." The reason Jess was half running was that she had just received word that one of the USU's members had overdosed in a room upstairs. Jess was rushing there with Narcan in the hope of saving the man's life. She responded to the woman: "I am and I want to talk but I can't stop right now." The admirer persisted and Jess was forced to tell her why she couldn't stop. "Someone is overdosing and I have to get to them," she said. To which the woman replied: "I promise, this will just take one second." Jess was dumbstruck. It was just one episode in a blur of bad news. "People's planes didn't come in at the right times," Jess says. "Rides didn't come through, banners didn't show up, we'd ordered all this swag and none of it came."

Louise and Jess were scheduled to speak in a total of four different conference sessions. Jess was coping with it all okay but Louise was not. It was only a few months earlier that she'd undergone her second amputation and she'd yet to be fitted with a new prosthetic. Don was there helping Louise, and the NHRC's leadership team had surprised her with an electric scooter that she was able to use for the weekend. But Louise was still hating every second of it. She was uncomfortable, a feeling that her intense sensitivity elevated from an inconvenience to unbearable. "I had no leg," she says. "We had organized a march and I didn't think I was going to be able to participate. I was working overtime when I was in the hospital, planning something that I wasn't going to be able to attend. I had mad feelings about that. I was really fucking sad. There was no part of me that even wanted to be at that conference. To go there with no leg and to stand up in front of people when I felt so fucking small and so not me, not okay, with such self-hatred and shame. People were wanting to talk and I wanted to hide." But she didn't.

On the third night of the conference, October 20, the USU and dozens of members of the harm reduction community met outside the Marriott to remember those who had passed away. Despite her anxiety, Louise was right at the center of it. USU members had built a barred cage for her that was attached to a bicycle. She would represent those victims of the drug war who remain alive but who languish in jails and prisons across America. "While you walk free, there are 2.3 million people in prison for nonviolent drug offenses," Louise shouted as the crowd outside the hotel's front door continued to grow.

There was still a lot of confusion that participants were sorting through. People weren't clear on where they were supposed to be. Part of the disorder was because there was a second NHRC-related event simultaneously taking place up on the hotel's 28th floor. This gathering was organized because, throughout the day, there had been rumors that the alt-right group the Proud Boys were in town for an unrelated event, had heard about the harm reduction conference, and planned to disrupt the USU's march and memorial that was about to get underway. The threat of a confrontation had made some conference attendees reluctant to participate, so Becki Brooks had put together a candlelight vigil in a room up on the 28th floor, where people who did not feel comfortable marching in the street could still take part in the evening's memorial and action on overdose deaths. "A lot of people took that option," Jess says. "They made a beautiful altar with candles. Becki did a really nice job."

But the possibility of a clash with the Proud Boys and the last-minute addition of a second memorial site created a lot of confusion, so much so that the march almost didn't happen. At one point, Jess suggested they concede the streets and move the entire evening's event into the hotel. But when Louise found out about that 10 minutes later, she freaked out and refused. Jess didn't require much convincing. "I immediately agreed with her," she says. "But by this point, I was just feeling beat down. We didn't have our banner, our parade route had been threatened, everything was just going to shit. But Louise and I said, 'Fuck it. We're doing it.'"

As the march prepared to depart from the conference site, Jess was one of those people still missing. She was rushing there as fast as she could, characteristically a few minutes late, but finally, she made it through the lobby and out onto the street, "And oh my god," she exclaims. More than 200 people were there together on the corner, each holding a lit candle, lending the crowd a warm glow. Most were somber, quiet, holding their candles with two hands near their chests with their heads bowed toward the ground. They called the action Light Up the Night because the overdose crisis had brought such darkness over the entire nation's community of drug users. Every person in attendance knew someone who had died of an overdose in recent years. Most knew many. They were romantic partners, best friends, and parents' children. Each death extinguished a source of light, and the Urban Survivors Union wanted to bring that light back into the world, if only for a night. Now it was happening. Brought together in New Orleans, the crowd glowed with the life of everyone they had lost. "I'll never forget that scene, outside the hotel and looking down the street," Jess says. Her eyes caught those of Louise. "We're actually doing this," Jess said. "It's happening." The two of them smiled at each other and the march began to move.

Standing next to Jess and Louise, Shilo raised a bullhorn and called the group to attention. "Everyone, do you know why we are here?" he shouted. "Because 72,000 people died last year of overdose. We have thousands of brothers and sisters who are in prison because of a faulty drug war. We have abandoned sex workers and their movement. It's time for us to stand together. We need to stand here and fight as one."

From the corner of Canal Street and Chartres, the march moved east. Shilo continued to project his voice through the bullhorn and a call-and-response chant united the crowd. "They talk," Shilo said. "We die," the crowd said back. "Fuck the drug war," everyone shouted together.

The night's energy caught Jess by surprise. "It was supposed to be a silent march but there was so much sadness and anger, and also hope. All of these voices rose up in chorus." Noisily, the group of drug users and harm reduction advocates walked down Canal Street until they reached the banks of the Mississippi River.

For the duration of the march, Louise looked around anxiously, waiting for Don. Jess similarly noticed that Albie was also missing. Finally, Don and Albie appeared together, just as the march arrived at the water. The pair of them had been left behind at the conference site, scrambling to replace the USU banner that was lost in the mail. They stole a tablecloth from the hotel and Don used his artistic talents to sketch out a message. Having caught up with everybody at the waterfront, they handed the banner to Jess, who unrolled it for display. "Light Up the Night," it read. "End the Drug War." The crowd was overcome by a wave of emotion. People held each other, crying. Others let themselves openly express anger. Some people smiled, fondly recalling memories of those who were represented by the candles they burned that night.

By this point, the crowd had thinned a bit. Some 100 people remained as the march morphed into a vigil on the water's edge. Upon their arrival there, the USU's sex-worker liaison, Caty Simon, took the megaphone and drew the crowd's attention to the myriad ways that she and the women standing with her are marginalized by the war on drugs and adjacent legislation that criminalizes prostitution. She added that, for sex workers, it often felt like they were the marginalized of the marginalized, as if no one within the larger harm reduction movement cared about them. "I am so happy that you are here for us right now," she said. "I need you to be there for us when you go home. For so long, sex workers have been showing up for harm reduction. All we want is for you to show up for us." Then Caty passed the microphone down a line of sex workers who each shared experiences from their respective cities and towns across America. "I'm Tamika Spellman and I'm representing Washington, DC," one transgender activist said. "The issue on the ground in the District of Columbia is safety. STDs are rising. Girls are on the street getting beaten, robbed, stabbed, and shot. That shit has to stop!" There was a roar of approval and the crowd shouted back: "Sex work is work."

After a few more speakers, the gathering fell quiet. The vigil's MC, the National Harm Reduction Coalition's Erica Poellot, took the microphone next. "Following a moment of silence, please join me in keeping alive the spirit of the beloved we have lost to overdose by calling them each by name," she said.

"Dan," "David," "John," "Conner," and "Adam," were the first names you could hear. Then there were so many spoken over one another that it became a cacophony. After a minute, the crowd returned to silence. "Say their names," someone shouted. And then a second wave began. "Laura," "Kevin," "Russel," "Mike," "Eva," and then again the names blended into one another. "We are witnesses," Erica called out. "Your name, your memory, they are ours. They are our way forward. A way that ignites, again and again."

Jess was supposed to address the crowd but couldn't bring herself to speak. She was crying, and then reached for a hug and was embraced in the arms of the woman next to her. Louise stepped in. "We are all here because we love each other," she began. "We love ourselves. We care about our health. We care about our lives. We care about one another, drug users, sex workers, loving one another, doing what they say we don't do. We do care about our health, we do care about our lives, we care about our families. We have so much love, we have so much to offer. We are here tonight with love. Love can heal us and love will heal us. This movement has healed me so many times and continues to sustain me. I love you all. Thank you for coming tonight. This is so fucking wonderful."

The crowd's energy began to shift again, from grief to anger and resolve. "This was put together by people that use drugs, people that sell sex, people that they say can't do these things," Louise continued. "We have done them and we will continue to do them and we will grow bigger and grow stronger. We will not stop until we are fucking free!"

Jess, her eyes still filled with tears, spoke now. "This movement was born out of months and months of love and dedication and put together by people who are sick of dying behind closed doors because stigma is killing us and killing people in our movement," she said. "We refuse to have it happen anymore."

A harm reduction activist from Boston named Angela Mae Ní Mháille had the final word of the evening. They used the space to issue a call for harm reduction.

"In the immediate, we *need* harm reduction," Angela said. "Supervised consumption spaces provide a necessary environment for those who consume illicit substances publicly in bathrooms or alleys. They provide an immediate point of contact between people who use drugs and professionals who care about their safety, who can offer them resources if they'd like but, at the bare minimum, can ensure that this hit will not lead to their death.

"Needle exchanges should be further funded, preventing the spread of blood-borne pathogens and giving people who use drugs access to the tools to keep themselves healthier. Expanded access to medication-assisted treatment to allow individuals to choose a regulated, pharmaceutical alternative to illicit substances while they address the conditions that informed their problematic use. We must make science-backed treatment available for free and on demand."

Angela concluded: "But beyond all these things, we must recognize that where there is poverty, where there is systemic injustice, patriarchal violence, racism, homo/transphobia, colonialism, and endless war at the expense of those abroad and at home, there will be trauma and problematic relationships to substances. If we want change, real meaningful change, our goals must be no shorter than a complete societal shift, with a caveat of 'preserve life by any means necessary' in the immediate. Opioids and overdoses are the symptom. The epidemic is far greater."

The crowd roared with approval and then quickly fell silent. The space maintained a solemn mood as individuals began to extinguish their candles and drift in separate directions. Jess allowed herself another moment to cry.

For Shilo, the night was pivotal. "It was one of the first things that we did as a national movement all by ourselves, and so it was incredibly powerful," he says. "This was a growing-up moment for the drug-user movement. Before, we were always housed as this sort of side project to harm reduction. Now, we've grown up, in the sense that we still want to work with harm reduction, but they are not the house that we live in. Drug-user organizing can stand on its own and have its own infrastructure. If the drug-user movement was in its infancy, it became a teenager at that moment."

Caty gives credit to Louise and Jess for welcoming sex workers into the drug-user movement in ways that produced tangible results. "They immediately changed their mission. They changed all the boilerplate language around how they describe themselves to include sex workers as people equally impacted by the drug war. That had never happened in a national drug-user union in any country before, to say, 'Drug users *and* sex workers,'" Caty says. "Drug-using sex workers have been an orphaned subgroup, not truly understood or served by either harm reduction or the sex-workers' rights movement, for too long. Now we're finally coming into our own."

Jess describes New Orleans as a moment of "trust," between her and Louise and the entire movement. "This was an oppressed, marginalized group of people who finally came together and made something happen," she says. "So many people, historically, they've let us down. And in that moment, we finally realized: we can't depend on them, so we are going to do this ourselves."

Monique Tula, who in 2016 the National Harm Reduction Coalition had just named its first Black executive director, thought the USU's successful event was a victory for women in the movement. But she was wary of its risks. "Louise and Jess stepped into a space that was primarily dominated by men, and that took some people back," Monique says. "It's risky. If they're going to be targeted and profiled, what is going to be the community response around this? Let's imagine they are in an advocacy space and are arrested for whatever. What is the harm reduction community's commitment to the two of them? And to the other drug-user members of their union?"

15

Drug-Induced Homicide

In 2018, the last year for which data are available, there were 6.4 million people under various carceral authorities' supervision in the United States, including prisons, jails, probation, and parole.[1] These numbers remain astronomically, reprehensibly high because of the persecution of people who use drugs. A full half of federal prisoners and one-third of state prisoners are incarcerated for crimes related to drugs.[2] Many, many more people are not in prison for drug crimes but have seen their lives significantly complicated by drug arrests. There were 1.6 million police apprehensions for drug-abuse violations in 2019 alone—more than any other category of arrest.[3]

There's a perception that the opioid epidemic is primarily a white problem, and that this has led policy makers and law enforcement toward a softer war on drugs, as compared to the so-called crack epidemic, whose harsh policies disproportionately targeted Blacks.[4] During the 1980s and early 1990s, police departments of cities like New York and Los Angeles patrolled Black neighborhoods with the force of an occupation, institutionalizing police harassment and regularly infringing on citizens' rights with impunity. In 1986, the Reagan administration passed the Anti–Drug Abuse Act, instituting mandatory minimum sentences for many drug crimes, including a five-year mandatory minimum sentence for trafficking five grams of crack (compared to five years for 500 grams of cocaine).[5] When the issue was crack, the nation's incarceration rate soared and an abhorrently disproportionate number of those thrown in prison were young Black men.[6] Meanwhile, compared to current drug policy makers' focus on fentanyl, heroin received relatively little attention when it was perceived as a Black problem. It was certainly never discussed as a health issue wherein people were deserving of treatment, as it is frequently today.[7] "It's been true throughout American history that when drugs penetrate into the middle class—the white middle class—politicians panic much more than they do when the drugs are concentrated in poor neighborhoods," Keith Humphreys, a senior policy advisor with the Obama administration's White House Office of National Drug Control Policy, told PBS's *Frontline* program in 2016. "It's not fair and it's not right, but that is the kind of country that we are living in."[8]

In its early years, the opioid epidemic *was* primarily a white problem, by certain measures. Fatal overdoses among low-income whites no doubt rose quickly through the 2000s, for example.[9] But Black people still consistently fared worse in terms of life expectancy and every sort of economic measure driving the overdose crisis.[10] And, by the overdose epidemic's second decade, the 2010s, the rate of Black people dying of drugs was rising much faster than that of whites. One study found that from 2011 to 2016, it increased a shocking average of 141 percent each year.[11] While America has taken its foot off the gas of the drug war in some ways—with some jurisdictions instructing police to refrain from arresting people caught with very small amounts of drugs, for example, and equipping officers with Narcan—in other ways, the drug war is now waged with greater intensity than ever before.

Incarceration numbers are only one piece of the picture: drug users are also caged beyond prison walls. In their book *Prison by Any Other Name: The Harmful Consequences of Popular Reforms*, journalists Maya Schenwar and Victoria Law detail how people caught with drugs can be coerced to attend and sometimes reside in addiction treatment facilities via an estimated 3,100 drug courts. Others are confined to their homes under house arrest or monitored with electronic ankle bracelets.[12]

At the same time, more old-fashioned aspects of the drug war—

conviction and confinement—remain alive and well today. The Drug Policy Alliance (DPA), the foremost nonprofit organization advocating for drug policy reform, maintains that in response to rising overdose deaths, "draconian policies have persisted" and, in many cases, actually expanded. Since 2011, 39 states plus Washington, DC, have passed legislation that increases penalties for drug crimes involving fentanyl. The new laws include mandatory minimum sentences, homicide charges, and provisions for mandatory commitment, among others. In response to fentanyl, "legislators have dusted off the drug war playbook," the DPA argues.[13]

In Washington, former president Donald Trump's White House instructed prosecutors to impose longer sentences for drug crimes and, in March 2018, threatened to use lethal force against high-level traffickers. "If we don't get tougher on drug dealers, we are wasting our time," Trump said, adding, "That toughness includes the death penalty."[14]

Louise's recovery from her second amputation was frustrating, painful, and long. Stuck in bed for weeks, she had a lot of time to read. During the preceding year, a number of USU members from around the country had emailed her news articles about something called a drug-induced homicide charge. Louise had flagged them to read later, and now, many months after receiving the first, she finally had time to go through them. Drug users were being charged with murder, she realized. With Don lying in bed next to her one night, Louise shared that she was feeling anxious. "What if I died of an overdose?" Louise asked him. "I don't want you to go to jail. I don't want anybody to go to jail."

A drug-induced homicide is a concept that American prosecutors and like-minded politicians invented in the 1980s. In June 1986, a University of Maryland student named Len Bias fulfilled a lifelong dream. He was drafted into the NBA, selected as the second overall pick by the Boston Celtics. He and his father were talking to Reebok about a sponsorship deal worth $1.6 million. There was a lot to celebrate. The night after he was drafted, Bias was out with friends at a party. They returned to Bias's campus dormitory between 2 a.m. and 3 a.m. the morning of July 19, where the party continued. Bias, childhood friend Brian Tribble, college basketball teammate Terry Long, and a couple of other guys shared a bag of cocaine. Shortly after 6 a.m., Bias experienced a seizure and stopped breathing. At 6:32 a.m., Tribble called 911, according to media reports.[15] His friends tried to revive him. Paramedics arrived and they tried to save Bias's life. The 22-year-old was taken to Leland Memorial Hospital and pronounced dead at 8:55 a.m. A few days later, more than 11,000 people attended a celebration of the young man's life. The Boston Celtics gifted his mother the number 30 jersey he would have worn for the upcoming NBA season.

Who was responsible for the death of this rising star who had just solidified such a bright future for himself? Somebody, the public outcry demanded. *Somebody* had to be held accountable. It turned out that was going to be Tribble, Bias's childhood friend and the person who had called 911 in an attempt to save Bias's life. Tribble was charged with possession of cocaine and possession with intent to distribute. Eventually, a jury acquitted him of all charges. But, roughly 30 years later, many others go to prison for alleged crimes just like the one for which Tribble was accused. Such cases are often spearheaded by parents whose children died of an overdose, and lawyers and politicians are only too happy to publicly side with a grieving mother.[16] The public is convinced that if someone decides to use drugs and dies after taking those drugs, someone else should be punished for it.

The Len Bias laws, as they collectively became known, set harsh sentences for anyone convicted of supplying drugs that result in an individual's death or serious injury. At the federal level, the 1986 Drug Abuse Act includes a mandatory minimum of 20 years for such a crime. In the decade that followed, more than 20 states passed similar legislation. Since fentanyl arrived in the mid-2010s, more states have joined them.

There is an understandable logic to the Len Bias laws. They say that if one person sells another person drugs, and the buyer dies of an overdose that is attributed to those drugs, the supplier should be held responsible for the death. Who could argue with that? Moreover, the laws weren't used very often. Until the 2010s, drug-induced-homicide laws—also called "death by distribution" and "drug delivery resulting in death," among other names that depend on the jurisdiction—were applied as lawmakers said they would be, almost exclusively against higher-level dealers and members of organized crime. But that changed when fentanyl began supplanting heroin. Pressured by parents to do something to stop the shocking increase in deaths—to do *anything*—authorities began deploying these charges and their stiffer penalties against street-level dealers, and then, in the second half of the 2010s, against drug users who were not "dealers" at all.

Louise and Jess began to receive calls and emails. "Any progress on Will? They're trying to get him on a murder charge for his friend's overdose death," one message reads. "What can I do? Do you have access to attorneys? Do you have a legal-aid fund?"

Will was not a drug dealer. He had simply purchased a small amount of heroin for himself and a friend. Fentanyl had contaminated the region's supply, they knew, and so they were using together in case one of them overdosed. Hard Drugs 101: never use alone. Then Will's friend did overdose, and, despite Will's best efforts, he wasn't able to save him. Now Will was charged with murder.

One of the first cases to draw attention to authorities' renewed interest in drug-induced-homicide laws was that of Louisiana's

Jarret McCasland.* In 2013, he was dating Flavia Cardenas. The two used heroin together and Flavia died of an overdose.[17] Then, in 2014 in Pennsylvania, Sean Harrington mailed heroin and cocaine to a friend, Elisif Bruun, who subsequently passed away at the treatment facility where she was staying in North Carolina.[18] There's a similar story about Michael Malcolm's family in Colorado. His eldest son died of an overdose in 2015 after ingesting drugs that his younger son had purchased for the pair of them.[19] And then there's Richard Gregoire of Illinois and his wife, Catherine Smith. The pair arranged a drug deal, went together to complete it, and Richard used the drugs first and overdosed. Catherine called 911 and tried to revive her husband but he never woke up.[20]

In each case—that of a girlfriend, friend, brother, and husband—authorities used some version of the Len Bias laws to hold the deceased's loved one responsible for their death.

Across America, 182 people using drugs faced similar indictments in 2013, according to an analysis of news coverage by Northeastern University's Health in Justice Action Lab, a research group focused on criminal-justice reform. Drug-induced-homicide charges increased each following year, with 495 in 2016.[21]

Northeastern University law professor Leo Beletsky, who runs the Health in Justice Action Lab, analyzed drug-induced-homicide prosecutions between 2000 and 2016 and found that in 50 percent of cases, it was not a "traditional" dealer who was charged; instead, it was a friend, family member, or romantic partner of the deceased.[22] "The people who are charged with these heinous crimes are not what the public's imagination defines as a dealer," Beletsky says. "Even without money changing hands, a person can be deemed a drug dealer. So the law is very ambiguous. The larg-

---

* There are earlier instances of a drug-induced-homicide law used to prosecute someone who supplied unknowingly lethal drugs to a friend or family member. Some of those cases date back as far as 2006. However, they were rare and it wasn't until 2013 that a trend began to emerge.

est group of people being subject to these prosecutions are not in fact drug dealers in the traditional sense; they are friends, family, romantic partners, and other people who had a preexisting relationship with the person who overdosed. So the idea that these prosecutions are being used to go after major drug dealers is just simply not reflected in the data."

Beletsky describes authorities' adoption of drug-induced-homicide laws as evidence that America's primary response to fentanyl is firmly rooted in prohibitionist ideology. "The war on drugs is not over. In spite of the rhetoric around authorities taking a public-health approach, that does not reflect reality. People are saying, 'We can't arrest our way out of this problem,' but in fact that is exactly what they are trying to do."

Drug-induced-homicide laws penalize people for selling fentanyl even when they do not know that that is what they are selling. There are plenty of documented cases in which the accused insisted in court that it was heroin they had shared with the deceased.[23] Lindsay LaSalle, a DPA senior staff attorney, says that, equally troubling, prosecutors use drug-induced-homicide laws to widen the net that authorities use to capture people involved with drugs.

"Anytime someone is picked up for a charge related to drugs—which could be possession, could be resisting arrest, could be property theft—prosecutors, as a matter of standard course, will threaten the highest charge they can possibly bring, even if there is actually no possibility of them meeting the requirements to get a guilty verdict in court," LaSalle explains. "Then very few of these cases actually end up in a courtroom because these cases carry a very high potential maximum penalty—much higher than your standard distribution charges and certainly much higher than possession with intent to sell. So people are going to plea down because they're potentially facing 25 years." This phenomenon is not captured in statistics related to drug-induced-homicide charges, LaSalle notes, because the drug-induced-homicide charge is used only as a threat that then translates into statistics for convictions that are less serious (but which still carry harsh penalties including prison time). "It's another tactic to really intimidate people and to get them to plea down," she says.

While more people go to prison and face longer sentences, there is no evidence to suggest that drug-induced-homicide laws prevent either the sale of drugs or overdose deaths. "In any of these places where we see really aggressive prosecutions of drug-induced homicide, we have not seen any reduction in the demand for drugs, the supply of drugs, or in overdose deaths," LaSalle says. Worse, these laws produce the opposite of what officials claim is their intended outcome. While in theory these laws were written to save lives, in practice, drug-induced-homicide laws result in greater numbers of deaths.

Generally speaking, a Good Samaritan law says that someone who calls 911 to save another person's life will not be prosecuted for small-time drug crimes. If someone is overdosing and you call 911, you will not be charged with possession of drugs, possession of drug paraphernalia, or, usually, violating parole. Both North Carolina and Massachusetts have Good Samaritan laws on the books, as do 44 other states.*[24] These laws' effectiveness, however, suffers from a lack of awareness. Both Louise and Jess have responded to overdoses where the victim's friend called them instead of dialing 911 because they feared the police. In addition, there are many consequences from which a Good Samaritan law cannot protect someone who's holding drugs. If they call 911 for an overdose and this makes authorities aware of their drug use, perhaps they won't be

---

* The five remaining states—Kansas, Maine, Oklahoma, Texas, and Wyoming—have laws stating that if a person caught with drugs seeks medical assistance for someone experiencing an overdose, that can be considered a mitigating factor during sentencing. Such laws are a positive step but fail to meet most drug policy advocates' definition of a Good Samaritan law.

arrested, but they could be kicked out of school, evicted from their apartment complex, or simply outed to their friends and family as someone who uses drugs. Still, the laws are a harm reduction success story. The existence of a Good Samaritan law in a state has been found to result in a 15 percent reduction in opioid overdose deaths; specific to African Americans, this number rises to 26 percent.[25] ("We found no evidence that these measures were associated with increased nonmedical opioid use," researchers note.)

It is these Good Samaritan laws, so effective in reducing overdose deaths, that LaSalle argues are hampered by drug-induced-homicide laws. "People are not going to call 911," she says. "The increased prosecution of drug-induced homicide completely undermines those laws. I mean, it almost makes them null and void. I don't think anyone cares that they're going to get immunity for possession if they're going to be charged with murder." Drug users agree. "This is in an overdose crisis wherein one of the major exacerbating factors for overdose risk is using alone," USU sex-worker liaison Caty Simon says. "Death-by-distribution laws undermine the Good Samaritan Act by fucking up people's ability to use with others."

The DPA has created regional profiles that detail where law enforcement officials have adopted death-by-distribution laws with the most enthusiasm. From 2011 to 2017, 50 percent of all such charges across the country were brought in just four states: Wisconsin, Ohio, Illinois, and Minnesota. Meanwhile, a trio of northeastern states—New York, New Jersey, and Pennsylvania—account for the fastest-rising numbers. The southern states of Tennessee, Louisiana, and Louise's home state of North Carolina similarly experienced sharp increases.[26]

If someone dies after taking drugs, Beletsky says it is very easy for prosecutors to turn possession into a drug-induced-homicide charge. "Pretty much all they have to show are text messages or electronic communication between the person who died and the person who is being prosecuted, and literally all they have to show is that drugs changed hands," he says. "That's why you see so many friends, families, partners, and other users charged. Because 'distribution' is being interpreted in the sense that it need not be a financial transaction. All they have to show are text messages." Anyone who shares drugs is vulnerable.

Jess and Louise followed Beletsky's work closely and this point about electronic communication really stuck in their minds. On the phone late one night, Jess told Louise a story. "Somebody overdosed. The girl who was involved called me, and she said, 'I erased all my texts.' People think that if you erase your texts, they're gone. But they're not. There is always a record."

Jess shared a couple of additional examples. Another member of the New England Users Union texted her, "Hey, I just bought heroin. Maybe. Do you know where I can get tester strips?" That text could get someone busted, Jess says. In virtually every media report that Louise and Jess found detailing a drug-induced-homicide case, it was always a series of text messages that led prosecutors to a successful conviction.

As they talked, the hour passed three in the morning—Louise's best time for brainstorming. "If you're texting, you're telling on yourself," she said to Jess. The pair of them turned that into the Urban Survivors Union's next social media campaign: "Your text is your tell."

They were beginning to poke at philosophical questions. Who is a dealer? What does that word mean? And what exactly is it for which a dealer should be held responsible? No matter how strongly she disagrees, Louise says she understands the logic and support behind a death-by-distribution charge. Drawing on the worst personal experience imaginable—the loss of her first daughter—Louise wrote a personal essay for the online publication *Filter* that gently argued that parents who support such laws should reconsider the direction of their anger.[27]

"Even though I have spent my life fighting against bad drug laws, and know in my heart what the problem truly is, I found myself right there," Louise wrote in December 2018. "I found myself blaming the wrong people. It was as if the grief and pain were too much to bear, but anger? Well, that felt better. It felt more powerful.

"Too many people know the pain I am talking about all too well, and have also experienced that same anger," she continued. "And politicians and prosecutors—rather than accepting responsibility for the consequences of their own failed policies—are increasingly exploiting this pain and anguish to make scapegoats of supposed 'drug dealers' through drug-induced-homicide laws.

"These powerful individuals are leveraging the debilitating powerlessness of people like myself, a parent who has lost a child to overdose, to justify charging individuals with murder or manslaughter. They mislead society into believing this response is necessary and appropriate, so our loved ones do not die in vain. *They* are the ones who truly deserve the anger of people like me.

"The outcome in drug-induced-homicide cases is two lives lost instead of one—and a false appearance of retribution, justice, and revenge."

16

Reframe the Blame

Louise wasn't provided painkillers immediately following her second amputation nor once she was discharged from the hospital. She returned to self-medicating with heroin. Don was using occasionally, too, and this got her thinking about the emails that USU members had sent her about authorities charging users with drug-induced homicide. Louise remained worried that if the worst occurred and she died of a drug overdose, that it might be Don who takes the blame. "If I died, I would hate it if you got arrested," she told him. "We have to fucking do something."

A couple of nights later, they got Jess on the phone. "What can we do?" Louise asked her. "I've sorta got this idea but I don't know what to do with it." Louise wanted to craft a USU response to prosecutors' increasing use of the drug-induced-homicide charge. She thought they could explain to the public that the people falling victim to these charges were not drug dealers, but rather were people who struggled with addictions of their own. If the public understood that the people who died of a drug overdose would not want their friend or family member charged with their death, this could erode popular support for the charge and thus discourage authorities from using it. Jess liked the idea so much that she took the next train down to Greensboro.

The trip did not get off to a good start. When Louise and Jess are together, they're able to maintain a productive relationship with drugs. "Yes, we're using, but we're very functional," Jess says. It was her first night staying with Louise and Don and the three of them were preparing a little heroin and a little cocaine to go with it. Jess was a little nervous. She was in a new city with a supply to which her body wasn't accustomed. In addition, the dope was a strange color she didn't like. Jess was about to do her first shot when Louise stopped her. "Let me try it out first, because the guy said it was strong," she said. Almost immediately, Louise was sick. Her body shook. She crawled on the floor toward the bathroom. "Call 911," Louise half mumbled, half shouted.

Don was scared. Louise would normally never, *ever* ask for authorities to get involved. In anything. Not ever. And now Louise had asked them to place a call that would likely result in the police showing up. "Weezie?" Don prodded her. Louise remained conscious but didn't seem to hear him. They moved her into the bathtub and soaked her in warm water, and, thankfully, Louise soon began to calm down. Jess rubbed her back and reassured her. "Finally, she just kind of fell asleep," Jess says. "And I continued to rub her back, taking her pulse and monitoring her."

Jess hated the situation so much. During this period, Louise was addicted and physically dependent on opioids, and prohibition forced her to inject her body with a substance that she could only hope was what she thought it was. "It was terrifying to watch her go through that and feeling helpless," Jess says. "All I could do was get her in the bathtub. She wasn't overdosing, but she thought she was dying."

"I did some fucked up dope that poisoned me," Louise says. She didn't blame the dealer. After they had gotten her into the bathtub, Don called the guy back to the house. He returned promptly, apologized profusely, and gave them back their money. And he pulled the rest of that batch off the street. "No way, I don't want to be responsible for a death," the dealer told them.

Louise and Jess blamed the war on drugs. "This is all a piece of the fentanyl-risk environment," Louise says. "And it is really, truly scary stuff. You can't tell what you got. People are cutting it with all kinds of stuff. And so it really is a terrifying environment to be a drug user in."

Thanks to prohibition, people who use hard drugs do not always know what they are putting into their bodies. A drug supply kept illegal means supply cannot be regulated, which means that when it comes to illicit drug consistency, there is only uncertainty.

The presence of fentanyl can serve as an indicator of a supply's unpredictability. Drugs on the street are seldom sold as fentanyl, and yet in Baltimore, for example, during the summer of 2019, police detected fentanyl in 75 percent of heroin seized.[1] Meanwhile, according to a study of take-home fentanyl test strips in Rhode Island in 2017, 50 percent of participants using hard drugs found fentanyl in the substance they'd purchased.[2] "The lack of regulation characteristic of illegal markets has formed the basis of movements for drug checking access and drug policy reform," the Baltimore researchers reported. "In other international settings, drug checking programs have aimed to reduce exposure to harmful adulterants as a method of harm reduction."[3]

So nothing was accomplished during Jess's first night in Greensboro. It was late into the following day before Louise was feeling better. By Jess's second night visiting, they got to work. And in the end, the first night wasn't a total waste. Louise's experience with that bad batch of drugs went into the project they were creating. If Don had given Louise drugs that led to an overdose, Louise didn't want Don to go to jail. And if Louise had died the night before, she didn't want that dealer to go to jail, either. The guy didn't know what he was selling. As soon as he did and realized it was something bad, he'd pulled it off the streets. How could they protect their friends like Don and protect guys like that dealer, too? How could Louise and Jess protect themselves?

With frequent phone calls to Becki Brooks and Caty Simon, Jess and Louise began their work with a series of questions. What was the problem? Who specifically did the problem affect? What solution could be most useful to USU chapters around the country? How would USU chapters deploy that solution?

On Jess's second night with Louise and Don in Greensboro, they had Becki on the phone and the four of them stayed up all night brainstorming. To slow the advancement of the drug-induced-homicide charge, they had to "reframe the blame," someone said. And that became the hashtag: #ReframeTheBlame. The initiative would counter what Louise and Jess maintain is the most significant intensification of the war on drugs that America has experienced in a generation.

The campaign—called "Reframe the Blame" for short but officially titled the "Last Will and Testament Project"—consists of two pieces. The first is largely about education, getting the word out that authorities are hitting small-time dealers and even casual users with a new kind of homicide charge. The second piece is a response to that development: an attempt to save people from potential prosecution.

"Drug use is a fact of many of our lives, as are related issues such as overdoses, health issues, and the myriad negative effects which result not from drug use itself, but rather from the prohibition of drugs," begins the Reframe the Blame tool kit that Jess and Louise drafted that week. "While we struggle with these issues, our problems are made significantly worse by the system that often claims it wants to help us. As we sell drugs to and procure drugs for other people, often to support our own habits or to help a friend or loved one out, we risk being targeted at the same time as we endure the trauma of losing a friend or loved one to overdose.

"It's time to reframe the blame; to shift it onto the shoulders of those at the other end of the ridiculous sentences, the beatings, the harassment, and the culture of fear and stigma that marginalizes our brothers and sisters. We are worthy of love and respect, and we will not stand by as people are thrown into prisons in our names."

The tool kit's concise 16 pages includes advice for local USU chapters on messaging, media engagement, leveraging social media, and event planning. It concludes with a quote attributed to Caty:

"If I die of an overdose, I demand that no one be prosecuted for my death. If you grieve for me and you seek vengeance, channel that rage to work to end the War on Drugs. It is criminalization that is killing us, not fellow drug users and low-end dealers struggling just like us to survive. It is the drug warriors who condemn us to death. I will not be a symbol for them. If I die, I refuse to be wielded as a weapon against other marginalized drug users in my community."

The tool kit is a compelling package, but the campaign's centerpiece is actually another document. In August 2018, the Urban Survivors Union advanced its Reframe the Blame campaign with the release of a symbolic contract that solidified Caty's wish that in the event of an overdose, no third party would be held responsible for her death. Called a "Do Not Prosecute Directive," or DNPD for short, it stands as a living will that asks for no one to be held responsible for a fatal overdose death beyond the individual who died.

"The DNPD is an advance directive to be used for instructing family members and for instructing law enforcement, district attorneys, judges, and other criminal justice system personnel to forgo prosecution attempts to all persons in the event of our unintentional overdose due to the ingestion of intoxicating substances," reads the document's preamble. "Charges to be withheld include those imposed under drug-induced homicide, felony murder, depraved heart, involuntary or voluntary manslaughter laws and any other malicious prosecution."

The Do Not Prosecute order acknowledges its own legal limitations but emphasizes that it describes the wishes of the deceased. "Courts are encouraged to honor this form in any situation where one has lost their life due to drug overdose," it reads. "While we understand this order is purely symbolic, it is a gesture to express our true intent and should be honored as such."

The order itself consists of a single page.* "If I die as a result of a drug overdose, I request that no one be charged, prosecuted, or

---

* See Appendix: Do Not Prosecute Directive.

held criminally responsible for my death," it reads. "This decision is being made to challenge the oppressive and often perpetuated false dichotomy between people who use drugs and people who sell drugs. We are, more often than not, one and the same."

It concludes: "I hereby agree to the Do Not Prosecute Directive." Below is a line for a signature and the signature of a witness plus the date.

Since the document's 2018 release, drug users have returned hundreds of signed copies to the USU's headquarters in Greensboro. They remain on file there, ready should they be needed in the event of a member's death.

Louise and Jess were expanding the Urban Survivors Union in multiple directions at once. They were integrating various communities that not only lacked a voice amongst the general public but were often overlooked even within the harm reduction and drug-user movements. Caty, for example, was a prominent writer and long-time activist in America's sex-worker community. Now she provided the USU with invaluable input on the Reframe the Blame tool kit. Jess and Louise pulled her further in.

Caty was born and raised in Massachusetts and had lived in Northampton for the last decade, so she and Jess had crossed paths several times before. "The first time I ever escorted, I was 19 years old and Patti Smith's 'Free Money' was ringing through my head," Caty says, continuing with a laugh: "The first time Jess saw me, I was dancing in front of the hotel where I was renting a room, in my nightgown or something." It was Louise, however, who chased after Caty and convinced her to fill in a leadership role within the USU. "She wanted a sex-worker liaison," Caty explains. "She saw the incredible failure that was the harm reduction movement not being a good ally to sex workers, and instead of doing an apology tour, Louise proactively wanted to start a sex-worker call that met as often as the drug-user call. And she sought me out to lead it."

On Reframe the Blame and sex workers, Louise and Jess were

smart enough to follow Caty's advice. They understood the intersection of drug use and sex work well, and knew that drug-induced-homicide laws placed sex workers at exceptional risk. But Reframe the Blame's Do Not Prosecute order was a complicated proposition. Working together on a Reframe the Blame PowerPoint presentation, Louise suggested including a slide instructing sex workers to ask their clients if they would sign a DNP order. Caty objected. "You know what, Louise? We're going to have to put a lot of modifiers in there because that is going to be basically impossible for most sex workers," she said. "It is not a strategy that makes sense when it comes to sex workers at all."

Caty presented the USU with an analysis of the case of Alix Tichelman, a woman based in Southern California who became Caty's pen pal after she was imprisoned for involuntary manslaughter. In November 2014, Tichelman was aboard the yacht of Google executive Forrest Hayes when he overdosed and died. Tichelman had procured heroin for the two of them and injected Hayes with the drug but, Caty emphasizes, he was obviously a willing participant to the couple's use. Tichelman also tried to revive Hayes, shaking him while crying in an attempt to wake him. It was an "accidental overdose between two consenting adults," Tichelman's lawyer said on the day his client was sentenced to six years in prison.[4]

Caty questioned how realistic it is to have expected Tichelman to discuss with Hayes what would happen to her in the event of his death. "Sex workers are often seen by this kind of man as their tour guides into leisure," Caty told the USU. "That includes drugs as well as sex. They have to cop for their clients in order to secure the date. So we are expected to guide them—middle-class men with no self-control and very little harm reduction knowledge—on these benders. But as our putative employers of the hour, we don't have an opportunity to tell them 'no.' Men don't like being told 'no' or to slow down when they're taking a load off. So I doubt Alix Tichelman had much of an opportunity to ask Forrest Hayes to sign anything or even to tell him that maybe his dose was too much."

For sex workers' clients, Caty and the USU ultimately decided that the Do Not Prosecute Directive was a poor fit. A client would likely interpret it as little more than evidence, Caty told them. "Clients see sex workers as part of their hidden double life, and most would never sign anything that would bring that double life to light," she explains. Still, Caty says the larger Reframe the Blame campaign has proven useful to sex workers, fostering cooperation between sex workers and drug users against laws that isolate and endanger both groups. "With Reframe the Blame, what I did was connect it thematically to similar themes in sex-worker activism and triangulate how it would affect sex workers specifically," Caty says. "As these death-by-distribution laws increase, and as the ones already on the books are used more often, we are seeing a lot of sex workers caught in this net."

The Reframe the Blame campaign also emphasizes the need to oppose racial components of the war on drugs and the ways in which drug-induced-homicide laws are already proving to amplify the racial disparities of prohibition.

Every aspect of the drug war impacts people of color worse than it does white people, and drug-induced-homicide laws are no exception. Northeastern professor Leo Beletsky explains how: "When these charges are brought, they are brought in situations involving a person of color who is the quote-unquote 'dealer' and the victim is white." The DPA's Lindsay LaSalle says the same: "The racist war on drugs is playing out under drug-induced homicide the same way it's played out under all of our drug laws." They both note that this conclusion is largely drawn from anecdotal reports, but both also state it as a certainty.

There is some data on the subject. A DPA analysis of federal sentencing for fentanyl trafficking, for example, shows that 75 percent of cases reviewed involved people of color.[5] LaSalle points to a study out of Minnesota that found that 80 percent of cases involving a drug-induced-homicide charge concerned a person of color, while people of color accounted for only 13 percent of the population there. Beletsky used media reports to quantify the disparity. "In our dataset, of the 47% of the cases that do involve drug distribution by a 'traditional' dealer, half of the individuals were either Black or Hispanic, and selling to a white drug user."[6] Beletsky also has rough calculations showing that a person of color charged with drug-induced homicide receives an average nine-year sentence compared to 5.5 years for whites.

"In other words, the drug war and its racial disparities are alive and well and the drug-induced-homicide paradigm is a clear illustration of that," Beletsky says. LaSalle agrees: "I think we can just extrapolate from history to know that obviously these laws are going to be enforced in racially disparate ways." In response to fentanyl, authorities have deployed new categories of crimes and punishment, and Black people remain the drug war's primary targets, feeling its burdens in disproportionate numbers, just as they always have.

Jess and Louise ensured their campaign took these realities into account. In addition to Caty, they consulted with a diverse range of drug users and integrated the views of other women and, notably, Dinah Ortiz and Robert Suarez, two newer USU members who had quickly proven themselves invaluable to the organization for the experiences they shared as Black people living through the drug war. "We stayed up for days writing that manual and that tool kit," Louise says.

At its core, Louise says Reframe the Blame was a response to fear and a manifestation of drug users' determination to fight back against that fear. "The police have always targeted me," she explains. "If anybody ever dies around me, I'm fucked. They are going to charge me with murder. And that is terrifying. And that's where the Reframe the Blame stuff came from: true fear."

Dan Bigg's death followed by the successful USU gathering in New Orleans and then the launch of Reframe the Blame made for an emotional roller coaster that only intensified toward the end of 2018. In Northampton, Jess and Albie continued with Harm Reduction Works, creating a space where harm reduction advocates could meet and collectively deal with their grief for the overdose crisis. Meanwhile, Louise and Don traveled to Europe, taking a very rare vacation that they had attached to a speaking engagement in Vienna.

They almost didn't make it. Don had found an idyllic little cottage on Airbnb, situated on a hill in Florence, Italy. But shortly after they made their reservation, Airbnb canceled their booking and then terminated Don's entire account. Just as Louise was beginning to feel like the USU was gaining a voice for drug users at the national level, she and Don received a harsh reminder of the fear and outright disgust with which mainstream society views people who use drugs.

Louise was livid and posted a rant on Facebook. "Just some more bullshit. Airbnb canceled and permanently deactivated my man's account due to drug charges on his record," she wrote. "We received no notice, just disabled accounts and a link to our criminal record online. Nice huh? I am so tired of the U.S. drug war. I am so tired of the discrimination that takes place surrounding drug use."

It is well-known that a criminal record can severely hinder job prospects and complicate options for housing. But there are countless other ways that a record can interfere with a person's life for years and even decades after they've completed a term in prison. For instance, parents with a criminal record (or even just a record of arrest) are more likely to opt out of school functions and avoid other volunteer positions, translating into a loss of social opportunities for their children.[7] Forfeitures also often include financial assistance, voting rights, firearms ownership, and eligibility for many occupational licenses.[8] Possibilities for college enrollment may also be adversely affected, as will access to student loans.[9] The list goes on. Don would discover that the three years he served in prison for cocaine would weigh him down for the rest of his life.

After a few hectic days rescheduling accommodations, he and Louise made it to Italy just in time for Christmas. On New Year's Eve, Don proposed.

"Loving my man," Louise wrote on Facebook the morning of January 2. "My best friend. Of course I said yes!"

Two hours later, she followed that up with another message. "Coming home ASAP," it begins. "Don's brother has died in a car accident."

Derek Jackson was 47 years old. A big guy, gentle in everything he did, he hung around the North Carolina Survivors Union's office on Grove Street and used the computer there. In recent months, he was helping out with external communications and producing videos that shared the organization's harm reduction work. "It really hit me, that we are in the middle of a fucking war," Louise says. "We call it an opioid epidemic, all these things. But it's the drug war. I'm watching everybody I love fucking die."

It took a few days for Don and Louise to figure out how to get home. They didn't have enough money to pay the exorbitant fees that airlines charge for last-minute flights. Louise launched a fundraising effort on social media, and harm reduction advocates from across the country chipped in to get the pair of them back to North Carolina.

"We will be there on the 9th," Louise wrote in another Facebook post. She continued with a short essay dedicated to Becki Brooks, the older drug-user organizer who helped Louise and Jess get the USU's national call going, organized the second vigil in New Orleans, and brainstormed with them on Reframe the Blame. An elder of America's harm reduction community known online by the nickname "Old Hippie Chic," Becki was house-sitting for Louise and Don while they were in Italy, taking care of their dog, Thai, and also helping run the NCSU needle exchange.

"Thank you so much Beck Brooks for taking care of my home, my dog, and our union," Louise wrote on Facebook while she and

Don waited for their flight back to Greensboro. "Your love and thoughtfulness is unmatched. In my busy busy rush rush I sometimes forget to formally thank the rocks in my life. Beck Brooks, you have talked with me night after night, cried with me, yelled with me, laughed with me. But mostly you have guided my hand, shared with me your amazing wisdom and allowed me to be your friend.

"I know in our world it is difficult to get close to people," the Facebook post continues. "So often it is dangerous to trust and painfully frightening to love. I must admit that I am not always easy to love, even more difficult to advise, and often downright impossible to disagree with but thank you. I love you more and respect you more each day. The National Movement would not be where it is without you and I need to say this to you and the world. We need harm reduction elders and mentors especially right now as we face all of these difficult hurdles. We need pragmatic individuals willing to really do the work. I am so excited about 2019 and scared at the same time. I know we have so much work to do."

It meant a lot to Becki. "Ah! speechless & appreciative," she wrote in response. "Thank you."

The last-minute flight home was a long one for Louise and Don. It was almost two full days of travel before they landed at Greensboro airport and then made it back to their home on the other side of town. Finally, exhausted and relieved, they walked through Louise's front door the morning of January 10. Becki greeted them with big hugs and they stayed up all night talking. Despite the tragic circumstances of their unexpected return, it was a joyful reunion. Then, in the early morning, Becki collapsed.

Don called an ambulance while Louise tried to revive her. She performed mouth-to-mouth and shot a dose of Narcan into her. But Becki didn't respond. The ambulance arrived and took her to the hospital. Louise and Don followed close behind.

Jess meant to meet them there the following day but fell into an incapacitating bout of depression. "I was supposed to fly down there," she says. Jess had known Becki for 20 years. She was one of her initial inspirations for a life in harm reduction. For days, Jess was paralyzed by the prospect of losing her. "I withdrew. I have a lot of regrets. I should have been there for Louise."

Becki passed away on January 14, 2019. The official cause of death was a heart attack. It remains unclear what role, if any, drugs played.

"Beck's cause of death has not been determined and toxicological analyses are still pending," Louise wrote on Facebook the following day. "This determination notwithstanding, people close to Beck know that she's been struggling with deep sadness and an enduring sense of unease due to the traumatic weight of consistently bearing witness to untold stories of death and despair caused by the current drug overdose epidemic. Her legacy will continue to motivate those of us on the front lines to remain doing lifesaving work in the communities that Beck spent her life serving."

There was a funeral for Derek Jackson at Aycock Fellowship Ministries on January 19. Becki's funeral was delayed because her family didn't have enough money to pay for her body's transport back to their home city of Tulsa, Oklahoma. "I just found out that our beloved Beck is still in NC," Jess wrote on Facebook. "She was a cornerstone to our movement. Please, if you have anything, even a dollar, please consider helping her get back home so she can be put to rest." Once again, the harm reduction community came through with donations. Jess and Louise raised more than $3,000 and Becki was cremated in Tulsa later that month.

"I feel so frustrated by our inability to get a break from the pain life seems to dish out," Louise wrote in an email that week. "It's been awful. Truly, awful."

17

A Labor of Radical Love

Fentanyl crept into America slowly at first. In 2000, there were 782 fentanyl-attributed deaths across the nation. In 2005, the number was 1,742, and then 3,007 in 2010. But by 2015, there were 9,580 fatal fentanyl overdoses, an increase of more than tenfold in 15 years. The rate would only grow. In 2019, the last year for which government data are available, there were 36,359 fentanyl overdose deaths.[1] Meanwhile, deaths attributed to prescription opioids and heroin both declined. Fentanyl supplanted the market. What's more, it did so to an even larger extent than the statistics reveal. CDC updates on overdose deaths warn that fentanyl analogs, such as acetyl fentanyl, furanyl fentanyl, and carfentanil—drugs similar in chemical structure to fentanyl but varying in potency—are often not included in coroners' analyses because specialized toxicology equipment is required to detect them.[2] Authorities' enthusiasm for drug-induced-homicide laws intensified as deaths attributed to fentanyl increased across the United States. From 2016 to 2017, the number of cases prosecuted as drug-induced homicides rose from 495 to 717.[3]

Jess and Louise were searching for a pragmatic approach to fentanyl's steady replacement of heroin, and one they hoped would bring tangible outcomes. This led them to G, a Greensboro drug dealer, and others like him.

"These guys are midlevel dealers. They're not users who are selling to support their habit, and still, everybody I talk to has no idea what they're selling," Jess says. "One guy, he trusts me, and we're showing him dilution and how to cut and what to cut with. And how to test for fentanyl." Often, it wasn't difficult to get a dealer involved, Jess says. She would tell them, "Hey, here's an idea: all that product you have, it's really strong. So instead of making 10 bundles out of it, let's make 20 bundles out of it."

"And you show them how. You get them thinking in terms of money and also in terms of not killing their customers. And then they're like, 'Ah, okay. This makes sense.'" You can't just tell a dealer to throw away anything that tests positive for fentanyl, she adds. That's just not going to happen.

Louise had experimented with working with dealers back when she was selling drugs herself, supporting her own habit while simultaneously pushing harm reduction with Wiggs. Now, she and Jess compared notes and improved strategies. They didn't view dealers as a bunch of evil predators, as mainstream media usually depicts them. The guys they knew didn't lurk in back alleys or hang out on street corners. Rather, Louise and Jess understood that people worked on the black market and sold substances of uncertain mixtures as a result of prohibition, because there were no regulations for their business. The majority of dealers disliked people overdosing on fentanyl just as much as the people doing the overdosing.

While Jess worked one-on-one with dealers in Northampton and surrounding towns, Louise got dealers involved in harm reduction work at the North Carolina Survivors Union's office on Grove Street. She first caught their interest with fentanyl test strips and then was able to convince some of them to distribute clean syringes and Narcan alongside the drugs they were selling. It turned out that a drug dealer making a house call to deliver a half-gram of heroin didn't mind packaging those drugs with a bag containing clean syringes and a Narcan kit. "Why would they?" Louise asks.

Surveys of drug users have found that dealers will often "go out of their way" to let customers know when a batch of fentanyl is moving through an area and make attempts to avoid selling drugs suspected of including fentanyl.[4] Researchers recommend that harm reduction organizations "engage" with dealers to distribute drug-testing equipment and help them better communicate with customers the contents of their drugs.[5]

One of Jess's guys even floated the idea of forming a drug dealers union, modeling the organization on Jess's New England Users Union, and using it to operate as a sort of co-op. If dealers banded together, combining their purchasing power, he reasoned, they could not only negotiate price but also purity, thus decreasing the risk of fentanyl (or at least knowing when a batch carried the risk of fentanyl). After another year of this work, G, one of Louise's longtime dealers who regularly dropped by the Grove Street exchange, even tagged along with Louise to a national harm reduction conference.

Jess believes they are making a difference. "The overdose rates in Hampshire County have actually dropped a little bit. I know it's not just me talking to dealers, but I'd like to think it is partly me, our participants, all the drug users who are passing out fentanyl test strips and talking about dilution and how to cut your product."

Through 2018 and 2019, a growing rift developed between America's harm reduction community and drug users' increasing demands for autonomy as a movement of their own. This wasn't outright hostility; rather, it was a fight within the family. Harm reduction organizations still sometimes stigmatized the users to whom they provided services, refusing to employ them, for example, as Jess knew only too well. They also penalized staff who were caught using drugs. Of course, there were prominent members of the harm reduction community who championed drug users and fought for their employment and integration into senior ranks of harm reduction programs and services: the late Dan Bigg, for example; Mark Kinzly, the Yale University researcher who defended Jess in Austin after she outed herself as someone who uses drugs; the National

Harm Reduction Coalition's new executive director Monique Tula; its former executive director Allan Clear; and its deputy director of policy and planning Dan Raymond, among others. But, USU members felt, there remained a long way to go.

Louise and Jess began reflecting on their own internalized stigma and arguing publicly that drug users like them could not only staff but actually run large organizations working to reduce overdose deaths. Their October 2018 march in New Orleans was a sign of a transition underway. In November 2019, the USU took a second step.

A Drug Policy Alliance conference was happening in St. Louis, Missouri, that month, and the USU seized the opportunity to convene an independent gathering of its own. The goal was to bring USU members face-to-face and work on structure and protocols that would build the organization to serve as a national voice for drug users. They called it a constitutional convening, and said this would begin the formalization of the USU as a special-interest group that operated at the federal level of American discourse.

Ahead of the conference, in September 2019, Jess and Louise met in Chicago and committed a few sleepless nights to early planning. They both arrived very late but met up anyway—they weren't going to lose any more time. It was 3 a.m. when they pulled their laptops out, so they had a solid four hours to get something done before meetings they both had scheduled for over breakfast. Louise stationed herself at the hotel room desk while Jess paced back and forth behind her. Louise's mind raced, firing off ideas in rapid succession that jolted the conversation in numerous directions at once. Jess picked up on the best of them, focused the conversation there, and strategized what was needed to bring them to fruition. The pair left Chicago with the beginnings of a plan in place for St. Louis, energized but anxious.

The St. Louis event was going to be significantly more complex than the USU's march in New Orleans. They intended to create a full day's program packed with detailed presentations and break-out groups that would lay initial groundwork for formalizing the USU's structure and decision-making processes. During Louise and Jess's initial meeting about all of this in Chicago, the task looked impossibly large, compounded by feelings of inadequacy. "I've been so hurt by people—people in our movement—and judged and stigmatized and persecuted in public health because I've admitted I used drugs," Jess says. "At the end of the day, I look in the mirror and I see a junkie . . . so I'm a hypocrite when I tell people, 'You have the right to use and drug use does not define you.' Drug policy and the drug war has fucked me up so badly."

Jon Zibbell, an old friend of Jess's who had retired from drug policy activism to work as a public health scientist, overheard these conversations in Chicago and wouldn't have it. "What you guys are doing has never been done before," he told them. "You are the two most powerful drug users in the United States. Other people see it. You guys need to see it." The number of people counting on them was growing.

Since the march in New Orleans, the USU's leadership team— Louise and Don, Jess, Shilo Jama, Caty Simon, harm reduction veterans like Mark Kinzly, and enthusiastic newcomers like Robert Suarez and Dinah Ortiz—had made a concerted effort to establish USU chapters in new cities. By now, the USU had grown from just one chapter in Seattle in 2009 to more than 20 chapters across America in 2019. Admittedly, a few of these chapters were little more than two or three friends coming together wherever they could find Wi-Fi, but they were trying, showing up on the USU's bimonthly calls and eager to learn. From these chapters spread out around the country, more than 50 USU members met in St. Louis the week of November 3, 2019.

Most used hard drugs like heroin and cocaine. Many lived in poverty. They were stuck with criminal records and marginalized in countless ways that pushed them to the edges of society.

The logistics were daunting. To be sure, pulling together a national event for active drug users didn't come without challenges. Each member needed somewhere to sleep in St. Louis. Hotels were expensive, while Airbnb conducts criminal-record checks and, as Louise and Don knew from their troubles in Italy, sometimes prohibits would-be renters who have a conviction for drugs. Transportation was similarly complicated. Some USU members had never flown before and were nervous about airports. Others were physically disabled. Most were actively addicted to drugs. In the months leading up to the convening, a dozen members of the USU's leadership team worked through these logistical details using online organizing platforms and encrypted messaging apps such as Signal. To lock down a space for the meeting, the USU had to negotiate with the Drug Policy Alliance. Louise worked to secure numerous grants that would subsidize expenses for as many attendees as possible. They scheduled speakers and facilitators, and drafted, printed, and assembled conference materials for each attendee. They debated desired outcomes.

"We had small, very reachable goals for this one," Louise says. "Get people there, let them see what we're doing, show them what the situation is, and bring everyone together. Show them it is possible for us to organize, giving people the reality of sitting in the same room together." Ahead of the convening, Louise barely slept for weeks.

It was understood that members would not stop using drugs while in St. Louis. Organizers therefore encouraged everyone who was going to use drugs to go slow—to first test their drugs by injecting a very small amount and then use less than their usual dose— and to never use alone in a new city with an unfamiliar supply. Other arrangements were made for those who wanted to receive opioid-substitution medications such as methadone or buprenorphine. It turned out that the nearest clinic offering those services to out-of-town patients was a 45-minute drive from the conference site. Ensuring those who needed it received medication-assisted treatment became one of the most challenging components of the entire affair.

At 9 a.m. on November 6, 2019, some 60 drug users met in a ground-floor meeting room at the Union Station Hotel. The day was facilitated by Robert Suarez, the Bronx-based organizer previously with VOCAL-NY who was now spending more time with the USU. He began the morning with an energetic rallying cry. "No longer are we going to wait for the slow ticktock of politics," Robert said. "We are organizing, we are building power, and we are going to take it to them."

Jess spoke next, offering a gentler welcome. "This is a labor of radical love," she began. "When I started doing drug-user organizing in 1998, there were just two of us in the room. And now, as a woman who injects drugs, I'm a little teary-eyed standing up here, looking out at a whole room full of people."

And then Louise: "We're doing this with a team-based system and sharing decision making—working together to build a national union that can get shit done."

Everyone who gathered in St. Louis had a story about how the war on drugs had harmed them: Jess was evicted from her apartment in Northampton after a friend suffered a nonfatal overdose there. More recently, her open identity as a drug user prevented her from gaining meaningful employment. Louise lost her leg to stigma intrinsic to the drug war. She was hit by a car and her history as an intravenous drug user led hospitals in Greensboro to treat her poorly. More than a year after the accident, an infection worsened and her leg was amputated. Shilo blamed the drug war for the fatal overdose that killed his friend in a vacant building in which the two of them were hiding. Caty knew countless sex workers whose clients had abused them and who subsequently suffered in silence, far too afraid of the police to go to them for help. Robert blamed prohibition for the death of his mother, who had contracted HIV from a dirty syringe back before there was a needle exchange in the Bronx. "If there had been harm reduction during her time, then she would not have been sharing needles," he says. "It's that simple. My mother would still be around."

In addition to reducing overdose deaths, it was those sorts of incidents that the USU decided it would organize to prevent. They would fight stigma. As with a labor union, the idea was to bring a strength-in-numbers approach to their cause. The group intended to function as an advocacy network, lobbying city, state, and federal governments to enact policies that would save drug users' lives and alleviate the worst harms of the persecution of people who use drugs.

"Nine-tenths of the pain I've experienced in my life was caused by the drug war," Jess says. "I can look back at so many periods of my life and say, 'My habit was totally manageable. It was the drug war that made me miserable.' It was a fear of arrest, fear of discrimination, fear of losing my job—a fear that had nothing to do with my job performance. That's what has always haunted me."

No group is more affected and simultaneously more often excluded from debates on drug policy than drug users themselves. The St. Louis convention was organized to change that. "Just sitting in a room with 60 drug users, that shit felt powerful," Louise says. "It felt like, 'We can do this.'"

Collectively, attendees agreed that the USU should maintain space for people who have entered recovery and no longer engage in regular drug use. In response to questions around how drug users' allies might interact with the organization, one idea was to create an advisory board composed of non–drug users, similar to the way public health authorities and research groups sometimes create advisory boards composed of drug users (flipping the common power structure on its head). There were also vocal demands for the guaranteed representation of marginalized communities, including sex workers, people who identify as transgender, visible minorities, and homeless people, among others.

The convening was a first-of-its-kind meeting to lay the ground-work for a coordinated response to America's war on drugs. At the same time, it was recognized that the St. Louis convening was only the second step (the first being New Orleans). Going forward in the long term, USU members determined they would need to address three basic questions: What is the Urban Survivors Union's mission? Who gets to be a member? And how should the national organization make decisions? It was planned for these conversations to continue online. "We're going to take two years to really make sure the structure works," Louise mentioned during an online meeting ahead of the conference. "This allows us some room. Then we're going to have quarterly meetings where major decisions around change can happen."

It was an exciting time but intensely stressful. "There are risks in all of this stuff," Louise says. She explains that with a movement of this nature—something that is the first of its kind—failure can remove a good idea from the table for a very long time. "We have got to make sure that active drug users stay at the forefront of this work," she says. "The time for this convening was now, but that took some convincing of the old guard. It was time to change that structure, and it's not easy to change structure. I'm not sure they freaking loved the idea, but it was time."

Shilo says their group tried to learn from past mistakes. "We had tried to organize different national drug-user unions before. There was always a lot of energy and then it just fizzled out. Someone would die, someone would get arrested, someone else would go to prison, someone would need to go get sober. Lots of things would happen and the core would collapse." St. Louis was different, he says.

Part of Shilo's inspiration for forming the original Seattle Urban Survivors Union was the Industrial Workers of the World, which secured concessions and improved conditions for those who as individuals held less relative power in society. "We're in a place now where the Urban Survivors Union has the ability to be that for drug-user unions," Shilo says. "A cause in Ohio, for example, with the drug-user union there, that can become a part of our national platform. We can all, collectively, start working and supporting each other. So there is huge potential to change policy and create new cohesive systems."

Caty was also in St. Louis with her contingent of drug-using sex workers. They'd made a lot of progress since first meeting one year earlier. "In between New Orleans and St. Louis, the sex-worker organizing group did a lot of networking. Calls are happening every two weeks and on at least every second call, we're hosting skill shares," Caty says. There were presentations on how to start a grassroots campaign—door knocking, for example—and how to create a bad-date sheet that warns of abusive men. "A year later, by the time St. Louis came around, I felt like we were ready for a national campaign." St. Louis was emblematic of the synergy building between sex workers and the larger drug-user activist movement. "We are both looking for the suspension of laws that criminalize us for committing victimless crimes."

Public demonstrations and larger advocacy campaigns were also on the agenda. While the USU's general membership set nothing in stone that week, the gathering gave attendees an opportunity to brainstorm ideas. For example, Jess made the case for drug users to demand a say in health care programs designed for those who use drugs. "A common thread that runs through every region where we've established a new chapter is a need for treatment on demand," Jess said in St. Louis. "We know that is the answer to ending overdoses: access to Suboxone and methadone, medication-assisted treatment." Jess added that the USU also intends to provide input on criminal-justice initiatives that have arisen out of the opioid epidemic. The Reframe the Blame campaign should be at the center of that effort, she said, challenging harsher sentencing laws favored by state legislators since the country's illicit-drug supply shifted from heroin to fentanyl.

Jess knew that during the HIV/AIDS epidemic of the 1980s and 1990s, public health authorities were initially reluctant to involve LGBTQ community leaders in decision-making roles. When they finally did, the expertise of people affected quickly proved invaluable to turning the tide on the crisis. "Drug-user unions are going to play a major role in ending this overdose epidemic," she says. "We have the knowledge and the tools to do that; we just don't have the money and the resources. But with sustainable unions across the country, we cannot be ignored any longer."

Caty echoes that sentiment. "This is the drug-user lobby," she says. "When we're writing grants, that's the language we're using lately. We're becoming a federal special-interest group: the voice of drug users."

18

Methadone in the Time of COVID

In March 2020, Louise was scheduled to attend a United Nations meeting in Vienna and, while there, do some work with the International Network of People Who Use Drugs (INPUD). Packing for the trip, she realized that something serious was happening. Some sort of a virus had jumped from China to the United States, and now people were talking about things like travel restrictions and "social distancing."

Louise only watches the news enough to keep up on politics related to her work. "I am deeply affected by the news. It does something horrible to me," she says. But this night, she was watching the news, lying in bed, on the phone with her mom. "Should I do this trip?" Louise asked. "Mom, I don't know what to do."

This was the start of the coronavirus pandemic. Sarah Beale was scared. Her daughter's immune system was fragile. Louise is prone to infection in the best of times, which, it was increasingly clear, this was not. Sarah told Louise to skip the Vienna trip or at least put it off until there was a better picture of what this COVID thing really was. "I give you permission not to go," Sarah told her. "I think it's a bad idea."

Louise was torn. On the one hand, a nightmare scenario played through her head. "I was scared to travel because I was scared I would get sick," she says. She had a source for methadone lined up in Vienna, but on her return trip, between Vienna and Greensboro, there was a long flight on which Louise was going to have to tough it out. "I was going to be dope sick," she says. Louise feared that, to a customs agent, dope sickness would look like COVID-19, and that would get her placed in some sort of government quarantine. "Being dope sick is frightening. Being dope sick in another country is mortifying. Being dope sick in quarantine—by our insane government—I can't even imagine." On the other hand, "This was a commitment. INPUD has one representative for the entire United States and that is me. So if I don't go, I'm going to eat myself alive. I might as well go because I'm going to be so goddamn mean to myself that there's no point in staying home."

Louise canceled her flight. Then she rescheduled it. Then she canceled it again, rescheduled it again, and then canceled it for a third time. As Don Jackson joined Sarah in begging Louise not to go, CNN reported that the entire city of Milan was under quarantine and other major cities across Europe were in the process of shutting down entirely. Finally, Louise left her flight canceled. "What the fuck is going on?" she thought.

By this time in Northampton, Jess and Albie Park had grown HRH413 into a fully operational needle exchange. They managed six outreach teams that offered syringes alongside other supplies like Narcan and fentanyl test strips. Team members were also trained in overdose response. They'd made 70 successful resuscitations since starting up six months earlier. "We always have about five people on and available, because we have situations where someone won't and cannot call 911," Jess says. "By which I mean, someone has Section 8 housing, has children in the house, or maybe lives in university housing. So they're not calling 911."

Business was booming, so to speak. And then Jess heard through a connection at the CDC about a deadly strain of the flu that was spreading in Washington State. "A little red flag went up," she says. "Within the next two weeks, everything was shut down. We had all these conferences coming up and they were canceled. All of my work, all of my contract work was canceled. Shit hit the fan." Jess had just returned from Washington, DC, where another COVID-19 outbreak was identified just six blocks from her hotel. In an effort to protect HRH413's clients—many of whom struggle with immunodeficiency issues—Jess went into a self-imposed two-week quarantine. "It killed me," she says. "I'm one of our team members who responds, even in the middle of the night. I'm usually out there unloading pallets of supplies. And all of that changed."

The Urban Survivors Union and Louise's local affiliate, the North Carolina Survivors Union, both took the coronavirus in stride. "I'm good in a crisis," she says. "I do well. A crisis kicks mania into gear." A lot of other people were falling apart. Everyone was watching the cable news networks 24/7 those days, and it was becoming apparent that this pandemic was a very serious thing. Louise and Don made a series of decisions. First, the Greensboro needle exchange was going to remain open, in some form. Second, its staff was going to get a break; Louise and Don would run things on their own. "We were determined to stay open," Louise says. "Don rock-starred it. He's been there every single shift. We've had the office cleaned like a motherfucker every week. This is one thing about drug users: we're so used to crisis and so used to coping with a crisis, that this was easy. We didn't have to think about it. It was just natural, like, 'We're going to do this, this, this, and this. We're going to make this happen. So let's go.'" The third decision that Louise and Don made was to maintain human contact. Connection was going to remain a part of what they did on Grove Street.

It's easy to miss how important the human aspect of an exchange is to its clients. This realization hit Louise in the context of COVID during a trip to the grocery store with Sarah. "My mom wouldn't give me a hug, because of social-distancing guidelines, and it made me cry. Because it felt like a feeling I'd had another time in my life, when I felt like my mom thought I was disgusting and didn't want to touch me. And so that really made me think about how COVID and all of this really impacts homeless people and people who are drug users. When someone acts like they don't want to touch a person who's a drug user, even if it's about COVID, it activates something in us that makes us feel like shit. So that was our reason to maintain face-to-face services. It became really important."

Jess and Louise had talked through COVID-19 over the phone and Jess and Albie arrived at the same conclusions as Louise and Don. They'd seen the harm reduction community sharing COVID-19 tips on Facebook, suggesting that outreach teams toss clients supplies through the air, or leave them on the ground and instruct clients to remain at a distance until outreach workers had left the area. "Much respect to you, but I'm not doing it that way," Jess thought. "Because the most important part of harm reduction, to me, as someone who has used outreach services when I was out there in chaotic use, is that three minutes—three minutes of human interaction, when someone genuinely cares about who you are and what you say." Jess and Albie looked for a happy medium. "Our participants are already treated like they are pariahs and ridden with disease," she says. "So for me, while I get that this social-distancing thing is precautionary, it perpetuates the stereotype that a drug user is dirty."

Louise and Don kept the Greensboro exchange open while the rest of the country shut down. Don cut the building's front door in half and turned it into a Dutch door, allowing participants to interact with the two of them while still serving as a barrier. They wore masks and gloves, of course, and maintained basic social-distancing protocols. "We just took precautions," Louise says. As other exchanges minimized hours or closed entirely, traffic at the Grove Street exchange tripled and then quadrupled. "Just because I can't touch somebody doesn't mean I can't look them in the eye, make full fucking eye contact, and pay attention to what they have to say."

Jess and Albie likewise stocked up on personal protective equipment and outfitted their teams with surgical masks, gloves, and hand sanitizer. Then they found their happy medium. HRH413 was primarily a mobile exchange service that met people wherever they were at, mentally and geographically. Supply drops continued, but with new and sensible restrictions. Hand-to-hands were discouraged. Instead, they had clients open bags they brought with them, and an HRH413 outreach worker would drop in a pack of syringes. There was no physical contact but eye contact continued. "You can meet with people, place supplies down or into their bag, and step back. There is no need to leave a bag and drive away," Jess says. "So our outreach teams are still running as they were before, just with slight adjustments."

In the months following the arrival of COVID-19, many other syringe service programs shut their doors, leading to drastic needle shortages in communities across the country. While official stats have yet to be released, both Louise and Jess provide anecdotal reports of increasing rates of hepatitis C and HIV. The closure of opioid-substitution programs similarly disrupted access to methadone and buprenorphine.

The first visit Louise made to a methadone clinic during COVID, she was pissed. "Everywhere else in the world, we're not allowed to have more than X amount of people somewhere. We're not even supposed to be leaving our houses. And then I go to the clinic and I'm in a room full of 50 people." Media reports from the early days of COVID confirm that Louise's experience was typical. "There were people wrapped around the building," one patient recounted from Tacoma, Washington. "We're standing in a line outside huddled together almost practically shoulder to shoulder."[1] Grocery stores extended hours for the elderly, restaurants erected tables outdoors, malls shut down entirely, and everyone else implemented revised occupancy limits; meanwhile, the country's methadone clinics continued with business as usual. "The doors aren't even open for air," Louise shouted at staff during that first visit during COVID. "Everything you guys are doing puts our health at risk. I'm walking out the door and I'm going to go use fentanyl."

Methadone and buprenorphine are the most effective tools we have to treat addictions to heroin, OxyContin, and fentanyl. They are the so-called "gold standard" for problematic opioid use.[2] They work by blocking or partially blocking the brain's opioid receptors, thus preventing feelings of euphoria, reducing cravings, and alleviating symptoms of withdrawal. Research shows that medication-assisted treatment (MAT) at least doubles opioid-dependent individuals' odds of successfully transitioning to abstinence compared to those who try to stop using drugs without the assistance of medication.[3] Going on MAT reduces the risk of contracting an infectious disease like HIV or hepatitis C, the risk of accidental overdose, and the risk of fatal overdose by 76 percent after three months of treatment and by 69 percent after 12 months, according to one study.[4]

Despite the benefits, it is not always easy for someone addicted to illicit opioids to get onto an opioid agonist like methadone or buprenorphine. According to an Urban Survivors Union presentation on treatment options, of 505 doctors contacted for a survey about addiction medicine, more than a quarter said they did not offer MAT. Of those who did, 72.3 percent said they had no openings for new patients; the remaining 27.7 percent reported average wait times of more than 16 days.[5] Another survey found that of 40,885 people diagnosed with an opioid-use disorder, just 12.5 percent were on MAT.[6]

The USU has an obvious interest in expanding access to methadone. In January 2020, Aaron Ferguson, a manager at an Austin treatment facility called Community Medical Services, stepped into the center of this effort. "I owe my life to harm reduction," he said. "I took methadone and buprenorphine when I was chaotic with heroin use." That was many years ago. Today, Aaron does outreach with methadone and other forms of medication-assisted treatment. But he remembers his journey and the difficulties he encountered working his own way through the treatment system, and remains sympathetic to those who struggle like he did. "The system really doesn't make treatment available to people in a way that's reasonable," Aaron says. "When you filter down to what's wrong with the addiction-treatment system, it's a general lack of and disregard for science and what actually works in favor of an ideological position about what addiction is and what the solution to it is."

There was a lot wrong with methadone distribution before the coronavirus. Everything, actually, if you ask Louise, Jess, and Aaron. Their first complaint is methadone's "liquid handcuffs." When you're on methadone, you're chained to a clinic. Generally, you have to visit the same location every single day and suffer the indignities of a technician witnessing you consume your medicine. It's a massive hassle, humiliating, and unique to methadone. It also makes it exceedingly difficult to travel beyond the driving range of that one clinic. "This medicine is regulated more heavily than any other in the world," Aaron says.

Everyone's second complaint is dosing hours. Many methadone clinics remain open only for a few hours early in the morning. If you miss the window, you miss your dose. That means one of two things: withdrawal, which is certain to be horrible, or the black market, which is completely uncertain and therefore dangerous. Furthermore, if a patient misses too many doses, as Louise concedes she often does on account of her hectic travel schedule, they can find themselves kicked out of the program entirely. "I've gone off methadone because there's no way for me to be on methadone and do my job," she says.

Complaint number three is "the piss test." Taking methadone usually means regular urine screens for illicit drugs, as if receiving the medication makes one a common criminal. Patients hate this indignity and unfortunately count it among many. Complaint number four is the general disrespect and otherwise poor treatment that Jess and Louise maintain is common at methadone clinics across the country. Number five is the lack of alternative options.

As terrible as the system is, if you want methadone, you're stuck with it.

"Methadone patients are among the most docile and subservient of patients," Jess says, "because they are terrified of having their medicine taken away. And so they get the shit kicked out of them." Aaron says it comes down to the simple fact that health care providers do not care about patients who are on methadone. "Ultimately, this industry has not been accountable to the individuals that it's supposed to be serving," he says.

COVID-19 placed new pressures on every aspect of this flawed system, exacerbating its arduous attendance requirements and intensifying every shortcoming. Just beginning to flex its muscle, the USU decided it would fight back and push for reforms.

In January 2020, Aaron delivered a presentation about challenges of the methadone system on one of the USU's biweekly conference calls. Since then, he, Louise, Jess, and a group of interested members had met regularly to discuss desired changes. Now they kicked into high gear. The USU drafted an open letter that demanded reforms in response to the coronavirus pandemic. "It was the people who signed the letter that made it important," Jess says. There were more than 50 initial signatories, among them the Drug Policy Alliance; National Council for Behavioral Health, the premiere organization of mental-health and addiction-care providers; and Open Society Foundations, the George Soros–led nonprofit, which is a major funder of harm reduction efforts. "We had organizations sign on that normally never would have sat in the same room together. Sure, drug users. But also conservative groups like medical journals were signing this letter, saying, 'We support it.'"

The USU letter on methadone reform is a concise list of demands. "While many regulators have argued that methadone and buprenorphine policies must be deliberately restrictive due to the risk of overdose, adverse medication effects, and medication diversion, the COVID-19 crisis has forced many regulating bodies to reevaluate these policies in order to comply with the urgent need for communities to practice social distancing and sheltering-in-place," it begins. "In order to reduce the risk of COVID-19 infection, involuntary withdrawal, and drug poisoning, the Urban Survivors Union and the undersigned organizations strongly recommend the following measures be taken immediately."

The list that follows calls for an immediate resumption of medication-assisted treatment programs that closed in response to COVID-19; dosage increases and the allowance of take-home doses in order to minimize required clinic visits; and a suspension of toxicology requirements (urine tests) for the duration of the pandemic. "Take-home exception privileges shall be expanded to the maximum extent possible, limited only by available supply and operations for delivery," the letter reads. "DEA [Drug Enforcement Administration] restrictions on mobile medication units shall be revised to accommodate delivery of medications to individuals who are sequestered in their homes." The letter concludes: "These recommendations outline a plan of primary prevention that will minimize the burden on our health care system and save lives during this national emergency."

To some USU members' surprise, the letter caught traction. Reforms in response to COVID-19 were underway before the letter's April 9, 2020, release. Notably, the U.S. Substance Abuse and Mental Health Services Administration (SAMHSA) had issued revised guidelines for methadone distribution that eased restrictions on take-home dosing. A March 16, 2020, SAMHSA notice instructs operators to provide 14-to-28-day take-homes in order to minimize clinic visits during COVID-19. But before the USU letter, these new coronavirus guidelines were not widely followed, Jess says. After the USU letter's release, "A lot of people took our letter into their clinic and within a couple of days, suddenly, across the board, clinic after clinic is falling into compliance. They're giving take-home bottles and no longer forcing people to come in to meet with their counselor every day." Jess and Louise call it a win for the USU, one of the first for the organization since it unified at the national level.

With the USU letter giving them a push, how did SAMHSA's reforms work out? Authorities' number-one stated fear was diversion: that so many methadone take-homes would result in a new supply of illicit opioids on the streets. But that never happened. "The world didn't end," Louise says. "Just look at me." The methadone clinic that Louise attends in Greensboro didn't go to 28-day take-homes or even 14-day take-homes. During the worst days of COVID, the biggest change it made was shutting down for the weekend, giving patients three-day take-homes to get them through to Monday. But even this modest reform meant the world, Louise says. "Because of that loosened regulation, I actually look like a stable patient. Just having the two days of freedom has made my life so much more manageable."

The next fight the USU has in the works is to push authorities to maintain their coronavirus-methadone reforms beyond the span of the pandemic. "We need change way past COVID," Louise says. "I don't understand how we plan to slow the opiate crisis until we fix methadone. It's the gold standard but it's totally motherfucking broken."

19

Creating Space

When COVID-19 arrived in March 2020, overdose deaths soared over and above anything that fentanyl and the larger drug epidemic had brought to date.

By August 2020, the Greensboro Police Department revealed that it had responded to 405 drug overdoses, 65 of them ending in deaths. "This year, we have lost more people to opioid overdoses than from homicide and traffic fatalities," the force reported. Greensboro firefighters similarly warned their overdose count was 36 percent above where it was at the same time the previous year. Louise is quoted in the newspaper: "The death toll that we have already seen, I'm not sure this community can stand it," she said. "We are resilient people, but this is a lot."[1]

At the time of writing, 2020 statistics for Northampton were not yet available. But state-level data showed that overdose deaths were rising in Massachusetts as a whole. After consecutive years of decline, the 12-month period ending in September 2020 came with a 7 percent increase in fatal overdoses compared to the previous year.[2] "People are using drugs in more isolated settings," an NPR affiliate report reads. "They fear becoming infected with COVID-19 if they seek treatment."[3]

It was the same story across the country, where NPR found that drug overdose deaths increased 27 percent during the first six months of 2020.[4] The CDC subsequently reported COVID had indeed exacerbated the crisis, resulting in 93,300 deaths by the end of the year.[5] According to the *New York Times*, "Several grim records were set: the most drug overdose deaths in a year; the most deaths from opioid overdoses; the most overdose deaths from stimulants like methamphetamine; the most deaths from the deadly class of synthetic opioids known as fentanyls."[6]

Louise describes a perfect storm. "In the midst of this pandemic, a lot of people are sort of falling apart. People are using because they don't have jobs, people are using because they have stimulus checks. There are a million people using for a million different reasons. Just look at what's going on in the world now. And the dope supply is a wreck. So overdoses are just going out of control."

There are ways to stop this, or at least to slow it down.

During Jess's time in New Orleans, she was busy with something else, beyond the public action she helped organize. She was running an underground injection site.

A public demonstration is exhausting to put together. Upon completion, people tend to be so burned out that it's common for organizers to go their separate ways and immediately fall asleep. That's what most of the USU's leadership team did after the New Orleans march. Except for Jess. After a slow and quiet walk back from the waterfront to the hotel, she had to go to work, taking a shift responding to overdoses.

There were a lot of overdoses at the 2018 New Orleans conference. Thankfully, no one died. That wasn't because of luck, though there was a little of that involved. People overdosed and no one died because drug users planned for overdoses. Conferences are a dangerous place for people who use drugs because they are in a new city, where the supply is inherently uncertain. So in New Orleans, drug users prepared, taking care of themselves in the context of prohibition, knowing that no one else would. Jess, along with Robert Suarez and Shilo Jama, created a designated space, off-site but close by the conference hotel, where people could use drugs under the watchful care of volunteers trained in overdose response.

"It was a don't-ask-don't-tell, word-of-mouth thing," Jess begins. "We called it the 'hospitality suite.' It's just a room where people can use safely. All the supplies are there. We've got everything from syringes, cotton, and Narcan, to an air bag and oximeter for the finger."

There was a basic set of rules under which the room operated. You were allowed in only if you identified as an active drug user— no exceptions. Everyone had to clean up after themselves. There was absolutely no fighting or confrontation of any kind. If anyone felt like they might overdose or felt anything out of the ordinary, they were to let someone know right away. "Total common-sense stuff," Jess says. "And no smoking." That one was a biggie. The last thing that anyone wanted was someone to get busted for heroin possession because someone else couldn't be bothered to take a walk outside for a cigarette.

Here's how the rest of it worked: Someone who didn't mind taking a risk with their credit card secured a hotel room that was large enough to serve as a meeting space. There was a sign-up sheet circulated online among those in the know, and everyone who could commit took a shift or two providing supervision. Volunteers were trained in overdose response. Two people worked together for two hours per shift. Every shift included at least one woman. Everything needed to inject drugs was kept tidy in one section of the room. There were clean syringes stocked in a variety of sizes, rubber tie-offs, cotton, cookers, alcohol swabs, and, of course, naloxone was kept ready. The bathroom was left available for people to use drugs with some privacy, though using in the bathroom was strongly discouraged. A towel was duct-taped around the doorknob so that the bathroom could not be locked, and it was primarily reserved for women who needed to inject in a part of their body they couldn't hit without removing some clothing.

If someone overdosed, everybody in the room was asked to remain calm and stay where they were. The two volunteers working the room then responded as they were trained. Meanwhile, some-one using the room called one of the hospitality suite's organizers. If the person overdosing had yet to completely lose consciousness, the volunteers would attempt to keep them awake with nonmedical measures. They'd give a strong grab on the shoulder and a knuckle rub along the sternum. They'd also repeatedly use the person's name and try to catch their attention that way. If there was still no response, the volunteers would raise their voices and threaten to administer Narcan. Since the overdose antidote works by essentially pushing opioid molecules off of the brain's opioid receptors, it has the effect of plunging someone addicted to opioids into withdrawal, and so is intensely unpleasant. A vocal threat of Narcan is therefore quite effective in snapping someone to attention.

If it's too late for any of that to work and the person overdosing has stopped breathing, the volunteers will immediately begin rescue breaths and administer naloxone, either in its intramuscular form or via the nasal spray. Rescue breaths continue and additional hits of naloxone follow as needed. By this point, one of the room's organizers will have arrived and decides whether to call 911. To date, this has never happened. But if the person overdosing could not be revived and it was deemed necessary to call 911, there are procedures for how to break the room down and make anything illegal disappear within minutes.

With extensive preparations in place, Jess and her team believed they had created a safe space for New Orleans conference attendees to use drugs. But right from the start, things didn't go exactly as planned. "Overdoses started happening," Jess says. "The first overdose that happened was a very experienced user. It speaks to just how badly our supply has been poisoned." The guy had a tolerance and loaded up his usual amount, but in New Orleans, that usual amount was too much. Every city's heroin is different, which is what makes travel a dangerous activity for someone addicted to opioids. "Whoa," the man said. Then he went down.

Jess and a couple of people using in the room lifted the man from the table where he sat and brought him down to the ground. "I open his eyelids and his pupils are tiny, constricted, and straight ahead," Jess continues. "I have a penlight in his eyes and I've got my watch, so let's go."

Jess shoved a dose of nasal Narcan into the man's nose and hit the plunger. Another woman placed a handheld oxygen pump over his face and began squeezing it to breathe for the man. A minute passed. Then two. There was no response. Jess grabbed a second dose of naloxone, this one an intramuscular syringe, and injected the man in the shoulder. "He was going blue and his pulse was fading out to nothing," Jess says. His eyes and mouth hung open but he remained unresponsive. "It was like looking at a dead body. There was just nothing there." They were getting worried, hiding panic. By now, it seemed an eternity had passed. Jess checked her watch. Exactly three minutes had gone by. "It always feels like a lifetime," Jess says. "Every time. Every time. But then he did come out of it." The old man's eyes flickered open and, after a moment of confusion, he figured out what had happened. "Fuck you," he said in a friendly way, playing it cool. "I'm sick." He let Jess give him a hug. "Thank you," he said to her.

"We thought we had found a pretty consistent source to go through for drugs while we were there, in New Orleans," Jess says. "Then we used it and . . . she trails off. "Something I've noticed over the past year or so is that I've become afraid of dope. That's something I hate about being in North Carolina, too. I'm terrified to do anything. Every batch that comes in is something different. You never know what you're getting."

Over the course of the four days and four nights that the hospitality suite ran in New Orleans, six people overdosed a total of eight times. Nobody died. "That's the thing," Jess says. "We can monitor people and then they stay alive. That's the beauty of a safe-consumption space. I think about how many people, if we didn't have that room, would have used alone in their hotel rooms and maybe would have died."

In the United States, it remains illegal to operate a space that is designed for the consumption of illicit drugs. According to Section 856 of the Controlled Substances Act, no one can "knowingly open, lease, rent, use, or maintain any place, whether permanently or temporarily, for the purpose of manufacturing, distributing, or using any controlled substance." Better known as the Crack House Statute, this law was designed to target your typical shooting gallery—the sort of ramshackle vacant row house you see in the movies where a bunch of homeless addicts nod off on a soiled mattress. But it could also forbid the establishment of a health care facility where nurses provide supervision for the ingestion of illegal drugs, and the sort of safe space that Jess and her team created in New Orleans.

The former Republican government in Washington insisted that is what it means. "It is a crime, not only to use illicit narcotics, but to manage and maintain sites on which such drugs are used and distributed," a December 2017 memo issued by the Department of Justice's U.S. Attorney's Office reads. "Thus, exposure to criminal charges would arise for users and SIF [supervised injection facility] workers and overseers. The properties that host SIFs would also be subject to federal forfeiture." The law interpreted this way has, however, never been tested in court, and legal scholars have questioned whether the Crack House Statute would apply to the operation of a health care facility.[7] A group in Philadelphia called Safehouse has publicly stated its intention to open a supervised injection facility and has initiated a case that could eventually see the U.S. Supreme Court issue a decision on the matter.* Such a definitive answer is, however, at a minimum several years away.

---

* Several states have groups working to open the United States' first sanctioned supervised injection facility. In addition to Pennsylvania, those that appear the closest are California, Washington, and New York. Updates on the Philadelphia effort are available at safehousephilly.org.

In the summer of 2019, Don Jackson walked down a long hallway, toward the back of the North Carolina Survivors Union's headquarters and needle exchange in Greensboro, into the small bathroom there. He was giving a tour to a pair of harm reduction activists visiting from the neighboring state of Virginia. With boyish enthusiasm, he pointed to a small piece of stainless steel that swung up off a hinge on the wall. Don grabbed it and flipped it into position, so that the shoebox-sized table was perpendicular to the wall, at a height of about three feet, positioned above and a few inches in front of the toilet seat. "Check it out!" This was not an injection site, as a matter of the law, but it might keep people alive, just the same.

Louise chooses her words carefully when talking about drug use at the NCSU. "We can talk about the ways in which we have to bend and twist and move to try to figure out how to operate inside and outside of the law," she says, "to try to help people."

That little steel table in the NCSU's bathroom is activists bending the law to keep their conduct within it. "We have a passcode and the door unlocks from the outside," Louise says. "We check on people every few minutes and ask them if they're okay. And people know that they can use our bathroom."

"This is not a safe consumption space," she continues. "We tell people, 'You cannot use drugs here. That is illegal.' But how should we handle this? We cannot forbid participants from using the bathroom. So much of what we do here is about giving people the dignity they are denied in so many other spaces. We cannot watch them while they're using the bathroom. And we know what goes on. So, what we can do is, let people know, 'You shouldn't use here. But if you are going to use, we are going to make sure that nothing happens to you here. We are going to check on you and we are going to keep you safe.'"

The NCSU's safe bathroom is somewhat more official than it looks. In an email, Louise shares a document labeled "NC Survivors Union Member Bathroom Policies & Procedures." Inside is a detailed breakdown of the bathroom, including structural components, staffing requirements, and operating instructions. "Upon witnessing opioid overdoses and improperly disposed syringes in the bathroom, our organization has determined certain measures must be taken to ensure the safety of members, staff, consultants, volunteers, peers, and custodial staff," the document reads. "It is recognized that bathrooms may serve a need to have a private space to use drugs and, in the absence of other safer options, are a stopgap service for participants of our organization."

The bathroom is open only when the NCSU has two staff on shift and both are trained in overdose response. Participants are allowed a maximum of 15 to 20 minutes inside. There is an intercom system that NCSU staff use to contact them every three minutes. "If a person does not respond, NCSU staff will enter the bathroom to check on the NCSU member," the document continues. In addition, the door was modified to open outward, so that no one inside the bathroom can prevent it from opening if they fall. There are also strict guidelines for maintenance and cleaning. "Overdose Drills should occur at minimum one time per quarter," it concludes.

The NCSU's bathroom is keeping people safe.

"Somebody said they hadn't used in some time," Louise recounts. "They went and used the bathroom, Don checked on them in three minutes, and nobody answered." Don shouted to let Louise know he was going in. He punched in the code for the door lock, opened the door outward, and saw the man lying on the ground, unconscious. Following NCSU procedures, Don first tried to wake the man with verbal cues and then quickly moved to try to shake him awake. Neither worked. Next came Narcan. Don pulled a capsule of the nasal spray out of his back pocket, tore away the package, placed the device into the man's nostril, and hit the plunger. A minute passed, during which time rescue breaths continued. Finally, there was the *woosh* of a large breath in. A moment later, the man's eyes flickered open. "You overdosed," Don told him as a matter of fact.

"So Don brought the guy back, we gave him a cup of coffee, sat and talked with him for a little bit, and that was that," Louise says. "If we hadn't had that safe bathroom, he would have used drugs down the street. He would have been alone, nobody would have known, and he would have died."

In Seattle, Shilo Jama has worked with supervised injection sites for a long time. "Some people call them track houses, some people call them shooting galleries," he begins. "In cities and communities that aren't yet overly gentrified, that still have abandoned buildings, these places always exist. There are always those spots. Years before we had all this talk [public debate] about supervised injection in the U.S., we were providing needles and Narcan in those places, making them safer."

Nothing more than a group of squatters can offer a lot of security, Shilo says. "People look out for one another." These days, he notes, in any vacant building where drug users settle in, there's usually a couple of people carrying Narcan. "And a mom and pop of the place, or whatever you want to call them," Shilo continues. "Someone who uses there and says something like, 'We don't have to be doing this in trash. Let's clean up.'"

Before long, what was once nothing more than a dusty vacant row house is getting organized. People who drop by regularly will get on board with a little bit of order and sanitation. Specific spots for used needles and other waste are designated, and the garbage is removed on a regular basis, every morning or two. If there's a needle exchange nearby, or someone like Shilo around, the place will be equipped with yellow bins designated for medical waste. "The first thing I did with a lot of those houses was, I put in 10 sharps containers, all over the place," Shilo says. "From then on, if someone drops a sharp or they throw and miss, someone else will be like, 'Why didn't you drop that into the sharps container?' It's funny—like most things harm reduction, you make doing the safer thing the easier thing."

Next someone brings in a table or something similar. Now there's a specific spot to inject. And now the mom and pop of the place are keeping that table clean, wiping it down and collecting any trash that accumulates there. Shilo's next step is to stock the place with harm reduction supplies: needles, Narcan, and everything else.

Shilo notes that people's behavior in these places has changed since fentanyl arrived. Back in the day, a lot of users would try to stake out an entire room for themselves and inject alone, in privacy. But now, a vacant building usually has one or two rooms specifically designated for injecting, and people are strongly discouraged from using anywhere else. "The rise in overdose rates kind of changed a lot of people's views on a lot of things," Shilo says.

Don't call it an injection site—that might violate the Crack House Statute. But by this point, Shilo's track house is looking somewhat official. "People are creating these sites for themselves," he says.

Just because the United States hasn't sanctioned a supervised injection facility, that doesn't mean there aren't many operating today. And just like their legal counterparts in Canada, Australia, and parts of Europe, where the debate on supervised injection largely ended in its favor many years ago, these unsanctioned sites are saving lives.

It raises the question, what is an injection site?

Perhaps the world's best-known official supervised injection facility is Insite, located at 138 East Hastings Street in downtown Vancouver, Canada. Insite works like this:

There are two doors, one for the entrance and the other for the exit. Inside, a series of rooms forms the shape of a U, facilitating the flow of traffic from the first door to the second. Upon entering, a friendly staff member greets participants and asks for a name (it doesn't have to be a real name) and the substance they are there to use. Then, sometimes after a short wait, clients proceed from the lobby to the injection room, better known as the IR. On one side, there's a raised desk staffed by a pair of registered nurses. On the remaining three walls, there's a semicircle of 11 booths, each with a chair and steel desk facing a wall-mounted mirror. At the nurses' station, there is everything one needs to inject drugs: packaged single syringes, ties, cotton, cookers, water, and alcohol pads. After collecting what one needs, a participant takes a seat at a booth, prepares their drugs, and injects themselves.

Insite does not supply drugs, and while its nurses can advise on how to inject, they cannot provide any sort of hands-on assistance. The nurses are there to provide supervision and respond in the event of an overdose. Staff can also connect clients with a detox program, treatment facility, and other health care services, if that is what a user wants. After injecting, a participant can hang out for a few minutes or proceed to the facility's third room, "the chill." In the chill, someone who has just injected drugs can hang out for a while longer, grab a cup of coffee, and, if they're not feeling well, remain under staff supervision until they're feeling right again. Then they can leave Insite and continue with the rest of their day.

From March 2004 to December 2019 (the period for which Insite's government partner was able to provide statistics), there were 7,884 drug overdoses at the supervised injection facility. Insite has never seen one death.[8]

Likewise, there has never been one death at Jess's hospitality suites, Louise's safe bathroom, or Shilo's various vacants and track houses.

A small mountain of academic papers further supports the establishment of supervised injection facilities. A *Lancet* evaluation of Insite's initial two years operating found a 35 percent decline in overdoses across the building's surrounding neighborhood.[9] A comprehensive evaluation also found a drop in HIV/AIDS, emphasizes the benefits of wound care at the facility, and notes there was an increase in community members entering detox programs for addictions to cocaine, methamphetamine, and heroin.[10] Looking at sites in Europe, a 2018 overview similarly found declines in the sharing of injection equipment, improved overall hygiene among clients, and low-barrier access to health care among populations that might otherwise not engage with health care systems.[11]

In the United States today, a few cities appear close to establishing official supervised injection facilities. Seattle, San Francisco, New York City, and, most promising, Philadelphia have all approved opening sites, in principle. It appears each jurisdiction hopes to be second, however. In each of these cities, neighborhood opposition has led to delay after delay, and federal threats appear to have left people with cold feet.[12] "Because federal law clearly prohibits injection sites, cities and counties should expect the Department of Justice to meet the opening of any injection site with swift and aggressive action," then–U.S. deputy attorney general Rod Rosenstein wrote in April 2018.[13] And so for years now, America's first sanctioned supervised injection facility has remained one or two years away.

But again, what is a supervised injection site? Jess, Louise, and Shilo no longer pay the debate much attention.

Shilo was once heavily involved in the campaign to establish a sanctioned site in Seattle. "I can tell you this: We're going to do this underground. We're going to just do it. That's how we've done everything else, from snorting kits to meth pipes. This [injection sites] was the first time we really slowed down and started to think about asking for permission. And that's my biggest regret."

Louise envisions supervised injection as a safe haven. "Where we don't criminalize people for using, where people feel like they are safe—that is so critically important," she says. Similar to Shilo, Louise has come to question whether such a place can exist if what's required to create it is the approval and involvement of the government. She explains that in countries like Canada, sanctioned facilities leave drug users cold. They come with onerous operating policies that let people inject drugs but ban the smoking of cigarettes, for example; prohibit assisted injection; and incorporate an overmedicalized environment that feels dehumanizing. "These things do better operating underground sometimes," Louise says. "By the time government gets its paws all over it, by the time they figure out what the rules and regulations of it are, why would anybody ever want to go in one?"

Underground works for Jess. She explains that, despite the name, a supervised injection site's most important function is not supervision. Rather, it is the space that such facilities create. "A space that drug users can call their own," she says. This space has tangible effects, Jess continues. Instead of a hurried shot in an alley, injection-site participants can take the time to look at what they are doing, prepare everything hygienically, and go slow with their drugs. But more than that, inside an injection site, people who use drugs can exist without fear of persecution by police. "It's a place where they don't have to hide from friends and family members, or from the shame that society forces on people who struggle with addictions. A space where you can be yourself." And for all of that, the underground might work better than a medicalized room on the ground floor of an austere government building, Jess concludes.

"It is so important for these programs to create this space, just so that drug users can sit down and stop running for five minutes," she says. "It really is all about creating space."

Epilogue

Louise's harm reduction running mate, Wiggs, passed away in June 2019. He was 35. The cause of death was complications related to endocarditis. However, it was an overdose that sent Wiggs to the hospital where he died, and so Louise remains confused about what actually happened. "That hospital is notorious for being awful to people who use drugs," she says. "What I'm sure of is, what needed to happen, didn't happen." She pauses for a moment. "I fucking miss him so much."

Jesse Harvey, a close friend of Jess's and a prominent harm reduction activist based out of Portland, Maine, died of an overdose in September 2020. "I am without words. Just a void of loss and anger," Jess wrote on Facebook. "We are all in shock. We lost four amazing young harm reductionists over the past month. The War on Drugs is killing us all. I refuse to stop fighting."

Meanwhile, prosecutors across the nation are using drug-induced-homicide laws to send low-level dealers and addicted users to prison for longer periods of time. In May 2019, a death-by-distribution bill was passed into law in North Carolina. It keeps Louise awake at night. With a drug-induced-homicide law on the books in her home state, she is convinced that if anyone dies around her, Greensboro police will finally have the tool they've wanted to send her to prison. "I live in fear," Louise says.

But people who use drugs are in the fight.

The Urban Survivors Union is becoming a proper special-interest group, giving drug users a unified voice at the national level for the first time. Since its march through the streets of New Orleans, the USU has held additional public demonstrations. Members are speaking out in the open as drug users, refusing to bow to the stigma that once kept them in the shadows. And since the constitutional convening in St. Louis, the USU has established new chapters in cities and towns across the country, bringing harm reduction to corners of America where something like a needle exchange has never been available. In users' collective response to the persecution they have now faced for so many decades, there is a map for social reform: a specific, realistic, and tangible path to limit the worst harms of the overdose crisis and America's war on drugs. This is harm reduction.

"Now that we know that we can get people together, now that we've got people interested, I feel like there is no stopping us," Louise says. "There are people that got a glimpse of this in New Orleans and St. Louis, and if it is anything like the glimpse that I got when I first started, if there are just a couple of people that felt the spark that I did when I first started, then we're doing good."

At her home in Northampton, Jess is busier than ever. With Albie Park, she's made a full-time job out of the Harm Reduction Works support group and its parent organization, HRH413. Jess and Albie lead HRW meetings on Zoom each week. And HRH413 continues to operate several outreach teams performing mobile needle exchange. The pair also run a number of underground supervised injection sites. These modest facilities are little more than spare rooms outfitted with the basic equipment one needs to inject drugs, plus naloxone and supervising volunteers ready to respond in the event of an overdose. But an injection site doesn't have to be as complicated as America seems to want to make it, Jess says. Her sites work. No one has died. They're saving lives, and creating space. "A space where people can catch their breath, eat something, and get some liquids into them," she adds. "A space where conversations can happen."

Despite the COVID-19 pandemic, Jess remains upbeat. She has an ambitious goal on the horizon. Jess is crafting a plan to bring "safe supply" to America.* She wants to make available known alternatives to street drugs, so that when you get a substance that is described as heroin or cocaine, you can be sure it is actually heroin or cocaine that you're taking. "With fentanyl, there's a point where no number of injection sites, no amount of drug testing, is going to change a poisoned supply. So why don't we talk about safe supply?" Jess asks.

What does that mean? Perhaps hard drugs could move into shops, similar to the cannabis dispensaries of states such as Colorado, California, and New York. More likely, safe supply could be medicalized, where one obtains a prescription for heroin or cocaine from a doctor. It's too early to guess. "We're going to be asking drug users, 'What should this look like for you? What do you want safe supply to look like?'" Jess says. Consultation is underway in only the most preliminary sense. But already Jess knows what she wants to accomplish with safe supply. "To end overdoses," she says. "And literally give drug users some agency over what it is we put in our bodies."

Louise struggled through the first year of COVID-19 and the restrictions that governments deployed in response to the pandemic. "It's been hard," she says. "I've got a lot going on, a lot of work stuff. People not coming into work. People are just struggling right now. Things have not been easy."

"We need interactions," Louise continues on a call. "There are things more dangerous than COVID, and social isolation is one of them. . . . The pandemic is fucking people up. The pandemic is just destroying people."

---

* The term "safe supply" is borrowed from drug-user groups in Canada, where the overdose crisis is almost as severe as it is in America. In Vancouver, activists convinced politicians that the medicalized distribution of pure drugs is required to reduce overdose deaths. In late 2021, authorities issued official guidelines for how regulated supplies of heroin (diacetylmorphine), cocaine, and methamphetamine could work under existing prohibition laws. Early trial programs are underway.

In November 2020, Louise's methadone clinic kicked her out and refused her pleas for readmission. They told her that her poor attendance record and a positive drug screen meant she was no longer "experiencing success" with their treatment program. Louise begged the clinic to take her back. "I have had success in my life. Whether you see positive drug screens or not, I am doing well in my life," she told them. "You guys are only looking at a drug screen and making decisions about my life. But you're not looking at the entirety of my life." The methadone clinic didn't care that Louise held a full-time job, ran her own nonprofit organization, and, with a master's degree in public health, regularly consulted as an expert on harm reduction. "The only way they see success is abstinence," Louise laments. "All they can see is the drug test."

The next methadone clinic that would take Louise as a patient was more than an hour away. She made the drive when she could, but when the clinic near her home kicked her out, it meant Louise effectively lost access to a medication that was working for her. "I am able to function on methadone and I am not able to function without it," she says. "It provides the stability that I need." Louise no longer has that stability.

"We talk about hitting rock bottom," she says. "Most of the time, we don't reach the bottom on our own. Most of the time, we're thrown to the bottom."

On what's next for the Urban Survivors Union, Louise says it's always been the same thing. Explaining, her mind wanders back more than 15 years, to the months she spent alone in a McDonald's bathroom. Louise had just lost both her children to their grandparents. Her parents had cut her off, withdrawing all support. She had criminal charges hanging over her head, filling every conscious moment with anxiety and dread. Her boyfriend was abusive in every way. She had nowhere to go. Louise was running, but with nowhere to run to. So, day after day, week after week, she huddled on the floor of a McDonald's bathroom, injecting heroin, desperately trying to shut out as much of the world as she could. "It's that loneliness that leads to my need to provide people with a safe spot," Louise says. "All I'm trying to do is give people somewhere where they can come and sit, just for a moment."

Since the coronavirus reached the United States, Louise's voice remained in a mumbled fog of intense fatigue. Now, for just a moment, it broke from that, and for the first time in months she sounded happy, or at least content. "Maybe I have created what I felt like I needed," she says. "Everything that I've wanted to create and everything I've wanted to provide was everything I didn't have," she adds. "A space where you can just come in and see, 'Oh, she understands.' And where we're not going to let shit happen to you here."

Afterword

A strange thing happens when you are caught using drugs. Instantly, your judgment no longer matters. Your knowledge, your opinions, your experience—none of it. You have been using drugs.

In many situations, distrust will be justified. Stigma forces people who use heroin to hide it from the world, including the people closest to them. And so family members and friends are lied to. I've never met a drug user who wanted to lie to their loved ones. But if they shared the truth, that they inject heroin or snort cocaine, the world might come crashing down, often with the heaviest of consequences. They could lose their marriage, the roof over their head, or their children. So people who use drugs do lie, many hating themselves for it, and some use more drugs to cover that pain.

I'm not just talking about a husband questioning their wife when she says she's only running to the corner store to grab a carton of milk. Every word is discounted, dismissed, or ignored. And everyone around the pair of them silently agrees that this is the way it should be. For the foreseeable future, no one is listening to anything you say.

To experience this is incredibly disorienting. You haven't changed. But in the time it took them to pull a flap of heroin from your discarded jeans pocket, what you say no longer matters. You no longer matter.

It feels like losing your mind, Louise tells me late one night at her home in Greensboro.

"If we do anything with this, I hope that we can speak some truth to power," she says. "Show people that we have a voice, and that we need to be heard and listened to."

In Jess's forested backyard in Northampton, she tells me about when the same thing happened to her. Eventually, she distanced herself from her family in order to preemptively avoid their mistrust, and her shame.

"When I look back and dissect why I felt a certain way during a given time, it was not my drug use," she says. "It was always what was imposed upon me by the constituents of my drug use. By the laws that I had to abide by, that I had to pee in a cup, and that I couldn't tell the truth about what I was doing. Once I was able to tell the truth about my drug use, it was so freeing. So much of my pain went away."

The lives of Louise and Jess reveal the harms of the drug war, laying bare how laws that criminalize drugs do more damage than the drugs themselves.

At some point, I lost count of the number of their friends and fellow activists who died during the writing of this book. Adam Wigglesworth, Jesse Harvey, Derek Jackson, Dan Bigg, Becki Brooks, Dylan Stanley, William Miller Sr., Aubri Esters . . .

There's no happy ending here. Fentanyl remains a threat, all but entirely replacing heroin in some parts of the country.

Roughly 365,000 people died after taking drugs in the United States during the last five years for which data are available (2016–2020)[1]. About 93,300 of them passed away in 2020 alone, more than 25 percent of the total[2]. Five or 10 or 20 years into the overdose crisis, depending on how you count it, things are only getting worse.

Most of these people did not die because they were using drugs. "This is the drug war," Jess tells me. "It is killing us. This is drug policy."

To evade authorities, traffickers want to smuggle more drugs in fewer packages, so potency rises and we eventually end up with fentanyl. A woman injecting in a back alley looks over her shoulder for police and rushes her shot, failing to take the time to properly measure her dose for fear of being arrested. A young man uses drugs in his parents' basement. He was told that if he's caught using again, he's kicked out. So he's alone, hiding what he's doing, preventing anyone who could save him from finding him in time. As a result of the government's refusal to regulate narcotics, people who are addicted to opioids—not using for fun, but physically dependent and mentally compelled to seek drugs—are forced to put something into their bodies without knowing what it is. Fentanyl and even stronger drugs like carfentanil make every shot a game of Russian roulette.

When regulated drugs are used in a clinical setting, as they are at a small number of facilities in a few progressive countries like Sweden and Canada, no one dies. At Crosstown Clinic in my hometown of Vancouver, for example, each patient receives a precise dose of diacetylmorphine (the medical term for heroin), uses it under the watchful care of nurses, and then exits the clinic and continues on with the rest of their day. Crosstown Clinic has offered prescription heroin since 2005 (first as an academic study and later as a government-funded experimental health care program). In more than 15 years, no one has died there. Just like no one has ever died at a supervised injection facility such as Vancouver's Insite.

The drugs themselves are not the reason that more than 93,000 people died in 2020. It is not the fault of the low-level dealers that authorities send to prison for decades with drug-induced homicide laws. The war on drugs is waged by the politicians who write its legislation and the law enforcement officials who blindly execute it on their behalf.

Across the country, cars are stopped, pedestrians are harassed, and homes are raided. People are imprisoned for years for nonviolent crimes that hurt no one but themselves. Families are broken, job prospects curtailed, and housing options limited. Black and brown Americans are disproportionately affected to an extent so extreme it calls into question the nation's very soul.

A realistic assessment of the U.S. war on drugs reveals that it is all but certain to continue for the foreseeable future. The rise of drug-induced homicide laws shows that despite Democratic administrations' softer rhetoric and some bipartisan support for shorter drug-crime sentences, the larger war continues unabated.

Activists will not end the drug war anytime soon, but they can begin to limit some of its harms.

At the front of this movement are drug users themselves. Their voices—until now left out of mainstream conversations around the opioid epidemic—are rising from unlikely locations. That's the story I tried to tell here.

Light Up the Night is a story about people who use drugs, told through their eyes, with no judgment of the decisions they have made. It is not a recovery memoir or self-help manual. It recounts the lives of two women, caught up in the drug war, struggling with an uncertain narcotics supply. They are organizing drug users and turning them into activists, saving lives in the face of an overdose crisis. A labor of radical love, in Jess's perfect words.

Beyond the lives of Louise and Jess, these pages tell small parts of much larger stories. This book cannot recount the complete history of harm reduction in America. Nor is it the entire story of drug-user organizing. Those tales are longer and more complex than the one here. Moreover, Louise and Jess are both white, and make no claim to share the drug war's heavier burdens endured by people of color. This is Louise and Jess's story, or at least my version of it, written humbly and in gratitude for the trust they have placed in me, conveyed as completely and accurately as I could.

Over years of interviews, we grew close, blurring lines of journalistic objectivity. It couldn't have happened any other way, I realize now. Jess and Louise pour everything they have into their work—every minute of every day and every ounce of energy they possess. Which makes their stories intensely personal, and a privilege for me to share.

I took up this project because I wanted to learn about how the arrival of fentanyl has affected drug users beyond the obvious impact of overdose deaths, about how it has changed the day-to-day lives of people who use cocaine and heroin. I wanted to see how America's drug war intersects with the overdose crisis to further endanger the lives of so many people. More than anything, I wanted to hear from drug users themselves, and amplify their voices so that America can learn from their experiences and expertise.

I discovered an underground movement, and a story of empowerment that demands the public listen. Jess and Louise, along with Shilo Jama, Robert Suarez, Dinah Ortiz, and every member of the Urban Survivors Union, are working together at the national level, expanding access to harm reduction services. It is a movement that is crucial to understand today because it understands the opioid epidemic and how to stop the country's skyrocketing rate of overdose deaths.

It is also a fight for civil liberties and for civil rights. Not one that is the same as feminism, Black power, or LGBTQ equality, although there are strong elements of all three within this fight. The activists who compose the Urban Survivors Union are demanding equal treatment despite the health conditions with which they struggle and the substances they choose to ingest as informed and capable adults.

The extent to which drug users are discriminated against is without parallel in America today. It is perfectly legal for a landlord to evict someone if drugs are found within their home, for an employer to fire someone who uses cocaine on weekends, and for child protective services to take a drug-using mother's baby from her, even if drugs are never used or found anywhere near the child and the care she provides is loving and flawless in every way.

This is discrimination on the basis of a health issue. A health issue is what society has agreed a drug addiction is, or at least how it collectively claims it regards an addiction. (Mainstream support for incarceration for drug crimes calls into question the genuineness of this claim, but if you ask people if they consider drug addiction a health issue, most will quickly say "yes.") And yet it is seldom questioned, let alone opposed, when someone is evicted, fired, or separated from their children for using drugs.

It was once acceptable to imprison those who struggled with a mental illness. I wonder if the persecution of people who use drugs will one day come to be regarded the same way; as counterproductive, cruel, and an unjust victimization of the marginalized and society's most vulnerable.

People who use drugs should not be fighting back against the war on drugs alone. As the opioid epidemic intensified through the 2010s and more families found themselves touched by addiction, learning through personal tragedy that drug users are not all deviants and thieves, opponents of the drug war gained allies and the movement grew in strength. Parents, for example, have emerged as strong allies of the Urban Survivors Union. Groups like Moms United and Moms Stop the Harm are holding anti-prohibition protests outside the White House and marching in the streets. But harm reduction activists need more help and deserve to receive it.

As I write the final sections of this book, Louise answers her phone less and responds to fewer emails and text messages. "How are you?" I ask each time we connect. "I've been struggling a little bit," she concedes on one call, obviously understating it. "Things have not been easy." It's toward the end of 2020–21's COVID lockdowns and Louise sounds exhausted, like the weight of the world is finally grinding her down. "Things have been hard," she says. "But I'm still here."

A week later, Jess sounds similar. She tells me she's worried about the toll this fight is taking on Louise, on herself, and on other advocates in the harm reduction movement. She knows they're not the only two who are using drugs to cope. In more than 20 years of activism, there's never been a year when she's known so many people who have died of overdoses. Alongside grief, there is frustration, so much so that it's turning to rage, she says. It reminds her of the stigmatizing looks she's received in hospitals and from police. Jess has countless good reasons to hate police. But she wonders to what extent so much anger is hurting her more than her enemies. The drug war has hardened each side against the other. "I've called this thing a labor of radical love," Jess says. "We've got to try to keep this about love." She means it, but sounds as if she's said it to remind herself. She sounds so tired.

Time passes and I don't connect with Jess again until after nearly a month of radio silence. "I lost three of my friends this week," she eventually texts me. Then nothing for several more weeks. Finally, she shares a quote.

"If we behave like those on the other side, then we are the other side. Instead of changing the world, all we'll achieve is a reflection of the one we want to destroy." —Jean Genet.

"I like it," I text back. "Take care of yourself. We need you."

Travis Lupick
August 2021

Acknowledgments

This book was written with the help of heroes walking among us. I'd like to make a second dedication, to the people this book is written about. It is for Jessica Tilley, Louise Vincent, Don Jackson, and the many activists alongside them. You gave me so much of your time and shared with me so much of your lives. The trust you've placed in me is incredible. It is a privilege to share your stories.

I want to express an equally great thank-you to Sarah Beale and Rebecca Rogovin, for giving me beds to rest in, sharing your tables with me, and making me feel welcome in your homes.

Along with Louise, Jess, Don, and their families, there is no one I want to thank more than the movement that welcomed me in. I owe gratitude to Aaron Ferguson, Albie Park, Andrew Bell, Caty Simon, Dinah Ortiz, Isaac Jackson, Jermaine Mondell, Knina Strichartz, Lindsay Roberts, Mark Kinzly, Mikey Gee, Mimi Cove, Mona Bennett, Monique Tula, Natty G, Reggie Thomas, Robert Suarez, Shannon Hicks, Shilo Jama, Tanya Koon, Terl Gleason, Thelma Wright, Tom Butler, and Will Miller Jr. There are more. For those whose names I am forgetting, I am sorry, and no less grateful.

Lucas Vrbsky, there is a night you spent with me on the phone in 2018. If it were not for that call, I doubt a word of this would have ever been written.

I also want to give a special thank-you to the activists who helped me with this book who are no longer with us. Adam Wiggleworth, Jesse Harvey, Derek Jackson, and Aubri Esters, thank you. You did not fight in vain.

Thank you to zakia henderson-brown for your invaluable first edit and always insightful advice, to Emily Albarillo and Cathy Dexter for your additional edits, and to everyone at The New Press who helped me get this out into the world. Thank you to Johann

Hari, Sean Baker and Samantha Quan, Dr. Carl Hart, Maia Sza-lavitz, Dr. Gabor Maté, Dr. Vincent Felitti, and Andrew Tatarsky for your kind support and generous time. And thank you to Robert Lecker for your guidance and so much help getting this project off the ground. As well, thank you to the Canada Council for the Arts for much needed financial aid. And to public libraries, thank you for giving me a warm place to work (and Wi-Fi) in no less than seven cities over the course of researching and writing this book.

Thank you to my parents, Sandy Stepien and Bruce Lupick, for your unconditional support for this venture and for everything I do; to Mallory Lupick for the website; to my wife, Cara Foster, for your early edits and frequent reassurance; to my son, Benjamin Lupick, for making breaks from work the best; and to Michele Foster for lending me your studio. Finally, thank you to Dan McLeod and Charlie Smith for giving me my start in journalism, now so many years ago.

Once more, thank you to the activists. For sharing your stories and for everything you do.

Appendix: The Urban Survivors Union Do Not Prosecute Directive

An Advance Request to Limit the Scope of Failed Drug War Policy

The Do Not Prosecute Directive

The Do Not Prosecute Directive (DNPD) / Last Will and Testament Project was developed by the Urban Survivors Union, the only authentic national drug user union in the United States. The DNPD is a symbolic gesture used by people who use drugs to underscore our conviction that, should we die of an unintentional overdose, that no person be held responsible, legally or otherwise, for our death.

The DNP Directive is an advanced order to be used for instructing family members, law enforcement, district attorneys, judges, and other criminal justice personnel, to forgo prosecution attempts against all persons in the event of our unintentional overdose due to the ingestion of intoxicating substances.

Charges to be withheld include those imposed under drug-induced homicide, felony murder, depraved heart, involuntary or voluntary manslaughter laws, and any other malicious prosecution aimed at incarcerating people who provide drugs for others, either for monetary gain or as a gesture of kindness.

America is experiencing an epidemic of drug overdose deaths. There is only one way to combat this crisis: The solutions require we fully listen to people who use drugs and implement evidence-based interventions. To combat this overdose/drug poisoning crisis, we must have full coverage for syringe service programs. We need naloxone access for everyone, safe supply for people who use drugs, medical heroin, methadone reform, low threshold methadone maintenance treatment, and access to buprenorphine. We need safe consumption spaces, full access to drug testing, and a complete end to the war on drugs, including decriminalization and full legalization and regulation.

Applicability

This form is to be used by organizations, drug user unions, individuals, and all activists and allies fighting against drug-induced homicide laws. It is designed to create dialogue amongst people who use drugs, their loved ones, and all allies, advocates, and activists. Other uses may include criminal justice settings. Courts are encouraged to honor this form in any situation where one has lost their life due to a drug overdose. While we understand this order is purely symbolic, it is a gesture to express our true intent and should be honored as such.

Instructions

The Do Not Prosecute Directive should be signed by any individual who wants to ensure that no person be charged or held responsible in the event of their unintentional overdose/drug poisoning death. We suggest that all people have conversations with their loved ones about this. There is no substitution for honest family dialogue. Share this information and have conversations about this DNP order.

The form that appears below should be kept by the person who signed the document. A second copy can be sent to the Urban Survivors Union to be retained at the organization's head office. Prosecution attempts may be initiated until the form is presented and the identity of the deceased is confirmed.

When you send the Urban Survivors Union a copy of the form, we suggest you make a donation to receive a DNPD bracelet or medallion inscribed with the words, "Do Not Prosecute." The Urban Survivors Union (1116 Grove St. Greensboro, NC, 27403) is a supplier of the aforementioned bracelets and medallions, which will be issued upon receipt of a properly completed Do Not Prosecute form, together with an enrollment form and the appropriate fee. Although optional, the use of a wrist bracelet or neck medallion facilitates the prompt identification of a person who is a willing participant in the ingestion of potentially deadly substances and avoids the problem of lost or misplaced forms. It is strongly encouraged.

Questions about the DNPD: The Urban Survivors Union will gladly discuss this form with any person who would like to better understand the need for such a document or learn more about how to use this document properly. Please contact the USU via its website at urbansurvivorsunion.org.

The Urban Survivors Union
Do Not Prosecute Directive

I _____ , request prosecutorial restraint as herein described.
Print current/former drug user's name

I understand that "do not prosecute" (DNP) means that if I die as a result of a drug overdose, I request that no one be charged, prosecuted, or held criminally responsible for my death.

I understand this decision is being made to challenge the oppressive and perpetuated false dichotomy between people who use drugs and people who sell drugs. We are, more often than not, one and the same.

I understand that I may revoke this directive at any time by destroying this form and any copies of this form, and by removing any DNP bracelets, medallions, or other regalia.

I give permission for this information to be given to law enforcement, attorneys, judges, and any criminal justice system personnel, as necessary to implement this directive.

I hereby agree to the Do Not Prosecute Directive.

_____   _____
Current/Former Drug User Signature   *Date*

I affirm that this person is making an informed decision and that this directive is their explicit desire.

In the event of death caused by an overdose of intoxicating drugs/substances, I will advocate for the deceased person's wishes as outlined in the DNPD.

_____   _____
Witness Signature   *Date*

_____   _____
Print Witness's Name   *Telephone (optional)*

Notes

Prelude

1. "Provisional Drug Overdose Death Counts," National Center for Health Statistics, Centers for Disease Control and Prevention (last modified July 14, 2021).

1: Tough Love

1. "Drug Overdose Mortality by State," National Center for Health Statistics, Centers for Disease Control and Prevention, www.cdc.gov/nchs /pressroom/sosmap/drug_poisoning_mortality/drug_poisoning.

2. Elliott Currie, "'It's Our Lives They're Dealing with Here': Some Adolescent Views of Residential Treatment," *Journal of Drug Issues* 33, no. 4 (October 2003): 833–64.

3. "The Science of Drug Use and Addiction: The Basics," National Institute on Drug Abuse (last modified July 2018), www.drugabuse.gov/publications /media-guide/science-drug-use-addiction-basics.

4. "Bipolar Disorder," National Institute of Mental Health, www.nimh.nih .gov/health/topics/bipolar-disorder/index.

5. "Comorbidity: Substance Use and Other Mental Disorders," National Institute on Drug Abuse (last modified August 15, 2018), www.drugabuse.gov /drug-topics/trends-statistics/infographics/comorbidity-substance-use-other -mental-disorders.

6. Substance Abuse and Mental Health Services Administration, *Results from the 2010 National Survey on Drug Use and Health: Summary of National Findings* (Rockville, MD: Substance Abuse and Mental Health Services Administration, 2011).

7. Lana Vornik and Sherwood Brown, "Management of Comorbid Bipolar Disorder and Substance Abuse," *Journal of Clinical Psychiatry* 67, no. 7 (2006): 24, pubmed.ncbi.nlm.nih.gov/16961421.

8. Icro Maremmani, Guilio Perugi, Matteo Pacini, and Hagop Akiskal, "Toward a Unitary Perspective on the Bipolar Spectrum and Substance Abuse: Opiate Addiction as a Paradigm," *Journal of Affective Disorders* 93, no. 1–3 (July 2006), doi.org/10.1016/j.jad.2006.02.022.

9. "Are You Self-Medicating with Substance, Drugs or Alcohol?" American Addiction Centers (last modified October 1, 2020), americanaddictioncenters

.org/adult-addiction-treatment-programs/self-medicating.

10. Michael A. Cerullo and Stephen Strakowski, "The Prevalence and Significance of Substance Use Disorders in Bipolar Type I and II Disorder," *Substance Abuse Treatment, Prevention, and Policy* 2, no. 29 (2007): doi.org/10.1186/1747-597X-2-29.

2: Trauma Was My Gateway Drug

1. Vincent Felitti, Robert Anda, Dale Nordenberg, David Williamson, Alison Spitz, Valerie Edwards, Mary Koss, and James Marks, "Relationship of Childhood Abuse and Household Dysfunction to Many of the Leading Causes of Death in Adults: The Adverse Childhood Experiences (ACE) Study," *American Journal of Preventive Medicine* 14, no. 4 (May 1998): 250, doi.org/10.1016/S0749-3797(98)00017-8.

2. Vincent Felitti and Robert Anda, "Origins and Essence of the Study," *ACE Report* 1, no. 1 (April 2003): 2.

3. Karen Heffernan, Marylene Cloitre, Kenneth Tardiff, Peter Marzuk, Laura Portera, and Andrew Leon, "Childhood Trauma as a Correlate of Lifetime Opiate Use in Psychiatric Patients," *Addictive Behaviors* 25, no. 5 (September–October 2000), https://doi.org/10.1016/S0306-4603(00)00066-6.

4. Karen Heffernan et al., "Childhood Trauma as a Correlate of Lifetime Opiate Use in Psychiatric Patients."

5. Michael Stein, Micah Conti, Shannon Kenney, Bradley Anderson, Jessica Flori, Megan Risi, and Genie Bailey, "Adverse Childhood Experience Effects on Opioid Use Initiation, Injection Drug Use, and Overdose Among Persons with Opioid Use Disorder," *Drug and Alcohol Dependence* 179 (October 2017): 325–29, doi.org/10.1016/j.drugalcdep.2017.07.007.

6. Gabor Maté, *In the Realm of Hungry Ghosts: Close Encounters with Addiction* (Toronto: Vintage Canada, 2009), 188.

7. Kimberly Sue, *Getting Wrecked: Women, Incarceration, and the American Opioid Crisis* (Oakland: University of California Press, 2019), 89.

8. Centers for Disease Control and Prevention, "Drug Overdose Mortality by State."

9. Matthew Desmond, *Evicted: Poverty and Profit in the American City* (New York: Crown, 2017), 190.

10. Alisha Jarwala and Sejal Singh, "When Disability Is a 'Nuisance': How Chronic Nuisance Ordinances Push Residents with Disabilities Out of Their Homes," *Harvard Civil Rights–Civil Liberties Law Review* 54 (July 2019): 908, ssrn.com/abstract=3415952.

11. Ashley Bradford and W. David Bradford, "The Effect of Evictions on Accidental Drug and Alcohol Mortality," *Health Services Research* 55, no. 1 (February 2020): 10, doi.org/10.1111/1475-6773.13256.

3: A Moment of Need

1. Laura Faherty, Ashley Kranz, Joshua Russell-Fritch, Stephen Patrick, Jonathan Cantor, Bradley Stein, "Association of Punitive and Reporting State Policies Related to Substance Use in Pregnancy with Rates of Neonatal Abstinence Syndrome," *JAMA Network Open* 2, no. 11 (November 2019), www.rand.org/pubs/external_publications/EP68010.

2. Jennifer Brown, "A Decade into the Opioid Crisis, Colorado Hospitals Have Changed the Way They Treat Opioid-Exposed Babies. And It's Helping," *Colorado Sun* (March 5, 2020), coloradosun.com/2020/03/05/substance-exposed-newborns.

3. Matthew Grossman, Matthew Lipshaw, Rachel Osborn, and Adam Berkwitt, "A Novel Approach to Assessing Infants with Neonatal Abstinence Syndrome," *Hospital Pediatrics* 8, no. 1 (January 2018), hosppeds.aappublications.org/content/hosppeds/8/1/1.full.pdf.

4. Eli Hager, "The Hidden Trauma of 'Short Stays' in Foster Care," *Marshall Project* (February 11, 2020), www.themarshallproject.org/2020/02/11/the-hidden-trauma-of-short-stays-in-foster-care.

5. William Hall, Mimi Chapman, Kent Lee, Yesenia Merino, Tainayah Thomas, B. Keith Payne, Eugenia Eng, Steven Day, and Tamera Coyne-Beasley, "Implicit Racial/Ethnic Bias Among Health Care Professionals and Its Influence on Health Care Outcomes: A Systematic Review," *American Journal of Public Health* 105, no. 12 (December 2015): 60, ncbi.nlm.nih.gov/pmc/articles/PMC4638275/pdf/AJPH.2015.302903.pdf.

6. Brigham and Women's Hospital, "Minority Patients Less Likely to Receive Analgesic Medications for Abdominal Pain," *ScienceDaily* 17 (November 2015), sciencedaily.com/releases/2015/11/151117143530.

7. Nora Volkow, "America's Addiction to Opioids: Heroin and Prescription Drug Abuse," National Institute on Drug Abuse (last modified May 14, 2014), archives.drugabuse.gov/testimonies/2014/americas-addiction-to-opioids-heroin-prescription-drug-abuse.

8. Josh Katz and Margot Sanger-Katz, "'The Numbers Are So Staggering.' Overdose Deaths Set a Record Last Year," *New York Times* (November 29, 2018), www.nytimes.com/interactive/2018/11/29/upshot/fentanyl-drug-overdose-deaths.html; "Overdose Death Rates," National Institute on Drug Abuse (last modified March 10, 2020), www.drugabuse.gov/drug-topics/trends-statistics/overdose-death-rates.

9. "Drilling Into the DEA's Pain Pill Database," *Washington Post* (January 17, 2020), www.washingtonpost.com/graphics/2019/investigations/dea-pain-pill-database.

10. Centers for Disease Control and Prevention, CDC Wonder, wonder.cdc.gov.

11. "Number of National Drug Overdose Deaths Involving Select Prescription and Illicit Drugs," National Institute on Drug Abuse.

12. Theodore Cicero, Matthew Ellis, and Hilary Surratt, "The Changing Face of Heroin Use in the United States," *JAMA Psychiatry* 71, no. 7 (July 2014), doi.org/10.1001/jamapsychiatry.2014.366.

13. Deni Carise, Karen Leggett Dugosh, A. Thomas McLellan, Amy Camilleri, George Woody, and Kevin Lynch, "Prescription OxyContin Abuse Among Patients Entering Addiction Treatment," *American Journal of Psychiatry* 164, no. 11 (November 2007): 1, www.ncbi.nlm.nih.gov/pmc/articles /PMC2785002/pdf/nihms128346.pdf.

14. Substance Abuse and Mental Health Services Administration, *Results from the 2014 National Survey on Drug Use and Health: Detailed Tables* (Rockville, MD: Substance Abuse and Mental Health Services Administration, 2015).

15. German Lopez, "The Rise in Meth and Cocaine Overdoses, Explained," *Vox* (January 30, 2020), www.vox.com/policy-and-politics/2020/1/9/21055113 /opioid-epidemic-stimulants-cocaine-meth-drug-overdose-death.

16. "20 Facts About U.S. Inequality That Everyone Should Know," Stanford Center on Poverty and Inequality, accessed April 1, 2021, inequality.stanford .edu/publications/20-facts-about-us-inequality-everyone-should-know.

17. David Cooper, Elise Gould, and Ben Zipperer, "Low-Wage Workers Are Suffering from a Decline in the Real Value of the Federal Minimum Wage," Economic Policy Institute (last updated August 27, 2019), www.epi.org /publication/labor-day-2019-minimum-wage.

18. Calvin Schermerhorn, "Why the Racial Wealth Gap Persists, More Than 150 Years After Emancipation," *Washington Post* (last updated June 19), 2019, www.washingtonpost.com/outlook/2019/06/19/why-racial-wealth-gap -persists-more-than-years-after-emancipation.

19. Bob Pisani, "Wealth Gap Grows as Rising Corporate Profits Boost Stock Holdings Controlled by Richest Households," CNBC (last modified August 27), 2020, www.cnbc.com/2020/08/27/wealth-gap-grows-as-rising-corporate-pro fits-boost-stock-holdings-controlled-by-richest-households.html.

20. John Harvey, "If Unemployment Is So Low Then Why Don't I Feel Better?," *Forbes* (last updated May 3, 2019), www.forbes.com/sites/johntharvey /2019/05/03/if-unemployment-is-so-low-then-why-dont-i-feel-better.

21. Anne Case and Angus Deaton, *Deaths of Despair and the Future of Capitalism* (Princeton: Princeton University Press, 2020), 40.

22. Elizabeth Arias and Jiaquan Xu, "United States Life Tables, 2017," *National Vital Statistics Reports* 68, no. 7 (June 24, 2019): 46, www.cdc.gov /nchs/data/nvsr/nvsr68/nvsr68_07-508.pdf.

23. Kelly Ray Knight, *addicted.pregnant.poor* (Durham, NC: Duke University Press, 2015), 145.

24. Joni Teoh Bing Fei, Anne Yee, Mohamad Hussain Bin Habil, and

Mahmoud Danaee, "Effectiveness of Methadone Maintenance Therapy and Improvement in Quality of Life Following a Decade of Implementation," *Journal of Substance Abuse Treatment* 69 (July 2016), pubmed.ncbi.nlm.nih.gov /27568510.

4: A Safe Space for People Who Use Drugs

1. Lance Dodes and Zachary Dodes, *The Sober Truth: Debunking the Bad Science Behind 12-Step Programs and the Rehab Industry* (Boston: Beacon Press, 2014), 16.

2. Michael Gossop, Duncan Stewart, and John Marsden, "Attendance at Narcotics Anonymous and Alcoholics Anonymous Meetings, Frequency of Attendance and Substance Use Outcomes After Residential Treatment for Drug Dependence: A 5-Year Follow-Up Study," *Addiction* 103, no. 1 (January 2008), doi.org/10.1111/j.1360-0443.2007.02050.x.

3. Jake Flanagin, "The Surprising Failures of 12 Steps," *Atlantic* (March 25, 2014), www.theatlantic.com/health/archive/2014/03/the-surprising-failures -of-12-steps/284616.

4. Dodes and Dodes, *The Sober Truth*, 16.

5. Ryan McNeil, Will Small, Evan Wood, and Thomas Kerr, "Hospitals as a 'Risk Environment': An Ethno-Epidemiological Study of Voluntary and Involuntary Discharge from Hospital Against Medical Advice Among People Who Inject Drugs," *Social Science and Medicine* 105 (March 2014), doi.org/10 .1016/j.socscimed.2014.01.010.

6. Joseph Merrill, Lorna Rhodes, Richard Deyo, G. Alan Marlatt, and Katharine Bradley, "Mutual Mistrust in the Medical Care of Drug Users," *Journal of General Internal Medicine* 17, no. 5 (May 2005), www.ncbi.nlm.nih .gov/pmc/articles/PMC1495051.

7. David Vlahov and Benjamin Junge, "The Role of Needle Exchange Programs in HIV Prevention," *Public Health Reports* 113, no. 1 (June 1998), www .ncbi.nlm.nih.gov/pmc/articles/PMC1307729.

8. Don Des Jarlais, Theresa Perlis, Kamyar Arasteh, Lucia Torian, Sara Beatrice, Judith Milliken, Donna Mildvan, Stanley Yancovitz, and Samuel Friedman, "HIV Incidence Among Injection Drug Users in New York City, 1990 to 2002," *American Journal of Public Health* 95, no. 8 (August 2005), doi .org/10.2105/AJPH.2003.036517.

9. Abu Abdul-Quader, Jonathan Feelemyer, Shilpa Modi, Ellen Stein, Alya Briceno, Salaam Semaan, Tara Horvath, Gail Kennedy, Don Des Jarlais, "Effectiveness of Structural-Level Needle/Syringe Programs to Reduce HCV and HIV Infection Among People Who Inject Drugs," *AIDS and Behavior* 17, no. 9 (November 2013), doi.org/10.1007/s10461-013-0593-y.

10. John Watters, Michelle Estilo, George Clark, and Jennifer Lorvick, "An Evaluation of Needle and Syringe Exchange in San Francisco," in *Proceedings: Workshop on Needle Exchange and Bleach Distribution Programs* (Washington, DC: National Academy Press, 1994), www.ncbi.nlm.nih.gov /books/NBK236639.

11. Ricky Bluthenthal, Aruna Gogineni, Doug Longshore, and Michael Stein, "Factors Associated with Readiness to Change Drug Use Among Needle-Exchange Users," *Drug and Alcohol Dependence* 62, no. 3 (May 2001), doi.org/10.1016/S0376-8716(00)00174-5.

12. Holly Hagan, James McGough, Hanne Thiede, Sharon Hopkins, Jeffrey Duchin, and E. Russell Alexander, "Reduced Injection Frequency and Increased Entry and Retention in Drug Treatment Associated with Needle-Exchange Participation in Seattle Drug Injectors," *Journal of Substance Abuse Treatment* 19, no. 3 (October 2000), doi.org/10.1016/S0740-5472(00)00104-5.

13. Hansel Tookes, Alex Kral, Lynn Wenger, Gabriel Cardenas, Alexis Martinez, Recinda Sherman, Margaret Pereyra, David Forrest, Marlene LaLota, and Lisa Metsch, "A Comparison of Syringe Disposal Practices Among Injection Drug Users in a City With versus a City Without Needle and Syringe Programs," *Drug and Alcohol Dependence* 123, no. 1–3 (June 2012), doi.org/10 .1016/j.drugalcdep.2011.12.001.

14. "Syringe Services Programs FAQs," Syringe Services Programs, Centers for Disease Control and Prevention (last modified May 23, 2019), www.cdc .gov/ssp/syringe-services-programs-faq.

15. "Syringe Exchange Programs," Opioid & Health Indicators Database, amfAR, opioid.amfar.org/indicator/num_SSPs.

5: The Wright Focus Group

1. Richard Eldredge, "Broadcast from the Bluff: Atlanta's Open-Air Heroin Supermarket," *Atlanta* (January 24, 2014).

2. Prasanthi Persad, Fairouz Saad, and Joann Schulte, "Comparison Between Needs-Based and One-for-One Models for Syringe Exchange Programs," Louisville Department of Public Health and Wellness, louisvilleky .gov/document/seprptneedsbasedvsoneforone2017pdf.

6: A Drug-User Union of One

1. Eliza Wheeler, Stephen Jones, Michael Gilbert, and Peter Davidson, "Opioid Overdose Prevention Programs Providing Naloxone to Laypersons—United States, 2014," *Morbidity and Mortality Weekly Report* 64, no. 23 (June 2015), cdc.gov/mmwr/preview/mmwrhtml/mm6423a2.htm.

2. Chandler McClellan, Barrot Lambdin, Mir Ali, Ryan Mutter, Corey

Davis, Eliza Wheeler, Michael Pemberton, and Alex Kral, "Opioid-Overdose Laws Association with Opioid Use and Overdose Mortality," *Addictive Behaviors* 86 (November 2018), doi.org/10.1016/j.addbeh.2018.03.014.

3. "Getting Off Right: A Safety Manual for Injection Drug Users," National Harm Reduction Coalition (last updated August 31, 2020), harmreduction.org/issues/safer-drug-use/injection-safety-manual.

7: All Practice up to Now

1. Maia Szalavitz, *Unbroken Brain: A Revolutionary New Way of Understanding Addiction* (New York: St. Martin's Press, 2016), 50, 119.

2. Theodore Cicero, Matthew Ellis, and Zachary Kasper, "Increased Use of Heroin as an Initiating Opioid of Abuse," *Addictive Behaviors* 74 (November 2017), doi.org/10.1016/j.addbeh.2017.05.030.

3. National Institute on Drug Abuse, "Overdose Death."

4. Julia Woo, Anuja Bhalerao, Monica Bawor, Meha Bhatt, Brittany Dennis, Natalia Mouravska, Laura Zielinski, and Zainab Samaan, "Don't Judge a Book by Its Cover: A Qualitative Study of Methadone Patients' Experiences of Stigma," *Substance Abuse: Research and Treatment* 1–12 (March 23, 2017), doi.org/10.1177/1178221816685087.

5. Wendy Sawyer, "The Gender Divide: Tracking Women's State Prison Growth," Prison Policy Initiative (last modified January 9, 2018), www.prisonpolicy.org/reports/women_overtime.html.

6. Sue, *Getting Wrecked*, 29.

7. Aleks Kajstura, "Women's Mass Incarceration: The Whole Pie 2019," *Prison Policy Initiative* (last modified October 29, 2019), www.prisonpolicy.org/reports/pie2019women.html.

8. Sawyer, "The Gender Divide."

9. Sue, *Getting Wrecked*, 90; Knight, *addicted.pregnant.poor*, 195.

8: A Period of Calm

1. Nicola Jeal, Rita Patel, Niamh Redmond, Joanna Kesten, Sophie Ramsden, John Macleod, Joanna Coast, Maggie Telfer, David Wilcox, Gill Nowland, and Jeremy Horwood, "Drug Use in Street Sex Workers Study Protocol," *BMJ Open* (November 2018), bmjopen.bmj.com/content/8/11/e022728.

2. Lisa Maher, Thomas Crewe Dixon, Pisith Phlong, Julie Mooney-Somers, Ellen Stein, and Kimberly Page, "Conflicting Rights: How the Prohibition of Human Trafficking and Sexual Exploitation Infringes the Right to Health of Female Sex Workers in Phnom Penh, Cambodia," *Health and Human Rights*

17, no. 1 (June 2015), www.jstor.org/stable/10.2307/healhumarigh.17.1.102.

3. Alison Bass, *Getting Screwed: Sex Workers and the Law* (Hanover, NH: University Press of New England, 2015), 113–14.

4. Alexandre Laudet, Jeffrey Becker, and William White, "Don't Wanna Go Through That Madness No More: Quality of Life Satisfaction as Predictor of Sustained Remission from Illicit Drug Misuse," *Substance Use and Misuse* 44, no. 2 (December 2008), europepmc.org/article/PMC/2629650.

5. Meenakshi Subbaraman and Jane Witbrodt, "Differences Between Abstinent and Non-abstinent Individuals in Recovery from Alcohol Use Disorders," *Addictive Behaviors* 39, no. 12 (July 2014), doi.org/10.1016/j.addbeh.2014.07.010.

6. Alan Davis and Harold Rosenberg, "Acceptance of Non-abstinence Goals by Addiction Professionals in the United States," *Psychology of Addictive Behaviors* 27, no. 4 (2013), doi.org/10.1037/a0030563.

9: The Urban Survivors Union

1. Stefan Kertesz and Sally Satel, "Some People Still Need Opioids," *Slate* (August 17, 2017), slate.com/technology/2017/08/cutting-down-on-opioids-has-made-life-miserable-for-chronic-pain-patients.

2. "Prescribing Practices," Opioid Overdose, Centers for Disease Control and Prevention (last modified August 13, 2019), www.cdc.gov/drugoverdose/data/prescribing/prescribing-practices.

3. Alex Vitale, *The End of Policing* (New York: Verso, 2017), 129.

10: Strange Dope on the Street

1. Danielle Ramo and Sandra Brown, "Classes of Substance Abuse Relapse Situations: A Comparison of Adolescents and Adults," *Psychology of Addictive Behaviors* 22, no. 3 (September 2008), doi.org/10.1037/0893-164X.22.3.372.

2. Ramo and Brown, "Classes of Substance Abuse Relapse Situations."

3. "Treatment and Recovery," *Drugs, Brains, and Behavior: The Science of Addiction*, National Institute on Drug Abuse (last modified July 2020), www.drugabuse.gov/publications/drugs-brains-behavior-science-addiction/treatment-recovery.

4. Michelle Rodriguez and Maurice Emsellem, *65 Million "Need Not Apply": The Case for Reforming Criminal Background Checks for Employment* (The National Employment Law Project, 2011), 3.

5. Jeffrey Selbin, Justin McCrary, and Joshua Epstein, "Unmarked? Criminal Record Clearing and Employment Outcomes," *Journal of Criminal Law and Criminology* 108, no. 1 (January 2018), doi.org/0091-4169/18/10801-0001.

6. Kai Wright, "Boxed In: How a Criminal Record Keeps You Unemployed for Life," *Nation* (November 6, 2013), www.thenation.com/article/archive/boxed-how-criminal-record-keeps-you-unemployed-life.

7. Dylan Minor, Nicola Persico, and Deborah Weiss, "Criminal Background and Job Performance," *IZA Journal of Labor Policy* 7, no. 8 (2018), doi.org/10.1186/s40173-018-0101-0.

8. Travis Lupick, "Prosecutorial Indiscretion: A Conversation with Emily Bazelon," *Los Angeles Review of Books* (August 10, 2019), lareviewofbooks.org/article/prosecutorial-indiscretion-a-conversation-with-emily-bazelon.

11: Narco Feminism

1. Mark Stevenson, "Mexico Opium Poppy Growers See Price Drop, Turn to Marijuana," *Associated Press* (June 21, 2018), apnews.com/article/cb4dac96eb24420697416c68ad92105e.

2. Ben Westhoff, "The Brazen Way a Chinese Company Pumped Fentanyl Ingredients into the U.S.," *Atlantic* (August 18, 2019), www.theatlantic.com/health/archive/2019/08/chinese-company-helping-fuel-opioid-epidemic/596254.

3. John Holman, "Mexican Drug Cartels, Poppy Farmers and the U.S. Fentanyl Crisis," *Al Jazeera English* (May 7, 2019), www.aljazeera.com/features/2019/05/07/mexican-drug-cartels-poppy-farmers-and-the-us-fentanyl-crisis.

4. Abby Goodnough, "In Cities Where It Once Reigned, Heroin Is Disappearing," *New York Times* (May 18, 2019), www.nytimes.com/2019/05/18/health/heroin-fentanyl-deaths-baltimore.

5. Josh Katz, "Drug Deaths in America Are Rising Faster Than Ever," *New York Times* (June 5, 2017), www.nytimes.com/interactive/2017/06/05/upshot/opioid-epidemic-drug-overdose-deaths-are-rising-faster-than-ever.

6. "Number of National Drug Overdose Deaths Involving Select Prescription and Illicit Drugs," National Institute on Drug Abuse.

7. Lisa Johnson, "A Grain of Sand: Why Fentanyl Is So Deadly," CBC News (September 15, 2016), www.cbc.ca/news/canada/british-columbia/fentanyl-science-potent-deadly-1.3760244.

8. Clayton Mosher and Scott Akins, *Drugs and Drug Policy: The Control of Consciousness Alteration* (New York: SAGE Publications, 2007), 308–9.

9. "Designation of Benzylfentanyl and 4-Anilinopiperidine, Precursor Chemicals Used in the Illicit Manufacture of Fentanyl, as List I Chemicals," Drug Enforcement Administration (last modified April 15, 2020), www.deadiversion.usdoj.gov/fed_regs/rules/2020/fr0415.

10. Azam Ahmed, "Drug That Killed Prince Is Making Mexican Cartels

Richer, U.S. Says," *New York Times* (June 9, 2016), www.nytimes.com/2016/06/10/world/americas/drug-that-killed-prince-is-making-mexican-cartels-richer-us-says.

11. Aubrey Whelan, "How Fentanyl, the Deadly Synthetic Opioid, Took Over Pennsylvania," *Philadelphia Enquirer* (October 24, 2018), www.inquirer.com/philly/health/fentanyl-synthetic-opioid-drug-overdoses-philadelphia-pennsylvania-20181024.

12. "3 First Responders Recovering After Possible Fentanyl Exposure During Traffic Stop," *Fox 35 Orlando* (May 8, 2019), www.fox35orlando.com/news/3-first-responders-recovering-after-possible-fentanyl-exposure-during-traffic-stop.

13. Jim Woods, "Officer Arresting Shoplifting Suspect Rendered Unconscious by Suspected Opioid Contact," *Columbus Dispatch* (January 22, 2019), www.dispatch.com/news/20190122/officer-arresting-shoplifting-suspect-rendered-unconscious-by-suspected-opioid-contact.

14. Bryan Passifiume, "Suspected Fentanyl Contamination Forces Calgary Police Station Evacuation," *Calgary Sun* (December 23, 2017), calgarysun.com/news/crime/suspected-fentanyl-contamination-forces-calgary-police-station-evacuation.

15. Kyle Hinton, "Hazmat Crew Finishes Decontamination After Fentanyl Exposure at Scott County Jail," *KFVS12* (September 2, 2018), www.kfvs12.com/2018/09/02/unknown-substance-sends-scott-county-jailers-hospital.

16. German Lopez, "You Can't Overdose on Fentanyl by Touching It," *Vox* (March 22, 2019), www.vox.com/science-and-health/2019/3/22/18277144/fentanyl-opioid-epidemic-touch-overdose.

17. Alex Kasprak, "Police Chief Warns of Fentanyl Overdose Risk from Residue on Shopping Carts," *Snopes* (November 10, 2017), www.snopes.com/fact-check/fentanyl-overdose-residue-shopping-cart.

18. Linda Cottler, Catina O'Leary, Katelin Nickel, Jennifer Reingle, and Daniel Isom, "Breaking the Blue Wall of Silence: Risk Factors for Experiencing Police Sexual Misconduct Among Female Offenders," *American Journal of Public Health* 104, no. 2 (February 2014), doi.org/10.2105/AJPH.2013.301513.

19. Nabila El-Bassel and Steffanie Strathdee, "Women Who Use or Inject Drugs: An Action Agenda for Women-Specific, Multilevel and Combination HIV Prevention and Research," *Journal of Acquired Immune Deficiency Syndromes* 69, no. 2 (June 2015), doi.org/10.1097/QAI.0000000000000628.

20. Amnesty International, *Criminalizing Pregnancy: Policing Pregnant Women Who Use Drugs in the USA* (London: Amnesty International, 2017), 14.

21. Fei, Yee, Habil, and Danaee, "Effectiveness of Methadone Maintenance Therapy."

22. Chris Barber, "Public Enemy Number One: A Pragmatic Approach to America's Drug Problem," Richard Nixon Foundation (last modified June 29, 2016), www.nixonfoundation.org/2016/06/26404.

23. Dan Baum, "Legalize It All," *Harper's Magazine*, June 2013.

24. "Trends in U.S. Corrections," The Sentencing Project, www.sentencingproject.org/wp-content/uploads/2020/08/Trends-in-US-Corrections.pdf; "Prisoners in 1980," *Bureau of Justice Statistics Bulletin* (May 1981): 1, www.bjs.gov/content/pub/pdf/p80.pdf.

25. "Prisoners in 1990," *Bureau of Justice Statistics Bulletin* (May 1991): 1, www.bjs.gov/content/pub/pdf/p90.pdf.

26. Paul Guerino, Paige Harrison, and William Sabol, "Prisoners in 2010," *Bureau of Justice Statistics Bulletin* (December 2011): 1, www.bjs.gov/content/pub/pdf/p10.pdf.

27. Nazgol Ghandnoosh, "U.S. Prison Population Trends: Massive Buildup and Modest Decline," The Sentencing Project (last updated September 17, 2019), www.sentencingproject.org/publications/u-s-prison-population-trends-massive-buildup-and-modest-decline.

28. Fareed Zakaria, "Incarceration Nation," *Time* (April 2, 2012), content.time.com/time/magazine/article/0,9171,2109777,00.

29. Jeffrey Miron, "Drug Prohibition and Violence," *Drug Issues* 493 (1985): 99.

30. "Rates of Drug Use and Sales, by Race; Rates of Drug Related Criminal Justice Measures, by Race," The Hamilton Project (last updated October 21, 2016), www.hamiltonproject.org/charts/rates_of_drug_use_and_sales_by_race_rates_of_drug_related_criminal_justice.

31. "The Drug War, Mass Incarceration and Race," Drug Policy Alliance (New York: 2018), 1.

32. Michelle Alexander, *The New Jim Crow: Mass Incarceration in the Age of Colorblindness* (New York: The New Press, 2010), 6.

33. Alexander, *The New Jim Crow*, 9.

34. Alexander, *The New Jim Crow*, 3, 17.

12: Blow the System Up

1. Patricia Freeman, Emily Hankosky, Michelle Lofwall, and Jeffery Talbert, "The Changing Landscape of Naloxone Availability in the United States, 2011–2017," *Drug and Alcohol Dependence* 191 (October 2018), doi.org/10.1016/j.drugalcdep.2018.07.017.

2. Ken Alltucker, "Clinton Foundation Works to Put Naloxone in Recovery Homes as Opioid Epidemic Is Overshadowed by COVID-19 Pandemic,"

USA Today (August 31, 2020), www.usatoday.com/story/news/health/2020 /08/31/clinton-foundation-joins-efforts-supply-naloxone-recovery-homes /5637522002.

13: Harm Reduction Works

1. "'They Don't Have to Be Alone in This': Drug Users Unions See Membership Increase," Here & Now, WUBR (June 6, 2018), www.wbur.org /hereandnow/2018/06/06/drug-users-unions.

2. Dennis Osmond, "Epidemiology of HIV/AIDS in the United States," HIV InSite, University of California San Francisco (last updated March 2003), hivinsite.ucsf.edu/InSite?page=kb-01-03.

3. "Provisional Drug Overdose Death Counts," National Center for Health Statistics, Centers for Disease Control and Prevention (last modified July 14, 2021).

4. Katrine Andersen and Cecilie Kallestrup, "Rejected by AA," *New Republic* (June 27, 2019), newrepublic.com/article/149398/rejected-aa.

14: Light Up the Night

1. Agnese Mariotti, "The Effects of Chronic Stress on Health: New Insights into the Molecular Mechanisms of Brain-Body Communication," *Future Science OA* 1, no. 3 (November 2015), www.ncbi.nlm.nih.gov/pmc/articles /PMC5137920.

2. Maia Szalavitz, *Undoing Drugs: The Untold Story of Harm Reduction and the Future of Addiction* (New York: Hachette Books, 2021), 311.

3. B.C. Coroners Service, *Illicit Drug Overdose Deaths in BC: Findings of Coroners' Investigations* (Victoria, BC: Ministry of Public Safety and Solicitor General, 2018): 5.

4. Anne Siegler, Ellenie Tuazon, Daniella Bradley O'Brien, Denise Paone, "Unintentional Opioid Overdose Deaths in New York City, 2005–2010: A Place-Based Approach to Reduce Risk," *International Journal of Drug Policy* 25, no. 3 (May 2014), pubmed.ncbi.nlm.nih.gov/24412006.

15: Drug-Induced Homicide

1. Laura Maruschak and Todd Minton, "Correctional Populations in the United States, 2017–2018," *Bureau of Justice Statistics Bulletin* (August 2020): 2, www.bjs.gov/content/pub/pdf/cpus1718.pdf.

2. Vitale, *The End of Policing*, 134.

3. "Arrests for Drug Abuse Violations," 2019 Crime in the United States,

Federal Bureau of Investigation, ucr.fbi.gov/crime-in-the-u.s/2019/crime-in
-the-u.s.-2019/topic-pages/persons-arrested.

4. Katharine Seelye, "In Heroin Crisis, White Families Seek Gentler War
on Drugs," *New York Times* (October 30, 2015), www.nytimes.com/2015/10
/31/us/heroin-war-on-drugs-parents.

5. Allison Graves, "Did Hillary Clinton Call African-American Youth
'Superpredators'?" PolitiFact (August 28, 2016), www.politifact.com/factche
cks/2016/aug/28/reince-priebus/did-hillary-clinton-call-african-american
-youth-su.

6. Elise Viebeck, "How an Early Biden Crime Bill Created the Sentencing
Disparity for Crack and Cocaine Trafficking," *Washington Post* (July 28, 2019),
www.washingtonpost.com/politics/how-an-early-biden-crime-bill-created
-the-sentencing-disparity-for-crack-and-cocaine-trafficking/2019/07/28
/5cbb4c98-9dcf-11e9-85d6-5211733f92c7_story.

7. Julie Netherland and Helena Hansen, "The War on Drugs That Wasn't:
Wasted Whiteness, 'Dirty Doctors,' and Race in Media Coverage of Prescription Opioid Misuse," *Culture, Medicine, and Psychiatry* 40, no. 4 (December
2016), www.ncbi.nlm.nih.gov/pmc/articles/PMC5121004.

8. "Transcript: Chasing Heroin," *Frontline*, PBS, February 23, 2016, www
.pbs.org/wgbh/frontline/film/chasing-heroin/transcript.

9. Anne Case and Angus Deaton, *Deaths of Despair and the Future of Capitalism* (Princeton: Princeton University Press, 2020), 40.

10. Christopher Ingraham and Heather Long, "The 'War on Whites'
Is a Myth—and an Ugly One," *Washington Post* (August 14, 2017), www
.washingtonpost.com/news/wonk/wp/2017/08/14/the-war-on-whites-is
-a-myth-and-an-ugly-one.

11. Joel Achenbach, "Fentanyl Drug Overdose Deaths Rising Most Sharp-
ly Among African Americans," *Washington Post* (March 20, 2019), www
.washingtonpost.com/national/health-science/fentanyl-drug-overdose
-deaths-rising-most-sharply-among-african-americans/2019/03/20/5cc94eba
-4b36-11e9-93d0-64dbcf38ba41_story.

12. Maya Schenwar and Victoria Law, *Prison by Any Other Name: The
Harmful Consequences of Popular Reforms* (New York: The New Press, 2020),
57.

13. Michael Collins and Sheila Vakharia, *Criminal Justice Reform in the
Fentanyl Era: One Step Forward, Two Steps Back* (New York: Drug Policy Alliance, 2020), 3.

14. Maggie Haberman, Abby Goodnough, and Katharine Seelye, "Trump
Offers Tough Talk but Few Details in Unveiling Plan to Combat Opioids,"
New York Times (March 19, 2018), www.nytimes.com/2018/03/19/us/politics
/trump-new-hampshire-opioid-plan.

15. Susan Schmidt and Tom Kenworthy, "Bias Died of Cocaine Intoxication," *Washington Post* (June 25, 1986), www.washingtonpost.com/archive/politics/1986/06/25/bias-died-of-cocaine-intoxication/180e831a-aaa5-4554-8208-73278e57d5ef.

16. "Why Are Drug Dealers Getting Away with Murder?" Drug Induced Homicide.org.

17. Jessica Pishko, "When Using Heroin with a Friend Gets You Charged with Murder," *Mother Jones* (December 2017), www.motherjones.com/crime-justice/2017/12/using-heroin-gets-you-charged-with-murder.

18. Daniel Denvir, "Heroin, Murder, and the New Front in the War on Drugs," *Vice* (September 27, 2015), www.vice.com/en/article/qbxwnp/heroin-murder-and-the-new-front-in-the-war-on-drugs-928.

19. Rosa Goldensohn, "They Shared Drugs. Someone Died. Does That Make Them Killers?" *New York Times* (May 25, 2018), www.nytimes.com/2018/05/25/us/drug-overdose-prosecution-crime.

20. Hannah Leone, "Drug-Induced Homicide Charge Is Complicated, for Families and Lawmakers," *Chicago Tribune* (December 19, 2016), www.chicagotribune.com/suburbs/aurora-beacon-news/ct-abn-drug-induced-homicide-st-1213-20161216-story.

21. "Drug-Induced Homicide," Health in Justice Action Lab, Northeastern University School of Law (last modified 2020), www.healthinjustice.org/drug-induced-homicide.

22. Leo Beletsky, "America's Favorite Antidote: Drug-Induced Homicide in the Age of the Overdose Crisis," *Utah Law Review* 2019, no. 4 (August 2018), dx.doi.org/10.2139/ssrn.3185180.

23. Lindsay LaSalle, *An Overdose Death Is Not Murder: Why Drug-Induced Homicide Laws Are Counterproductive and Inhumane* (New York: Drug Policy Alliance, 2017), 17.

24. "Good Samaritan Overdose Prevention Laws," Prescription Drug Abuse Policy System (last modified July 1, 2018), pdaps.org/datasets/good-samaritan-overdose-laws-1501695153.

25. McClellan et al., "Opioid-Overdose Laws."

26. LaSalle, *An Overdose Death Is Not Murder*, 11.

27. Louise Vincent, "The Rage of Overdose Grief Makes It All Too Easy to Misdirect Blame," *Filter* (December 5, 2018), filtermag.org/the-rage-of-overdose-grief-makes-it-all-too-easy-to-misdirect-blame.

16: Reframe the Blame

1. Noelle Weicker, Jill Owczarzak, Glenna Urquhart, Ju Nyeong Park, Saba Rouhani, Rui Ling, Miles Morris, and Susan G. Sherman, "Agency in the Fen-

tanyl Era: Exploring the Utility of Fentanyl Test Strips in an Opaque Drug Market," *International Journal of Drug Policy* 84 (October 2020), doi.org/10.1016/j.drugpo.2020.102900.

2. Maxwell Krieger, William Goedel, Jane Buxton, Mark Lysyshyn, Edward Bernstein, Susan Sherman, Josiah Rich, Scott Hadland, Traci Green, and Brandon Marshall, "Use of Rapid Fentanyl Test Strips Among Young Adults Who Use Drugs," *International Journal of Drug Policy* 61 (November 2018), doi.org/10.1016/j.drugpo.2018.09.009.

3. Weicker et al., "Agency in the Fentanyl Era."

4. "Alix Tichelman, Woman Charged in Google Exec's Death, Sentenced to Six Years," KSBW, NBC Bay Area (May 19, 2015), www.nbcbayarea.com/news/local/alix-tichelman-woman-charged-in-google-execs-death-sentenced-to-six-years/69116.

5. Collins and Vakharia, *Criminal Justice Reform in the Fentanyl Era*, 3.

6. Beletsky, "America's Favorite Antidote," 874.

7. Sarah Lageson, "Found Out and Opting Out: The Consequences of Online Criminal Records for Families," *ANNALS of the American Academy of Political and Social Science* 655 (May 2016), doi.org/10.1177/0002716215625053.

8. James Jacobs, *The Eternal Criminal Record* (Cambridge, MA: Harvard University Press, 2015): 3–4.

9. David Kirk and Robert Sampson, "Juvenile Arrest and Collateral Educational Damage in the Transition to Adulthood," *Sociology of Education* 86, no. 1 (January 2013), doi.org/10.1177/0038040712448862.

17: A Labor of Radical Love

1. National Institute on Drug Abuse, "Overdose Death Rates."

2. "Synthetic Opioid Overdose Data," Opioid Overdose, Centers for Disease Control and Prevention (last modified March 19, 2020), www.cdc.gov/drugoverdose/data/fentanyl.

3. "Drug-Induced Homicide," Health in Justice Action Lab, Northeastern University School of Law (last modified 2020), www.healthinjustice.org/drug-induced-homicide.

4. Jennifer Carroll, Josiah Rich, and Traci Green, "The Protective Effect of Trusted Dealers Against Opioid Overdose in the U.S.," *International Journal of Drug Policy* 78 (April 2020), doi.org/10.1016/j.drugpo.2020.102695.

5. Geoff Bardwell, Jade Boyd, Jaime Arredondo, Ryan McNeil, and Thomas Kerr, "Trusting the Source: The Potential Role of Drug Dealers in Reducing Drug-Related Harms via Drug Checking," *Drug and Alcohol Dependence* 198 (May 2019), doi.org/10.1016/j.drugalcdep.2019.01.035.

18: Methadone in the Time of COVID

1. Elizabeth Brico, "Methadone Rules Requiring In-Person Visits Are Putting Patients at Risk of Coronavirus," *Appeal* (April 15, 2020), theappeal.org /methadone-rules-requiring-in-person-visits-are-putting-patients-at-risk-of -coronavirus.

2. Hilary Smith Connery, "Medication-Assisted Treatment of Opioid Use Disorder," *Harvard Review of Psychiatry* 23, no. 2 (March/April 2015), doi.org /10.1097/HRP.0000000000000075.

3. Connery, "Medication-Assisted Treatment of Opioid Use Disorder."

4. Sarah Wakeman, Marc Larochelle, Omid Ameli, Christine Chaisson, Jeffrey McPheeters, William Crown, Francisca Azocar, and Darshak Sanghavi, "Comparative Effectiveness of Different Treatment Pathways for Opioid Use Disorder," *JAMA Network Open* 3, no. 2 (February 2020), doi.org/10.1001 /jamanetworkopen.2019.20622.

5. Wakeman et al., "Comparative Effectiveness of Different Treatment Pathways for Opioid Use Disorder."

6. Wakeman, et al., "Comparative Effectiveness of Different Treatment Pathways for Opioid Use Disorder."

19: Creating Space

1. Daniel Pierce, "Opioid Deaths and Overdoses Up in Parts of the Triad," Fox 8 (August 27, 2020), myfox8.com/news/opioid-deaths-and-overdoses-up -in-parts-of-the-triad.

2. Jim Morelli, "CDC Report Finds Big Jump in Pandemic Drug Overdose Deaths," Boston 25 News (April 14, 2021), www.boston25news.com/news /health/cdc-report-finds-big-jump-pandemic-drug-overdose-deaths.

3. Martha Bebinger, "Overdose Deaths Have Risen in Mass. Amid Pandemic, State Data Show," WBUR (November 18, 2020), www.wbur.org /commonhealth/2020/11/18/coronavirus-opioid-overdoses-death-data.

4. Brian Mann, "Drug Overdose Deaths Spiked to 88,000 During the Pandemic, White House Says," NPR (April 1, 2020), www.npr.org/2021/04 /01/983414684/white-house-says-drug-overdose-deaths-spiked-to-88-000 -during-the-pandemic.

5. "Provisional Drug Overdose Death Counts," National Center for Health Statistics, Centers for Disease Control and Prevention (last modified July 14, 2021).

6. Josh Katz and Margot Sanger-Katz, "'It's Huge, It's Historic, It's Unheard-of': Drug Overdose Deaths Spike," *New York Times* (July 14, 2021).

7. Alex Kreit, "Safe Injection Sites and the Federal 'Crack House' Statute,"

Boston College Law Review 60, no. 2 (2019), lawdigitalcommons.bc.edu/bclr
/vol60/iss2/2.

    8. B.C. Information Access Operations, email to the author, April 2, 2020.

    9. Brandon Marshall, M-J Milloy, Evan Wood, Julio Montaner, and Thomas Kerr, "Reduction in Overdose Mortality After the Opening of North America's First Medically Supervised Safer Injecting Facility: A Retrospective Population-Based Study," *Lancet* 377, no. 9775 (April 2011), doi.org/10.1016 /S0140-6736(10)62353-7.

    10. Urban Health Research Initiative, *Insight into Insite* (Vancouver: BC Centre for Excellence in HIV/AIDS, 2010).

    11. European Monitoring Centre for Drugs and Drug Addiction, *Drug Consumption Rooms: An Overview of Provision and Evidence* (Lisbon: European Union, 2018).

    12. German Lopez, "Trump's Justice Department Is Threatening Cities That Allow Safe Injection Sites," *Vox* (August 30, 2018), www.vox.com/policy-and -politics/2018/8/30/17800028/safe-injection-site-justice-department-trump.

    13. Rod Rosenstein, "Fight Drug Abuse, Don't Subsidize It," *New York Times* (August 27, 2018), www.nytimes.com/2018/08/27/opinion/opioids-heroin -injection-sites.

Afterword

    1. "Overdose Death Rates," National Institute on Drug Abuse (last modified January 2021): www.drugabuse.gov/drug-topics/trends-statistics /overdose-death-rates.

    2. "Provisional Drug Overdose Death Counts," National Center for Health Statistics, Centers for Disease Control and Prevention: www.cdc.gov/nchs /nvss/vsrr/drug-overdose-data.htm.

About the Author

Travis Lupick is an award-winning journalist who has written for the *Los Angeles Times*, *Los Angeles Review of Books*, *VICE* magazine, *Toronto Star*, and *Globe and Mail*, among others. He is the author of *Fighting for Space: How a Group of Drug Users Transformed One City's Struggle with Addiction* and has worked as a journalist in Sierra Leone, Liberia, Malawi, Nepal, Bhutan, Peru, and Honduras. Follow him on Twitter: @tlupick.